STAY
HUNGRY
STAY
FOOLISH

STAY
HUNGRY
STAY
FOOLISH

The inspiring stories of 25 IIM
Ahmedabad graduates who chose
to tread a path of their own making

RASHMI BANSAL

westland ltd
Venkat Towers, 165, P.H. Road, Maduravoyal, Chennai 600 095
No. 38/10 (New No.5), Raghava Nagar, New Timber Yard Layout, Bangalore 560 026
Survey No. A - 9, II Floor, Moula Ali Industrial Area, Moula Ali, Hyderabad 500 040
23/181, Anand Nagar, Nehru Road, Santacruz East, Mumbai 400 055
4322/3, Ansari Road, Daryaganj, New Delhi 110 002

First published in India by CIIE, IIM Ahmedabad 2008

First published by westland ltd 2012

Copyright © CIIE, IIM Ahmedabad, India 2008

10 9 8 7 6 5 4 3 2 1

ISBN: 978-93-81626-71-9

CONTENT AND PAGE DESIGN BY
JAM Venture Publishing Pvt Ltd.

Cover Design by Amrit Vatsa

Typesetting by Ram Das Lal

Printed at Manipal Technologies Ltd., Manipal

ACKNOWLEDGEMENTS

This book is a labour of love supported by the Centre for Innovation Incubation and Entrepreneurship (CIIE) at IIM Ahmedabad and the Wadhwani Foundation. I would like to thank the following people for making it possible:

Prof Rakesh Basant and Kunal Upadhyay at CIIE for believing in me.

Laura Parkin at the Wadhwani Foundation for the funding.

My friend Piyul Mukherjee for her valuable feedback and comments on every chapter.

Anjan Mukherjee, for coming up with the title for this book and Amrit Vatsa, for conceiving the cover.

The team at JAM for giving me time off from work to focus on writing.

Priyanka Sharma, for her brilliant design and Madan Mohan for the layout.

Swastik Nigam, Arjun Ravi and Tamanna Jaisinghani for proofreading.

My husband Yatin and daughter Nivedita, for giving me a high-five for every chapter and keeping me going.

And finally, all the entrepreneurs who shared their thoughts and experiences so generously and honestly.

I know that you will be as inspired by their stories as I was.

That holding this book in your hands will be like meeting each one of these amazing people in person.

ACKNOWLEDGEMENTS

FOREWORD

It is indeed very satisfying to write the foreword for a very different kind of book, one on the entrepreneurship of the alumni of IIM Ahmedabad. The Institute is already well known globally for the quality of the post-graduate programmes in management it offers. It is now increasingly getting recognised for the innovativeness and the entrepreneurship of its alumni. In this book, Rashmi Bansal, herself an alumnus of IIMA, describes how twenty-five alumni of the Institute chose the path less trodden and successfully built new businesses and organisations. Written in a conversational style, the book lucidly captures how these individuals, with fire in their bellies and stars in their eyes, overcame the odds to realise their dreams of being their own masters as they ventured into uncharted territories, some with little else than a belief in themselves. The book should be a 'must read' not just for students of management but for all youngsters as it would inspire them to dream the forbidden and achieve the impossible.

The book was commissioned by the Centre for Innovation, Incubation and Entrepreneurship (CIIE), IIMA. The funding for the project was provided by the Wadhwani Foundation. On behalf of the Institute I thank the Foundation for providing the funding support.

Even as I pen the foreword, I realise that many more alumni of IIMA have become entrepreneurs. This is the first attempt to document the insights and experiences of IIMA entrepreneurs. The Institute will continue such endeavours through books, cases, documentaries and other modes of communication to inspire and instill the 'can do' spirit of entrepreneurship in the younger generations.

Samir K Barua
Director
IIM Ahmedabad

AUTHOR'S NOTE

Of all the questions we leave unanswered the one that comes back to haunt us the most is : 'What if…'

What if I'd married my college sweetheart?

What if I had the good sense not to?

What if I had been born in this job market?

What if…

What if I'd planned a little less?

What if I'd lived a little more?

What if I'd chucked it all and started my own company?

'What ifs' are never idle fantasy. These are our hopes, dreams and desires.

Logic and reason are the naphthalene balls we use to pack them away into a *sandook* called 'Some day'. But when that day comes we are too old, too poor, too tired or too lazy.

This book is for all those people who seized their moment. So they would not wake up one day with regrets.Of course they saw markets and opportunities and need gaps. But more importantly, they stood in front of the mirror and saw their true selves.

That self told them it was meaningless to sell soap just because you're paid well to do so.

That being a corporate slave was the easy option, but not the one that felt right.

That there was something bigger and better to do with their talents.

So they did the things others thought were foolish.

And they stayed hungry for that something more.

Stay Hungry, Stay Foolish is what Steve Jobs advised the graduating class of Stanford University in his commencement address to the class of 2005. And that is the motto by which all the entrepreneurs I have met for this book have lived.

AUTHOR'S NOTE

Each story may be different but at another level they are all the same. The entrepreneur took a leap of faith. Then struggled and strived for years. Before finally achieving a size and scale which made the effort what we call a 'success'.

For every such story there are several who are still out there, struggling, striving. This book will give them renewed hope and vigour.

And for those who look at themselves in the mirror each morning, before they head out to sell those soaps, I hope you catch in it a glimpse.

A glimpse of your hungry and foolish true self.

Rashmi Bansal

Mumbai, May 2010

CONTENTS

THE BELIEVERS

People who knew entrepreneurship was the Chosen Path. They took the plunge straight after their MBA or after working barely a couple of years. And they persevered until they made it big!

PGP is the two-year Post Graduate Programme in Management at IIM Ahmedabad. The year denotes when the student graduated.

CONTENTS

THE BELIEVERS

People who knew entrepreneurship was the Chosen Path. They took the plunge straight after their MBA or after working barely a couple of years. And they persevered until they made it big!

CONTENTS

THE OPPORTUNISTS

These entrepreneurs did not plan to take this path but when opportunity knocked they seized it. Their stories go to show that you don't have to be 'born with it', you can develop an entrepreneurial bent of mind at any age.

CONTENTS

THE OPPORTUNISTS

These entrepreneurs did not plan to take this path but when opportunity knocked they seized it. Their stories go to show that you don't have to be 'born with it', you can develop an entrepreneurial bent of mind at any age.

CONTENTS

THE ALTERNATE
VISION

These individuals are using entrepreneurship to create a social impact. Or as a platform which allows them creative expression.

CONTENTS

THE BELIEVERS

People who knew entrepreneurship was the Chosen Path. They took the plunge straight after their MBA or after working barely a couple of years. And they persevered until they made it big!

THE BOOK

OF JOB

Sanjeev Bikhchandani (PGP '89), naukri.com

Sanjeev is India's most successful internet entrepreneur. For close to a decade he struggled on the sidelines but never gave up on his Big Idea. In 2006, naukri.com became the first dotcom to IPO on an Indian stock exchange.

Sanjeev Bikhchandani is a man with a lot of energy. He strides into my office for the interview, makes himself comfortable and spends the first 40 minutes giving *gyaan* on how I should run my business.

Whatever he says makes perfect sense. The entrepreneur in me is taking mental notes, but the writer exclaims, "Gosh, this guy talks a lot!" Like the Energiser bunny he can go on and on and on. And that's actually an apt metaphor for India's most successful internet entrepreneur. The guy started early and simply never ran out of juice.

Not when he couldn't pay himself a salary for six years.

Not when he had to take up a second job to support the family.

Not when he got funded but the whole dotcom dream went bust.

The thing is, entrepreneurship was not one of many options for Sanjeev, it was the *only* one. But did Sanjeev imagine that one day his company Info Edge (commonly known as naukri.com) would be a darling of the stock markets? An industry leader with a market capitalisation of $1 billion (₹ 4,300 crore) at its peak,* and an absolutely scorching pace of growth?

The answer, Sanjeev honestly admits, is "Not really." The reason for starting his own company was independence. You are your own boss – doing your own thing, setting your own priorities. There was the urge to create something, do something different.

Success came along the way, but even through the days he ran a tiny business out of the servant's quarter, Sanjeev was happy. And that's what makes it such a fascinating story.

* As of May 2008, the market capitalisation stands at $630 mn.

THE BOOK
OF JOB

Sanjeev Bikhchandani (PGP '89),
naukri.com

"I have spent most of my life in Delhi. My father was in the government, he was a doctor. My mother was a housewife; there was no business person in the family."

Nothing out of the ordinary and yet Sanjeev, at age 12, had more or less decided which direction his career would take. "At that stage, the idea started forming in my head that, look, somewhere along the way, I should be starting a company of my own."

Sanjeev went on to study economics at St Stephen's college. The interesting thing is that he had got admission to IIT but did not take it.

"I thought it was a five-year course whereas BA was a three-year course, so let me study economics instead. Then, let me work for two years and go to IIM Ahmedabad."

The truth is, he wasn't inspired by engineering. Like most middle class kids living in government colonies, he just took the exam. But unlike others he had a mind of his own and the careless confidence to buck the trend. A trait you commonly find in entrepreneurs!

Sanjeev worked for three years and then got into IIMA. "While on campus, there was a group of us who would talk about entrepreneurship, think entrepreneurship. I took a few courses like LEM and PPID, which are more oriented towards entrepreneurship."

The plan was to work for a year or two and then start a company.

"I was clear that I was going to be in Delhi because my parents had a home – there was a safety net. I didn't have any capital. I thought I would work for while, look for an opportunity and then branch out on my own."

There was a desire to be different but Sanjeev did not actually do something different when he first started out. Except for the act of leaving a fairly comfortable job marketing Horlicks at HMM (now known as GlaxoSmithKline). Along with a partner, Sanjeev set up two companies – Indmark and Info Edge. The first specialised in pharmaceutical trademarks and the second produced salary surveys and reports.

But the thrill of doing one's own thing was palpable.

The company started life in the servant's quarter of his father's house, at a modest rent of 800 rupees per month. There were employees to be paid and often, a cashflow crisis on the 29th – just before payday. Sanjeev's own pay-cheque came from teaching at a couple of business schools over the weekend.

Luckily, there was an 'angel investor': Sanjeev's wife – and batchmate – who was working with Nestle. That's how they managed to run the house.

What I like is how he says this, matter-of-factly. "I had told Surabhi, even before we got married that I would soon quit and become an entrepreneur. I had told her that we will be living off your salary for quite a while. She was cool with it."

The more important bit: *he* was cool with it. Not all men are.

The thing with entrepreneurship is you can't afford to have a big ego. You want to stay in business, you do every bit of business that comes along. You want to keep the dream afloat, you don't care what the neighbours and relatives have to say about who wears the pants in your house.

And all the while you keep searching.

For that one idea, that one product or service which is going to make your company something more than a writer of reports, a doer of projects.

> **"I could see my future, had I continued as a manager in the corporate sector. If I was lucky, at the end of 5 years I'll be a senior product manager, in 8 years I'll be marketing manager... In 25 years I might be at CEO somewhere. All this if I am really good. I used to ask myself: Is this what I want in life?"**

That one idea which makes you a brand.

Ideas can come from anywhere. You could be sitting in a tub and have a eureka moment. Or in a bus or at your dining table. And so it was with the idea of a job database.

Sitting around in the open-plan HMM office Sanjeev would see colleagues flipping through *Business India*, the leading business magazine of that era. In those days the back of the magazine carried 35 to 40 pages of appointment ads and Sanjeev noticed that everyone read the magazine *back* to front.

The eureka moment?

"Everyone likes to be in the know on jobs."

Even at a company like HMM – a good employer – people were keen to track what else was out there. You may not be looking FOR a job but you would look AT a job. That was a valuable insight and Sanjeev just knew it had an application somewhere.

To top it all, every week headhunters would call and offer jobs that weren't ever advertised.

So there was a bunch of jobs out there and people interested in knowing about those jobs. If somebody were to aggregate this database and keep it current and live, you would have a product which solved a problem. And it could somehow be monetised.

Except there was no way to compile such a database and make it accessible easily and cheaply to users. And so it became one of those 'file and forget' ideas.

Until one fine morning an advertisement issued by the Department of Telecom appeared in the paper. The ad talked about 'Videotex' – a service where people would be able to access information stored on a central server from terminals all across Delhi.

The ad invited private players to create and maintain these databases, on a revenue share basis. And Sanjeev said, "Hey, why don't we make a job database on this platform?" Info Edge was shortlisted. A detailed project report with screens, navigation and UI was submitted. Alas, DoT shelved the project.

The year is 1993 and there are other things to worry about.

Sanjeev and his partner decide to go separate ways. Each partner kept one company, and half the employees and assets. Sanjeev was left with Info Edge. And the 'job database' idea came with it.

But life went back to the usual – reports, databases, market studies. Standardised stuff sold at a cheap price. Info Edge shifted back to the servant's quarters from the office in south Delhi it had inhabited for a brief while.

On a lower cost model, Info Edge made some money and Sanjeev managed to get construction work done at his residence. Once again the company shifted – this time into the second floor of his own house.

"As an MBA from Ahmedabad, we all have a hunger for multinational companies. Because it's prestigious. But to my mind, it is false prestige. You are a prisoner of your visiting card and the logo on it, a prisoner of your EMIs... Taking a risk becomes all the more difficult."

So things were okay. Not too good, not too bad. Business was growing, but slowly. And then Sanjeev visited an exhibition at Pragati Maidan called 'IT Asia'. Here, he was introduced to the internet for the very first time.

It was a defining moment. Just talking about it, recounting how it happened, Sanjeev gets all animated.

"I saw a stall titled WWW. I was intrigued."

I said, "What is this?"

He said, "Sir, this is the World Wide Web."

"What is the World Wide Web?"

"This is the internet."

"What is the internet?" I had never heard of it.

He said, "Sir, you can send and receive emails."

The stall was a reseller of VSNL internet accounts and mainly interested in selling an email id bundled with an internet connection. But Sanjeev didn't know anyone who had an email ID, so he didn't see the point. Whom would he communicate with?

Then, the guy added, "Sir, with the internet you can access a lot of information."

"On what?" Sanjeev asked. And the reseller gave a demo, on a rudimentary B & W monitor, on an interface which looked similar to DOS. He opened a site called 'Yahoo!' and typed a keyword search.

"Like this, sir, you can go and search for any information."

By now Sanjeev's mind was ticking. He thought, "Hey, that old idea that you shelved! This may be the medium for that."

He approached the reseller, "Look, I want to set up a website. How do I do it?"

He said, "Sorry sir, I can't help you. For that you need a server and all servers are in the US."

Sanjeev said "Fine, thank you."

> **"I didn't want to sign complex agreements, have somebody breathing down my neck and be under pressure for growth. I was comfortable, leading an uncomplicated life."**

But a thought had been set into motion – a way would be found. He went home and called his brother Sushil. Seven years his senior, an IIMA grad and a professor at UCLA.

I said, "Look I want to start a website on the internet. Have you heard of the internet?"

He started laughing. "Of course, we use it every day."

"I said, 'Okay, but it has come to India now, and I want to start a website but all servers are in the US. I need a server.'"

My brother said, "Yeah, sure."

I said, "But I don't have any money."

It was October '96 and the recession had hit. The company was back in the red. With one kid in the family and another on the way, Surabhi had also taken a break. By then Sanjeev had taken up a second job at the *Pioneer* newspaper as consulting editor of the career supplement.

When he explained the predicament, *bhai* said, "Don't worry, I will pay for your server until you are able to do it."

The shared server cost 25 dollars a month. In return, Sanjeev gave his brother a 5% share in the company. "He didn't ask for it, but I just thought it was fair."

Sanjeev then invited VN Saroja (PGP 1990) from IIMA on board. Saroja looked after operations in the start up team and got a 9% stake.

Now Sanjeev went to Anil Lall, a friend who was a very good programmer and worked from home on freelance projects. "I said, 'Look, I want a website.'"

Anil said he knew nothing about the internet.

Sanjeev said, "Never mind, I am sure you will be able to figure it out somehow."

In a week Anil called and said, "I can do it." And thus Anil became a founding partner of naukri.com with a stake of 7%.

Meanwhile, Sanjeev had got the classifieds of recognised newspapers from all over the country. He went to two data entry operators in the company sitting idle because business was low (remember, there was a recession!).

He pulled out the old file with a detailed structure of the jobs database and said, "I want you to input the jobs in your own words in this data structure."

In three days, they had 1,000 jobs. Within a week there was a server. The database and a navigation UI was handed over to Anil. Within a week, a website was ready. And naukri.com was up and running by late March '97.

Now at the time many people warned Sanjeev that 'naukri', 'naukar', etc was downmarket. But something told him it was distinctive, unique. He went with his gut and stuck to the name. "Today, it's one of our greatest assets."

Entrepreneurship is about dozens of small leaps of faith like this. Taken every day. Often, you have to take a contrarian stand. You can't say why but this feels right. And you have to have it your way.

The very act of becoming an entrepreneur is contrarian to 'middle class values'; study hard, get a good job, be happy with a secure income and steady salary.

"For the first six months we did not have an internet connection. We would go to Anil Lall's house with two floppies and he would upload the site. And our promise then was 1,000 jobs minimum on the site. Live and current. No job older then 30 days, all jobs taken from the newspapers."

Soon enough the site started getting traffic because it was one of the few sites targeting Indians living in India. Most catered to the NRI audience.

> "We knew how difficult it was to make money on the internet. We knew the value of money because we had always been short of money."

There were only 14,000 internet accounts in the country when naukri.com launched but to Sanjeev it looked like a large number.

Then naukri began to get press coverage. Because journalists were writing for the Indian audience. And when they wanted to quote, they would invariably quote naukri, because there was no one else. That became a big asset. The site got a great deal of press coverage in the first two years without even trying.

Not that he is trying too hard, even now. In the midst of our interview, Sanjeev gets a call from a journalist. He rolls his eyes and excuses himself. A ten minute conversation on 'job trends' follows. Sanjeev handles a lot of this stuff even now. *Karna padta hai*. Free publicity is the oxygen of any business. 10 cms of editorial coverage is worth a 100 cc of paid advertising.

The secret is that you – and your company – should be the 'go to' person for that industry. Any journalist writing on jobs will call Sanjeev. And he will be available.

The other asset which worked brilliantly for naukri was its own users. When folks began sending out covering letters referring to 'Your ad on naukri.com' recruiters took notice. *Yeh kaun si nayi cheez hai?*

Within six months of launch, a direct mail letter was sent out to 3,000 HR managers and recruiters. For 350 rupees you could list a job on the site. For 6,000 rupees you could get annual subscription which gave you unlimited listings through the year.

And thus, naukri.com began to get business. Low business, maybe ₹ 2-2.5 lakh, but in year two, more direct mails were sent out. "Revenues increased between 8-9 times in one year. I had not seen any of our products respond like that!" exults Sanjeev.

Suddenly, naukri was bigger than the rest of the company in terms of revenue, although it was still not profitable. Then, it broke even at ₹ 18 lakh a year. Sanjeev decided to shut down every other activity – no more reports, no more databases. "I put all people, all resources to naukri, and said: 'This is the future.'"

"I figured that perhaps this is the Big Idea. India is a large country, large working population, internationally growing."

Sanjeev was right. The world was soon caught up in a frenzy called the 'dotcom boom'.

The year was 1999. Investment bankers were throwing off their ties and setting up somethingsomething.com. Armed with four page business plans, they promised world domination of anyone, anywhere and anything online – subject to the receipt of 10 million dollars in venture capital funds. And some of them actually got it.

Sanjeev too started getting feelers. "We would like to invest in your company," they said.

His initial reaction: "I don't need your money… We are breaking even now. Next year, we will continue to grow, bring in Rs 50-60 lakh and make a profit. And I will be happy."

The truth was he was happy as a small company, operating from home. After years of struggle, he could finally see the word profit in the horizon.

"I didn't want to sign complex agreements, have somebody breathing down my neck and be under pressure for growth. I was comfortable, leading an uncomplicated life."

Around that time, he came across international magazines talking about dotcoms, Yahoo! IPO, valuations. "I figured something is happening in here. But I said I don't want the money anyway, no matter what the valuation."

But then, funded competition was launched. The advertising budget of jobsahead.com – just the launch – was twice as large as naukri's annual turnover. They had deep pockets. When that happened, Sanjeev realised the game had changed.

"You can't be a bootstrapped small company – 50 lakh turnover, five lakh profit. You gotta be a five-crore company with 50 lakh profit. To migrate from this orbit to that orbit, you need funding because there will be losses in the interim. Without those investments, you can't migrate from orbit 'A' to orbit 'B'."

A quick call was made to the investment bankers.

"We told them, look, we have changed our minds. They said, fantastic, great! Why don't you write a business plan? We quickly put together our business plan, which now looks very embarrassing."

Info Edge got funding from ICICI Venture in April, 2000. The company, with a ₹ 36 lakh turnover received a ₹ 45 crore valuation (which in those bubble days seemed modest). A month later, the market crashed.

"We also got lucky in many ways," muses Sanjeev. "We got the money just before the market meltdown. So, we didn't get time to spend it foolishly. We just put it in a fixed deposit. And through the meltdown, we spent the money on technology, products, people, offices, the sales team, getting new clients, trying to cut the losses."

This is when the importance of building good teams kicked in.

"Some of the people who joined at that time – just before VC money and just after the VC came in – have probably contributed more to building the company than I have," muses Sanjeev.

"I may have been the founder, led the bootstrap years from 1990 to 2000. But post 2000, a lot of the credit goes to so many others...."

One such person is Hitesh Oberoi, the COO. Sanjeev refers to him as the 'de facto CEO'. An IIM Bangalore graduate, Hitesh was working in Delhi in Hindustan Lever and joined naukri in the pre-VC phase. How did he manage to pull that off, I wonder? Ah, but those were the bubble days. Everyone and their uncle wanted to work for a dotcom!

Hitesh actually came to Sanjeev for advice. He had got an offer from another start up. Sanjeev talked to him for about 2-3 hours about life in a dotcom, what to look at, what the offer is like. At the end he said, "*Yeh sab theek hai*. But why don't you join us instead? You will be happier here because we will give you less money and salary but we will give you more stock."

Hitesh joined. He got a lot more stock (and ain't he happy about that today!). The other company collapsed a few months later.

Post VC funding, of course, Info Edge was able to hire more people, as there was money in the bank. And after the dotcom meltdown, when people were leaving dotcoms, naukri was one of the few which kept its eggs in the internet basket. It kept the faith, kept recruiting.

When you truly believe in the fundamental value of a business, it's not about cyclical ups and downs. People need to eat, they need to bathe, they need to get jobs. When the market crashed the bankers put away their jeans and brought back the ties. But the entrepreneur simply rolls up his sleeve and works twice as hard.

That is what naukri.com focused on: building a solid business. The company had money in the bank, and spent it slowly and strategically. There was a dotcom meltdown, an IT meltdown, general economic recession. There was 9/11. But right through that period, naukri kept growing.

Of course, it was a scary period. All around, dotcoms were shutting down, VCs were pulling the plug. But ICICI was patient.

The money came in tranches and incredibly enough, it was not linked to performance.

To their credit, ICICI did not hold back anything. The last tranche came one and a half years after the first one. But

"When I am talking to entrepreneurs, I always say base your business on deep customer insights, the way naukri was formed."

there was no renegotiation of the valuation.

"We kept growing but of course there were tough times. There was a point when we were losing ₹ 25 lakh a month in cash. And we had about 18 months of money left. That was the lowest point – in late 2001."

This mindset of frugality helped Info Edge. "We knew how difficult it was to make money on the internet. We knew the value of money because we had always been short of money. So when this 7 crore came in, we were very careful about how we spent it."

Now generally, you invest, costs climb and revenues climb later. But the encouraging thing here was that revenue kept climbing as the company executed very well on sales. And this, Sanjeev says, happened largely because of Hitesh.

Hitesh had no sales experience – he was a commercial manager in Levers. But this was probably a good thing. He had no preconceived notions on 'how sales should be done'. No cobwebs.

The company adopted a 'common sense approach'. A salesperson costs the company ₹ 10,000 rupees salary plus a mobile phone plus conveyance plus office space and use of the computer. All in all, 20,000 bucks a month.

So if this salesman can recover ₹ 25,000 a month, he is contributing. Then, you keep on hiring more and more sales guys, build structure and systems, open new branches and new markets. And that's what Info Edge did.

Every branch kept breaking even in six months, and before they knew it, Info Edge was a 300-person sales organisation with 10-12 offices all over India. There were two years of losses and then the company broke even at ₹ 9.5 crore. Along the way, Info Edge moved into a larger, swankier office in Noida, opened several branches, invested in techonology platforms and people.

Today, Info Edge has 1,650 people of which 1,200 are in sales.

Post break even, the company diversified. There was already an executive search operation. The company added Jeevansathi (a matrimony site), 99acres and allcheckdeals.com (property sites), naukrigulf (on local job trends in the Middle East), Brijj.com which is a social networking site and most recently, asknaukri, and an education portal, shiksha.com.

There are multiple lines of business but naukri is still the flagship brand, the one people have heard of the most.

As the company grew and became more and more profitable, it became increasingly logical by 2005 to do an IPO. In November 2006, Info Edge became the first pure Indian dotcom to conduct a successful IPO. At the time it had revenues of ₹ 84 crore and profits of ₹ 13 crore.

A year after its IPO, Info Edge is still growing at a crazy pace. In the year 2007-08, revenues stood at ₹ 239 crore with post-tax profits of ₹ 55 crore. The company's current market capitalisation is $630 million (over ₹ 2,500 crore).*

Many companies go through a phase of high growth. But the Info Edge story is way beyond that. In 2002, the annual turnover was a mere ₹ 3 crore with losses of ₹ 1.1 crore.

"In the year we made ₹ 84 crore (2005-06), our business plan had said we will make ₹ 12 crore. So we had *massively* underestimated our growth. The good bit was that whenever there was an audit in ICICI, on who committed what and is delivering what, we came out smelling like roses."

Of course, it's also about being in the right place at the right time. As the economy once again went into a growth phase and confidence in the internet was restored, naukri.com took

* As of May 2008

strong advantage of the opportunity.

But let me qualify that by right place and right time I don't mean he simply got 'lucky'. There was a fundamental belief in the product. And the genuine need gap it addressed.

"When I am talking to entrepreneurs, I always say base your business on deep customer insights, the way naukri was formed."

Let's say you have such an idea or insight. But it does not work right now, perhaps it is ahead of its time... Keep it, at the back of your mind. As the environment changes, as technology changes, you might be able to 'join the dots'. To connect different pieces of the puzzle and bring your concept to life.

Going to IT Asia was a wonderful break, but it was not something that just 'happened'. Sanjeev went to the expo every year, just to look around, get new ideas. He even had a strategy: avoid stalls of large companies, visit the small ones – they're more interesting.

Seek, and ye shall find!

Entrepreneurs are seekers. And they are always open to change. There are different kind of pressures operating at each stage – you evolve, and learn to cope with them.

"There was a certain pressure when you were not breaking even... There was a certain pressure when you took the VC money and the market melted down and you had to deliver growth... There are more pressures when your financials become more complex and another set of pressures when you do an IPO."

For Sanjeev, and most other entrepreneurs in the scale-up phase, the key personal transformation area was learning to delegate. It wasn't easy. "I had to learn to understand that it is not my company alone, anymore."

When you're going for that kind of growth it's all about getting good people, aligning them to a larger goal and making things work. When you have smart people, they will demand their space. They will demand respect. You have to empower them and get out the way.

But 'what if.'

What if Sanjeev hadn't got funding at the right time?

What if the dotcom industry had remained in the doldrums?

What if he was still trying to figure out how to connect those dots?

How long does one hang in there? 5 years, 8 years, 10 years… At what point would the entrepreneur throw in the towel? Decide to give up?

"Never," says Sanjeev.

"I could have quit any time in the first 10 years, and I would have been a failed entrepreneur. Why did I keep going? Because I wasn't chasing money. And if you chase something long enough, sooner or later you will get lucky. If you are really lucky then you will do it in 5 years, if you are moderately lucky then you will do it in 10 years, if you are terribly unlucky you will do it in 15 years."

"But if we had missed this bus, I would have continued working at what I was doing and maybe I would have succeeded at something else 5-6 years hence. The point is to try long enough and hard enough. I think persistence is a quality that you have to have, to be a successful entrepreneur."

If you love your work, and it gives your life meaning, then you will have fun through the difficult times. You will find it in your heart to keep going. You will never lose hope.

You see, there is no such thing as a failed entrepreneur. You are a failed entrepreneur only when you quit. Until then, you are simply not successful… yet.

ADVICE TO YOUNG ENTREPRENEURS

Be early. You can make your mistakes while it is cheap to make them, when there is no competition.

Do not exaggerate in your business plan. Undercommit and overdeliver.

Get great people – sell them the vision, the idea and share the wealth, be generous with offering stock.

If you are starting a business to make money, don't do it. Chances are that you will fail, because there WILL be hard times. And if your motivation is not something beyond money, those hard times will test you. You will quit and go back to your job. But if you are doing something other than money, you will rough it through the hard times.

I spotted the opportunity but I didn't know how big it was, how big it was going to be. I just said this is a smart idea, I love it! And it happened to be the right idea, at the right place, at the right time... If you are in enough places, enough times and long enough, you get your breaks in some form or the other. You just have to be smart enough to take them.

Scaling up is also a lot about letting go. Get smart people. If they are truly smart and if they have their self belief, they will create their own space and they will do stuff that maybe you can't do. Or may be you haven't thought of.

And do keep in mind that every choice you make impacts the family. If you live in a particular part of town, it will obviously impact the kind of school your kids go to. Frankly, these were the choices, the implications of which I did not consider. Thankfully, things have turned out well; the children also, the family also.

ROCK WITH IT, ROLL WITH IT

Shantanu Prakash (PGP '88), Educomp

Despite a regular middle class upbringing, Shantanu went into business while doing his BCom. The entrepreneurial streak continued after the MBA from IIM Ahmedabad. His company Educomp is today the leading provider of digital content for schools across India.

Are entrepreneurs born or made? Did they always know this is what they wanted from life or did an opportunity come up and light the way?

Shantanu Prakash grew up in an "absolutely typical middle class background." But he knew entrepreneurship was his calling, early in life. He founded a company while still in college and started another one right after graduating from IIM Ahmedabad.

And this was in the late '80s, years before entrepreneurship was in fashion.

The thing about Shantanu that strikes you is how much at ease he is as he relates the story. It's not like he made it big overnight, it's actually taken close to two decades. But through the hard times, the weak sales, the poor cashflows, he says it was "never difficult."

"When I look back, every single year of my life, I thought, was the coolest year of my life."

Sitting with him in the coffee shop of the amazing Trident Hotel in Gurgaon, a part of me said: "This guy is definitely lying. *Aisa kaise ho sakta hai...*" But at a deeper level, what he said seemed to ring true.

Your reality is what you make of it. If you see life with an 'all is wonderful in this world' pair of lenses, that's how it is.

This is against conventional wisdom. The middle class ethic of being careful and completely realistic about the big, bad world around you. But all I can say is the formula seems to have worked for Shantanu. His company Educomp works with 9,000 schools and six million students across India, US and Singapore, generating revenues of ₹ 276 crore in FY '07-08. Its market capitalisation is ₹ 7,000 crore. *

But like I said, it's the attitude with which it's been built which is more interesting than the building itself.

As of May 2008

ROCK WITH IT, ROLL WITH IT

Shantanu Prakash (PGP '88), Educomp

Shantanu Prakash was born in Rourkela, a small town with only one notable feature – the steel plant. Dad in SAIL, mom a school teacher, an upbringing no different from thousands of steel town kids in the 1970s.

After class 10, the family shifted to Delhi and he enrolled in DPS, a "shiny, big-city school." A reasonably good student, Shantanu joined Shri Ram College of Commerce. And that's when it first became evident, 'this guy is different.'

"Whenever my dad used to travel, he used to buy me books. In fact, I don't remember getting any presents except books. I used to read voraciously. And probably that unlocked something in the mind. Big thinking, big horizon and so on."

"Secondly, when my dad retired and wanted to come and settle down in Delhi, he found that he didn't have enough money to buy even a DDA flat. Right! So somewhere at the back of my mind I thought that if I need to make money, then working in a job is probably not going to do it for me."

While at SRCC, Shantanu started a company along with a friend. The business was organising rock music concerts. Not that he had any particular fascination for rock music but it was a good opportunity.

"We used to collect sponsorship from companies, do these events and shows in hotels and sell tickets. We made a lot of money."

How much? ₹ 4-5 lakh – truly a lot of money 20 years ago!

"I thought I was completely rich. And then the stock market bug bit me. So I used to be on the floor of the Delhi Stock Exchange, every single day for almost two years. Till I lost all the money! And I thought it was really cool you know – we were not going to college, doing things which were more 'adult'. It was just a completely different rush."

Shantanu got into IIM Ahmedabad although he was actually more keen on FMS Delhi.

"(Laughs) Honestly at that time I didn't know what this whole MBA thing meant... Someone from our event management company flew down to deposit the form in Ahmedabad, because it was too late to post it. So it was all a last minute kind of a thing."

Shantanu joined IIMA, even as the event management business back in Delhi continued to flourish. A contract had been signed with Thums Up to do a series of concerts all over India. A concert in Bombay was yet to be staged.

"Every weekend, in the first year of IIM Ahmedabad, I used to go down to Bombay and work with my friend organising this concert. It was a great hit. We got Remo to perform, it was held in a hotel in Bombay and one time when I came back, I had this board outside my dorm room in D-14, saying 'Visiting Student.'"

"So I had a complete ball during the two years in IIM Ahmedabad. Honestly, I didn't take it very seriously in the first year. Then in the second year, I said okay, let's see the curriculum, what it's all about. I always had this *bindaas* outlook. Why are these kids studying so hard, what is there to take so seriously here, you know! That sort of a thing."

And at the time salaries from campus weren't exactly stratospheric. Shantanu recalls that 17 of his batchmates joined Citibank at salaries of ₹ 7-8,000 a month in 1988.

Not surprisingly, Shantanu did not go for placements at all. With his friend and partner from the event management business he launched a company focused on education.

> **"You don't need any capital to start, you can start with zero capital. If you have capital, great. If you don't, it doesn't mean you can't start."**

The idea was to set up computer labs for schools. The business model was innovative – the schools did not invest. They only paid a monthly fee for every student who used the lab and signed a multi-year contract.

"That was the time when IT was coming into schools. So there was this whole mystery around IT. When we went and spoke to school principals, they welcomed us with open arms saying these guys know more about how to retrofit a computer lab in the school than we do. So we actually got off to a great start. Lots of schools."

In two years, the company did 50-60 schools and boasted a couple of hundred employees. The turnover was ₹ 4-5 crore. Again, huge for 1990.

But, there were ideological differences among the partners.

"I wanted the company to go in one direction, he wanted to go in another. But we were great friends, we are still very thick."

Shantanu decided to do something on his own. The partner kept the company and pretty much all the money, while he made a fresh start. The year was 1992.

Educomp started very small. And with a different focus. Instead of hardware, Educomp went into software. The first product it launched was a 'School Management System', an ERP of sorts for schools which took two years to build.

On paper it seemed like a phenomenal market to automate schools – there is a real pain that you are trying to address. But it wasn't a very successful product. After getting the product into 10 schools Shantanu realised that every school wants customisation. And they don't want to pay for the customisation.

"All the stuff they teach you in terms of case studies at IIM Ahmedabad, all that is really relevant. But while on campus you appreciate none of it because you haven't gone through the grind. Not understanding what running a business means, you later relearn all those lessons the hard way."

Besides, Educomp started its life with zero capital base.

"So one day you just opened shop, sat in one room with a computer and started?" I ask.

"Yeah, almost like that. I had two employees in the very beginning."

"What about the two years that went into developing the product?"

"A few school computer lab contracts kept some cash coming in," he says.

"But the focus was on building this piece of intellectual property. Even before it was fully developed, we started going to the market and selling the product. And I think I am quite a good salesperson. So I managed to convince a number of schools to buy it and business started growing."

Eventually the product was abandoned and Educomp expanded into digital content for schools, and subsequently into e-learning. Today if you look at the product portfolio, the company has footprints in almost every space from KG to class 12.

"But you are making it sound so easy," I protest. "From 1992 to 2006 (when Educomp got publicly listed) what was the process that you went through?"

> "Entrepreneurs are smart people, they manage the risk-reward equation very well. With an IIM Ahmedabad degree, the risk is not much. You can always go and start something. If it doesn't work out, somebody will give you a job..."

"Honestly speaking, for me it wasn't a difficult process at all. And I think it's more a mindset issue than anything else."

"I remember, the first office didn't even have a fan. But I didn't seem to mind at all at that point in time. I was so completely obsessed with what I was doing and what I was building. So every single year of my life when I look back, I thought, that was the coolest year of my life. That I was doing the most significant things that I could ever hope to do."

"And that basically translates into being happy. So one way to describe myself would be, you know, an eternal optimist. When you are an optimist some of the external environment stuff doesn't really bother you. It never bothered me."

Getting into the details of how the company grew, it was slow. Very slow initially.

In 1998, six years after starting, Educomp's revenues stood at ₹ 3.5 crore. Then the company started growing. In the year 2000, the topline was around ₹ 12 crore. Then it really took off and in FY '07-08, Educomp clocked revenues of ₹ 276 crore, with net profits of ₹ 70 crore.

Did something happen at the ₹ 4 crore level, due to which the company started growing 50-60%? Because a lot of people start a business but most of them are never able to work that scale-up magic.

Shantanu believes there are two questions which need to be asked:

a) Is the business inherently scalable?

b) Is the market opportunity large enough?

"In our case, the solutions that we were offering were technology based, so they could easily be scaled up. Secondly, the universe of opportunity in India is phenomenal. There are 220 million kids going to school. There are one million schools, five million teachers, all of that stuff."

"So even today, the market penetration levels are less than two per cent. And Educomp can keep growing 100 per cent over the next 10 years. Without reaching a saturation point."

> **"It's all about being an eternal, insane optimist. I never had the dilemma: Am I doing the right thing? Should I just shut this down and go take up a job? Never!"**

Additionally, the market started responding favourably to digital content.

"It could have happened 3-4 years earlier, it could have happened 3-4 years later. As far as we were concerned, we were passionate about it and believed this was the way to improve the quality of education." 75% of Educomp's revenues today come from licensing content to schools – helping teachers do their job better.

To grow, you need people. Good people. Of course all companies start with just a few, with the founder managing all the strategic functions. The question every entrepreneur grapples with then is, how can I get more people as good, or better than me?

"I wanted to work with high-quality, smart people. But the problem was, the high-quality smart people didn't want to work with me... So it was a lot of struggle."

One of the many reasons Educomp was eventually able to attract talent was because people easily become passionate about education.

"The trick is to identify the DNA in a person, where he or she wants to do something different, and wants to be differently incentivised. It means not just a big fat salary cheque, but things like stock options, the feeling of partnership, being part of a start-up organisation, fast growth, all of that. That's how I was able to get some really good people as partners."

Almost all of whom are still with the company. There are 4,000 employees at Educomp but the attrition rate is amazingly low, at less than three per cent.

Aisa kyun?

"People are happy, I would like to believe that. And the company is growing 100 per cent a year, we are now five times larger than our nearest competitor in India in this space... so where do you want to go!"

With the company going public, Educomp today has at least 25 employees who are dollar millionaires. Like all new-generation entrepreneurs, the secret sauce of stickiness lies in sharing the wealth. And the heat of growth is fuelled by a timely dose of venture capital.

Educomp received $2.5 million of venture capital in June 2000. It wasn't much of a struggle given the IT and dotcom boom at the time. The funding was wrapped up in two months.

Did life change after the funding?

"Practically – nothing. The canvas was always large. With more money you can just buy more paint and do a better painting."

Six years later when more funds were needed for expansion, Educomp decided to raise the money through an IPO.

"Our company had reached a critical size, and we thought that capital markets are ready. A lot of people ask us, 'Why did you take your company public at the small size that you had?' ₹ 50 crore in sales. We are very happy we took the company public rather than take private equity money."

The important thing is that Educomp went IPO at the right time in its growth curve. Since then the company has been growing 100% a year.

But 20 years into the business, isn't a sense of fatigue setting in?

"No, my role is changing, the company is changing, we have a phenomenal growth opportunity in front of us. Educomp is valued at about one and a half billion dollars (as of May 2008). I think we can be a ten billion dollar company in the next three years. So I am certainly there, in charge, driving growth for the company."

"Being an entrepreneur is the art and science of creating value."

There are new thrust areas. For example, Educomp is now building schools. The company will invest ₹ 3,000 crore in the next 2-3 years to set up 150-odd schools in India. The company is planning to get into higher education as well as making acquisitions outside of India. "So again, this is the most exciting year that we have ever had. But I felt the same way in 1995!"

There's the whole romantic aspect of taking your company, your creation to new heights. The desire to see your company doing better and better and better. And there is always a 'next milestone'.

"Milestones certainly keep one active and moving. But I think for me personally, understanding how value is created is a very fascinating subject. Studying consumer behaviour, getting new products out into the market, working with really smart people, it's a rush."

"Every single day of my life, I experience that and I go out of my way to create those experiences that give me the challenge of being alive, driving something, doing something meaningful. Especially in the business that I run, which is education, it's so easy to feel that you are contributing to society."

Wonderful! But have there been any sacrifices on the family front?

"I think my family said this guy is crazy. So let him do whatever he wants... When I got married, certainly I was an entrepreneur at that time, my wife was understanding. But business every year has become more and more demanding of my personal time."

"More than the monetary sacrifice, it is really the sacrifice of time when you are an entrepreneur. And that is a much more expensive sacrifice than money."

Shantanu admits he works 24x7. Even this interview is scheduled on a Sunday afternoon, right after lunch.

"My life is completely unidimensional. Yes, had I been working in a job, I would have been very conscious of leisure time, very conscious of how much I am working. Here I am working for myself. I had decided a long time ago that the next 10 years of my life I am completely going to devote to building up my company."

The family has learnt to be okay with it.

"But you don't *see* it as a sacrifice as such?" I persist.

"It is a sacrifice, no doubt about that. Maybe I am not intelligent enough to balance or do this right, I am not proud of the fact. I think the ideal situation is to be successful professionally and take out enough time for your family and for other vocations, hobbies."

"I have this nice little picture, it has not happened to me. That's something that I guess I will have to learn."

We all have to, actually.

ADVICE TO YOUNG ENTREPRENEURS

The risk-reward equation is completely in favour of the entrepreneur. There is no way that you will be economically rewarded less for being an entrepreneur than by taking up a job.

Recently, Educomp invested in an online tutoring company. This company, Three Bricks E-Services, was started by three very young IIMA entrepreneurs. Chandan Aggarwal, Riju and Mohit. They were in business for a year and a half and then Educomp acquired a 76% stake in their company.

In a short period of two years, each of these people, if you value their 24% stake in the company, would be worth at least ₹ 15-20 crore each. There is no way you can do that if you are doing a job. Impossible!

Two years you may struggle. If the average salary is ₹ 15-18 lakh p.a. (gross) how much do you make in five years? 18 x 5, right? After tax, you make some 50 lakh. In 5 years, I can guarantee you, any business you do, will earn you that. Assuming that you are at least a little bit intelligent, within a year, the valuation of your business itself will exceed fifty lakh. No matter what you do.

So if a 24-year-old entrepreneur came to me, I would say choose anything that you want, that interests you, the internal passion you have.

How to choose what to do? I came from a background where I did my Bachelors in Commerce from SRCC and then my MBA – no 'skills', right? So I could have chosen any domain, but you have to keep some of those key principles in mind – 'Is the opportunity big enough, are you able to make a contribution and fundamentally change something that generates value?'

THE CAT WITH NINE LIVES

Vinayak Chatterjee (PGP '81), Feedback Ventures

Vinayak quit his job at Pond's because he didn't see the point of selling soap for the rest of his life. Originally set up as a market research company, over the years, Feedback Ventures morphed into India's leading infrastructure advisory and engineering firm.

I am late for the interview – the Feedback office in Panchsheel Park, Delhi, is difficult to find. Miss a particular turning and you have to go several kilometres in the wrong direction, until you find your way back.

Kind of like what happens in life. You make a plan, even a roadmap. But there could be a vehicle coming at you at full speed from right around the bend.

Vinayak Chatterjee has faced these bends with courage and recovered from accidents of fate. Feedback Ventures had a near-death experience. Not once, but three times. Each time Vinayak managed to save it from extinction and hang in there, eventually taking the company to new heights.

Vinayak's story tells you that ability matters, determination matters, but ultimately so does destiny.

When life deals you a rough hand, it's not about how smart you are but how many people out there believe in you. It's the relationships you've built and the trust you've deposited in the Goodwill Bank which you will draw on. To get that second lease of life.

THE CAT WITH
NINE LIVES

Vinayak Chatterjee (PGP '81),
Feedback Ventures

Vinayak Chatterjee was brought up in a small town, about 40 kilometres outside Calcutta. His father was a production supervisor in a jute factory.

"Those were good days in jute, the factory was owned by the Scottish, so we had a good life – compound, swimming pool, all of that. My mother was a lecturer in Calcutta University, she taught economics and political science. So a reasonably middle class life, very small-town upbringing, only child."

Like so many middle class Bengali families, the Chatterjees were in the corporate world and teaching, but there was no history of anybody in the family having anything to do with business.

After schooling in Calcutta, Vinayak decided to go to Delhi for higher studies.

"It was the height of the Naxalite movement in Calcutta. I am talking about the mid '70s. In any case, because I lived far away, I had to stay in a hostel. I had some seniors, cousins from whom I had heard of St Stephen's. I applied and got in."

The college experience widened his perspective and exposed him to people from varied backgrounds, including those from elite schools. Instead of being diffident about it, Vinayak meshed in extremely well there, forged some deep friendships and became extremely confident. "I thrived in the open society that St Stephen's is! Certainly a valuable three years!"

Vinayak was very clear that he wanted to do economics. Even if he hadn't come to Stephen's, he would have pursued economics at Presidency College in Calcutta.

The prevailing value system in a middle class Bengali family for a child who does economics is to emulate Amartya Sen. Vinayak would have been happy enough to complete graduation and then go on to the Delhi School of Economics. He would have probably tried for the Indian Foreign Service and if that didn't work out, got a PhD and become a lecturer.

But then Vinayak sat for the CAT exam, mainly because of his best friend at Stephen's – Ajay Banga. Ajay was the younger brother of Vindi Banga, who had done extremely well at IIMA and joined HLL. So the entire gang sat for CAT with barely any preparation, and Vinayak made it to Ahmedabad. But then there was the dilemma: D School (Delhi School of Economics) or B-school.

Vinayak had almost rejected the IIMA option until his friends pointed out, "You can always come back to D School. But if you don't go take admission to IIMA, you are closing the gate. Take a look!"

As it turned out, Ahmedabad was good for Vinayak, although he hated the quanti courses and didn't quite take to production.

"First and second term, I really hated IIMA. Not for the grades and all that but for the quality of what I thought were puerile courses." By the third term, Vinayak warmed up to what management had to offer. He enjoyed courses such as business policy and marketing which had a wider perspective.

But Vinayak still didn't know what he wanted to do in life. So he followed the herd into summer training at Pond's. It was a high-profile job and Vinayak took the pre-placement offer that came his way.

Pond's treated him extremely well and confirmed Vinayak as Area Sales Manager just six months after joining. Two weeks after getting the confirmation letter, Vinayak told his boss he wanted to resign.

"Something in me revolted. I can't put a finger on it even now. But I just didn't feel my job had any content. I couldn't get excited selling Pond's cold cream or Cutex nail polish remover. It meant nothing. I looked at myself in the mirror and said that if these products don't mean anything to me, I am probably being untrue both to myself as well as to my employers to hang around in the job."

Not that he had any clear alternative. But Vinayak was clear about what he *didn't* want. Which is a start. "It wasn't an easy decision but it was a call of the heart that said if you don't like something, nobody is forcing you to do it." It was January 1982 and Vinayak was on the rough road to 'finding himself.'

Vinayak could have stayed on in Bombay, but chose to go back to the small town where he grew up, in West Bengal.

"I spent one month with my parents. I am an only child. They said, we told you to go to D School and do economics. Why did you go to IIMA and chase this... what they called the '*Maya Mrigaya*', the golden deer of money in the corporate world."

So, no great pressure from his parents to go back and bring in the bucks. But it was important to do *something*. Something respectable.

Vinayak had always enjoyed writing. He'd been part of the Stephen's magazine and also editor of the IIMA mag *Synergy*. So he thought, why not combine the business degree with journalism? There was an offer from C R Irani, to start the business section of *Statesman* in Calcutta. And an offer from Ashok Advani, to become the Bombay correspondent for the recently set up *Business India*.

But Mrs Chatterjee was more keen that Vinayak go back to IIMA and complete his PhD. She said, "You are 21, you can come out as a PhD at 23-24. So there is no hurry to take up a job." Vinayak did just that. He went back and joined the fellow programme (FPM) at IIMA.

"I remember putting my steel trunk and hold-all on the Ahmedabad-Howrah Express, the 48-hour journey, again

"In looking back it seems, we were in step with the turning in the economy. ... The truth is, it all just happened. In hindsight, you can call it strategy."

back in dorm 17, got my room. I chose the business policy area and started library work."

Then something interesting happened. Professor V L Mote called Vinayak to his house. And there he met Raunaq Singh, chairman of the Apollo group. Vinayak hadn't heard of him back then. Prof Mote introduced Raunaq, saying he had a company called Apollo Tyres which was badly in debt because the government had nationalised it. (There is a long history to this – the company was given back to the family after a Supreme Court judgement in 1981.)

But essentially, the chairman wanted an MBA to turn around the company. Prof Mote said, "Vinayak, we know you are back here to do a PhD but do you want this option of joining as executive assistant to Raunaq Singh?"

It was one of those uncertain phases in life. "One side of my mind was very clear that I don't want a multinational FMCG job. The other half was still not clear what I wanted to do with life. But picking up ideas, picking up opportunities, some being created, some coming my way, picking, moving on."

Vinayak decided to take the offer. He joined what was known as the 'Raunaq Group' in those days consisting of Bharat Steel Tubes, Bharat Gears and Apollo Tyres – a fairly large north Indian set-up. The next three years – 1982 to 1985 – were extremely challenging. Because in those years, Apollo Tyres actually turned around."

"It was not just me," Vinayak clarifies. "There was a very small team – one of them is currently the MD of Ceat Tyres, Paras Choudhary – and the other is now the chairman of Apollo Tyres, Omkar Kanwar." However, at 22, Vinayak was the youngest person of the lot.

The work was hectic but satisfying. Very different from selling more cold cream. This was all about being part of the big picture – getting your hands dirty, taking small and big decisions which re-engineered the very DNA of the company.

"I was flying from Delhi to Cochin every Monday, visiting the plant at Thrissur in Kerala. Revamping 22 branch offices, product development, marketing. But to cut a long story short, I actually learnt 'real time' management. There was a lot of environment management in those days – licensing, pacing the corridors for loans from IDBI, industry meetings, tyre industry associations." Raunaq Singh was the chairman of Assocham, so Vinayak's job included writing his speeches.

"Those 3-4 years were brilliant. I got *dhakkaoed* but I learnt a lot. In many senses, Apollo Tyres was my finishing school. They grounded me in practical management *ki Hindustan mein business chalaane mein kya hota hai.*"

Something which every fresh MBA definitely needs to learn!

The other thing was that having seen the world top-down, from the chairman's office, Vinayak realised that he still wasn't excited by the proverbial rat race. "At the age of 45, if I am damn good, I will be the MD of Apollo Tyres. So what?"

It seemed like a pretty easy thing to achieve, where was the challenge? And that's what sparked the idea of becoming an entrepreneur.

As it happened, Vinayak's wife Rumjhum worked with the well known research agency IMRB. It was she who brought to his notice a business opportunity. Dorab Sopariwala and Titu Ahluwalia had broken away from IMRB and started MARG in Bombay. It was the first real competition IMRB had tasted. But there was nothing like MARG in Delhi.

By this time Vinayak felt it was time to do something new. He was all of 26.

"I realised that I had some weaknesses. I am not a details guy. I am better at strategy, marketing and networking than operations. In those days I believed I didn't know finance also. So I said if you have to start a business, let's put together a group of like-minded people who also complement each other's strengths."

Vinayak roped in some of his batchmates – B K Jain (the batch topper) and Ram Subramaniam. Also his wife Rumjhum, who was a Calcutta University psychology graduate. And a very good friend from Stephen's – Rashmi Malik – an IIMA batchmate who had worked with AF Ferguson.

Each member of the team brought in some special skills. Ram, for example, was an IIT engineer, MBA and CA who had worked with Prof SK Bhattacharya, in management structural systems. He is the current vice chairman of Feedback Ventures. Jain and Rashmi Malik are no longer with the company.

The team decided that starting a market research firm made sense and put in ₹ 15,000 each as start-up capital. At that time, 'Feedback' seemed a very logical name. That name has stayed, though the company has nothing to do with marketing anymore.

The first thing the young entrepreneurs did was meet Prakash Tandon and ask him to be their honorary chairman. To celebrate this, Feedback threw a large party and blew up half of its initial capital! But luckily, clients were not hard to find. Batchmates from IIMA had reached managerial level. Someone was with Nestle, somebody in AmEx. Market research projects started coming in.

"So we were in business. The market research business... but you know in this line, events overtake you." The story of how Feedback went from a market research agency to an infrastructure company is more accident than design. Serendipity, not a well-chalked-out strategy.

Vinayak's old employer Raunaq Singh came to him and said, "There is a group called Booker (the same people who give the Booker Prize) who want to set up a factory. Will you do it?" He agreed.

Feedback went in as market research consultants. "But they saw in us a capacity to help them build up a project in India where they did not have management. So we ended up building a factory. Then word spread that this group of guys from IIMA, professional ethical chaps are available to do this kind of work."

It was 1991. Narasimha Rao was the Prime Minister, India was opening up. FDI had just started coming in and with delicensing, many new multinationals were entering the

"What management education does is provide you a perspective. But it doesn't force you to work for anybody else. It's an education degree, that's all."

country. Feedback helped set up the Coca Cola plant, General Motors plant and several other industrial plants. And the business model shifted. Feedback vacated the market research space to focus on setting up factories.

"We ran the MR business for five years – from 1985 to 1990. We were number four in the country, with 4-5 branch offices, good clients. It was a good business but we somehow got more excited by the project's story." Market research services had become boring. Soap *ka* colour, toothpaste *ka* taste – that kind of thing. But to get into land, FIPB, industrial policy, civil engineering, machinery clearances, import licences – the value chain seemed far more exciting and interesting.

"That has always been important to you – that what you do should be exciting?" I ask.

"True... Money is a by-product. Business growth, turnover, bottomline is a by-product of what your heart and head want you to do. So if you follow that, money will follow. *Woh Gandhi waali baat hai.* 'Find purpose and the means will follow.' That has held true for us. I saw that hoarding in Bombay a few years ago and said, 'Ah, that applies to our lives'!"

Find something you want to do, that you are passionate about and *paisa to koi na koi dega*. Unless it's a stupid idea!

The switch to projects happened easily and naturally for Feedback, there was no real sacrifice involved. Word spread and work flowed in. Then a state government heard about Feedback.

"By a very interesting quirk of fate again, we got called by the government of Tamil Nadu to do India's first private sector industrial park in Chennai, which today is, incidentally, called Mahindra World City. So by the mid-nineties, we got into industrial parks from factories."

And a company of 5-10 people grew and grew until it reached its current strength of a thousand professionals. The plan is to ramp up to 5,000 in the next 3-4 years. But surely there must have been some bumps on this road? Some tipping point?

"Well, one more point of inflection for us – we took the infrastructure position in 1997. And that happened because of a meeting with Mr Deepak Parekh. And he, in many senses, has been a mentor for me, personally, as well as for the company."

Feedback's first real outside shareholders were HDFC. Now there is also IDFC. These are the two biggest shareholders and the chairman is common – Deepak Parekh. And he took a lot of interest in Feedback, guided the company, suggested it should go for private equity. One piece of advice from him which Feedback took was: 'position the company as an infrastructure specialist'. And it wasn't so fashionable back then either.

"Everybody said *kya kar rahe ho, mar jaaoge. Factory banaa rahe the.*" Nevertheless, Feedback gave up factories and got into hardcore industrial projects – parks, roads, highways.

But is it necessary to vacate an existing space to capture a new one? Don't many companies somehow manage both? Well, many do but Feedback has always just moved from one thing to the next.

"See, our infrastructure position is such a wide umbrella. We are putting up 5,000 kms of roads and SEZs, even hospitals. We do advisory but our biggest volume business now is engineering. We have 600 engineers and we do everything from fundamental engineering and designing to construction, supervision and project management."

Feedback describes itself as 70% engineering, 30% consultant.

Consulting comes easy to MBAs, but hardcore engineering and execution of mega projects is a whole different cup of coffee. How did that happen? Well, Vinayak traces it back to a chance meeting with the then Malaysian High Commissioner, Mr Nambiar.

He asked, "What do you do?"

I said, "We are doing infrastructure advisory."

He said, "Isn't engineering an option?"

I said, "Yes."

He said, "There is a Malaysian company which wants to enter India."

So Vinayak and Ram went and met the company, liked them and did an on-the-spot 50:50 joint venture. The company was called HSS Integrated. Basically, they brought in pre-qualification, or PQ, and in a few years Feedback bought them out.

The question is which came first, the chicken or the egg? The infrastructure position or the JV?

"The position came first, the JV follows. There is something called destiny also that comes into play. Of course, one has to be a little opportunistic. We didn't think that much. When doing the JV, Ram and me both said, '*Mistake hua to dekha jaayega*.' And today Feedback is one of the top ten engineering companies of the country. With 5,000 kilometres of roads, bridges and industrial parks to its credit.

But the company is a little low profile. Is that a conscious choice?

"You know, every time someone thinks of a project in infrastructure, my phone rings. We don't require brand equity more than that. I can't even handle the traffic today – my order books are bursting."

An IPO will happen but in 2-3 years time. There is no immediate hurry as the company is adequately capitalised with new shareholders like L&T coming in. But the original promoters still hold 40% of the company. The plan for the next few years is 'ORRU'; which sounds straight out of a Phantom comic but basically means 'Organic Rapid Ramp Up'. Increase market penetration, market share, market size in existing lines of business.

But it wasn't a smooth ride all the way. There was, in fact, a point when the company almost shut down.

"Somewhere in '98-99, we built up overheads far higher than our order book. We had negative cash flows." It was the second last day of the month and there was no money to pay salaries.

Vinayak boarded a flight to Mumbai, went to Deepak Parekh and cried, "Sir, I really need some help." I am drowning and need to be rescued was more like it! And Parekh lowered a lifeline.

"There are people who believe in you. He looked me straight in the eye and said, 'You will be able to get out of this mess if I bail you out now?'" Five minutes later Vinayak walked out of the office with a cheque in his hands.

Again it sounds like 'oh this was meant to be' in hindsight but there were some very tough years, around '98-99. Some divisions were shut, people were asked to leave. Also the transition from advisory to infrastructure was not taken very kindly by some of the senior management.

To cut a long story short, three times in its history, for reasons of bad business planning, or wrong decisions, Feedback came close to liquidation. If some friends or institutional assistance had not bailed the company out, put in money without any security or collateral, purely on faith... Feedback would have been history.

"And that is a debt that I can never repay in my life.The financial debt is cleared, we are debt-free today, but it is a very humbling experience. Because today if anybody calls and says, 'Oh you are successful today', I know in my heart of hearts there were three occasions when I have made such stupid mistakes, that I was almost on the road."

"And somewhere you realise it is divine intervention. You realise, that *apni aukaat se* you can only do so much, and you will make mistakes in life. But if you are honest to your purpose, you've never cheated anybody and you show clear focus, commitment, there are people in society who will go out of their way to back you."

So Feedback, in a sense, has been a very philosophical experience. Of course, there were hard decisions but always a sense of fair play. *"Aisa nahin ki cost control kiya to apna salary aadha nahin kaata. Sab ka salary kaata."*

Three times the company 'almost' died. Each time the mistake was a different one?

"One time it was to do with a very high ramp-up. Then at one point we got tempted to think we could be developers. So we took a licence to develop a 100-acre township, put a lot of time and effort behind it and then realised that we were inadequately capitalised."

"Also there is a thing called DNA. Everybody can't do everything. And we realised that it was not in our DNA to be a developer. We could be very good knowledge providers to developers like L&T or DLF."

The third near-miss was in the early '90s. Each time it was tough. But once you come out of it, you are stronger. You have learnt the meaning of 'taking a risk'.

Speaking of which, time and again people talk of the 'risk' of quitting a job and going into business. But every entrepreneur I meet scoffs at the idea.

"What risk? At most the partners would lose the ₹ 15,000 capital. A reasonable amount in those days but well worth it. There was no livelihood risk – jobs would always be available. And a 2-3 year blip in your early 20s would hardly mean losing the rat race."

"The real issues that bothered us was the peer group, what your friends and family will say if you fail. We just decided to be thick-skinned about it."

The interesting thing about Vinayak – and so many entrepreneurs – is that sense of self-awareness. The knowledge that hey, I may have bagged one of the 'most wanted' jobs on campus but that does not define me. I am more than my visiting card or salary slip.

"In our time, FMCG marketing jobs were held as Totem Poles of managerial success. There was excessive hype and glamour about multinationals but I just never got what's so great about selling Dreamflower talc in rural India. I care a damn!"

The trick is to find something you care about and do a damn good job of it. And that applies to just about anything.

ADVICE TO YOUNG ENTREPRENEURS

My only advice is, be true to your inner voice. *Joh karna hai tumhe zindagi mein, woh karo*. If your inner voice says you really love the rat race and can be great in the rat race, please do it. Just don't attach any value systems to it. Many of my batchmates have made great careers for themselves, built great brand equity, done well as global managers. If your inner voice says, that's my route, go for it!

If your inner voice says, my route is social entrepreneurship, do it. If your inner voice says, I want to be an author, journalist, write books, please do it! I had a colleague from St Stephen's, Ramchandra Guha, who did economics and became a noted historian. And look at the brand equity that he has today.

What I find is many people hear that inner voice but just don't have the conviction to act upon it.

Don't get too concerned about peer pressure. You may be successful, you may be unsuccessful, but in the philosophical market, what is success and what is failure? At least you will have the pleasure when you face yourself in the mirror to say "I did what my inner voice told me!" *Koi phikr nahin hai, tu apna kaam kar*!

I don't want to put a premium on entrepreneurship. It's not a fad or fashion to follow.

So my only piece of advice is find a purpose, the means will follow. Life's journey will take you wherever it is. Don't worry about the fruits. *Woh Gita wali baat hai – nishkaam karmayoga* – duty without desire.

But be prepared to stick it out. Remember Narayana Murthy's quote: "It has taken me 25 years to become an overnight wonder."

SOFTWARE
COWBOYS

Ashank Desai (PGP '79),
Mastek

In the early '80s, much before IT was a buzzword, Ashank Desai set up Mastek along with a couple of friends. Mastek was the first company to focus on India as a market and is today one of the top 15 IT companies in the country.

Jab chaar yaar mil jaayein it can be an all night drinking session, or a $200 million dollar company. That is the story of Mastek.

Mastek may not be the biggest Indian IT company in terms of size or scale, but it is certainly one with a lesson for many an entrepreneur wanting to start a company with his college buddies. More than friends getting together though, it is friends *staying* together for 25 years that is intriguing. Because partnerships which endure are such a rare thing in today's world!

Many a dream is born on an IIM campus, only to die out when faced with the real world. However Ashank, Ketan and Sundar kept that dream alive and made it happen. What's more, they did this in an era when it took, on average, 15 years to get a telephone connection. And you could start an IT company, but forget about owning a PC. In fact, the 'PC' was not even in the market, technically speaking.

But life in the Doordarshan era was kinder and gentler. There was less pressure to perform, and leeway to make some mistakes. The team was young and flexible, and figured out a way. And they had patience, which is another commodity in short supply today!

It takes a bit of patience to reach the Mastek office in SEEPZ, where I am to meet Ashank. I have to 'declare' all the electronic equipment I am carrying – none of which is re-checked on the way out of the place! I may not have managed to smuggle out anything of value to customs, but two hours with Ashank left me feeling richer for the experience.

SOFTWARE COWBOYS

Ashank Desai (PGP '79), Mastek

--Ashank Desai came from a family where becoming a professor, doctor or engineer was the ultimate goal. Yet he had the *keeda* of entrepreneurship somewhere, at the back of his mind.

"When I was at IIT I thought I should 'do something'... Then I worked for some time and I said, 'Yeah, I should do something.' But I think somewhere in IIM it got crystallised," recalls Ashank. This was in the year 1978.

There are always stories about how rock bands get formed. And it's the same with companies. How do the founders actually come together? Usually they are classmates, colleagues or old friends.

The core group at Mastek was formed on the IIMA campus – Ashank, Ketan Mehta, Sundar and Wasan. The group would sit and discuss what kind of venture they could take up after passing out. They decided to make use of a course called PPID (Project Planning Implementation and Development) to actually put together a workable plan.

The team took up a project based on 'IT' which at that time was a little known concept. They took advantage of being IIMA students and contacted very senior bureaucrats in Delhi and IIMA alumni.

"We sent out mailers which said, 'We want to start this

business, would you please help us?' And some of the people contacted, such as Kishore Kher and Arun Nanda, actually responded positively."

So inspiration, advice, contacts, all that happened in IIMA. And to top all that there was the support of IIMA professors, in particular Prof Mohan Kaul and Nitin Patel from the IT department. Their interest in the project indicated to the team that they were on the right track.

Placement was not on Ashank's mind because he had taken study leave from Godrej and hence, had a 'moral commitment' to return to the company. Keeping in mind the 'IT' business plan, Sunder joined HCL and Wasan went to IDM, while Ketan took up a job with NOCIL.

Of course, there was this feeling that it's fine to plan but once you get a job, once you get married, all this will be over. Yet somehow they managed to keep the spark alive.

Ashank's employer, Godrej, offered the advantage of a house. So the friends literally 'stayed together'. "I tell Jamshyd Godrej that you are indirectly responsible for starting Mastek," grins Ashank. The flatmates spent most nights chatting away till 2 am, discussing their business plans. In fact neighbours remarked, *"Kya karte ho tum log, baatein karte rehte ho!"*

The options considered included market research, voltage stabilisers and even manufacturing computers (they were not called PCs at the time though!). But finally they settled on IT because it required less investment, no manufacturing and also, it was a field they were comfortable with. The other big decision was to be based in Mumbai, for reasons of both head and heart.

But did Mastek actually see the full potential of IT? The way in which it would transform all our lives? Yes and no. This was the era when computer data was stored on 'tapes' and Ashank admits they had no clue about the PC revolution which lay ahead. But they did know IT was important to companies at a strategic level; software as a field would grow.

"We genuinely believed, and still believe, that IT should help with management decisions, it should offer solutions. That's why we didn't call ourselves Software Technologies, or Information Systems, but 'Management and Software Technologies' (Mastek, in short)."

Sundar was the first to leave his job, followed by Ketan. By this time Ashank was married and so he was the last to quit, six months later. The year was 1982. Mastek was born in Ghatkopar, where Ketan had a house. The total investment was ₹ 15,000. Business started coming in through friends and contacts. Sundar's stint at HCL helped, and the first big contract Mastek secured was from Richardson Hindustan (now Procter & Gamble), through IIMA classmates.

It was a classic management problem. Richardson Hindustan were manufacturers of Vicks. It was a product whose peak demand was in June, July and August (the cough and cold season, so to speak). The dilemma they faced was whether to manufacture in advance and stock goods or produce just in time. There were costs and benefits associated with each option. Other consultants had tried to tackle the issue but hadn't come up with a satisfactory solution so they said, "Let's try these guys. They're young and might have a fresh approach."

Using a computer lying in their laboratory, Mastek built a complete model based on the transportation algorithm. "I remember we found it very challenging and we solved that problem very well. I am very proud of that, although it is so small compared to our size as a company today. But I still feel good about it and in fact, I talk about that example when I address new recruits."

In those days there was no concept of 'user interface' – it had to be created by writing a 'C' code. Luckily, Wasan was good at that. That first contract was worth ₹ 30,000 and also fetched Mastek a bonus for completing the work ahead of time.

Like many other MBAs who take up entrepreneurship, Mastek capitalised on the intellectual capital of its founding team to get into the game. How you leverage this advantage and take the company to the next level is the crux of every success story.

"When Mastek had its IPO, software was not known to brokers. Many of them asked, 'Do you make floppy disks?'!"

Mastek quickly moved out of Ketan's drawing room to Nariman Point because they wanted a 'good address'. It was a 35-square-foot office, but it was in the prestigious Mittal Towers. The other problem was that there was no phone in Ghatkopar – it used to take 15 years to get a connection in those days!

A jeweller friend agreed to take their calls, but he stopped when there were one too many! Sounds like science fiction in today's day and age but it tells you the kind of 'true grit' one needed to get into business in pre-liberalised India.

"We started business with a public phone. We did not have a computer for the first five years, can you imagine that?", grins Ashank. The business was executed at the customer's office, on their machines. "But it was a difficult time. Like all new businesses, it took time to stabilise. We were not earning money..."

The partners took ₹ 1-2,000 as 'salary', after meeting all expenses. At this point, friends and batchmates working for multinational companies were 'moving up in life' while the Mastek team was travelling second class. So, once in a while, the thought of closing down and getting back to a job did come to mind. But what carried the team was two things – moral support from the family and the vision of building an institution.

Mastek had, in fact, started hiring people soon after it started operations. It was clear that the company did not want to be a 'boutique' based on the skills of a few individuals.

One of the important people who joined Mastek early on was Sudhakar. He was working with Rediffusion, a client of Mastek, and was so impressed with the young company that he asked to come on board as a partner. Meanwhile one of the founders, Wasan, moved on.

An exhibition by CSI (Computer Society of India) proved to be a turning point of sorts. The PC had just been launched and Mastek was the only software company to advertise there. The company bagged orders from companies like Citibank and Hindustan Lever through its visibility at this event. So Mastek started getting some kind of traction in the market and somewhere, the IIM brand also helped. But the 'struggle phase' lasted six years.

"I came across a management book which said the average time required to stabilise a business is 6-7 years. They reached this conclusion after studying 10,000 companies," says Ashank. "By stabilise I mean a sense of constant inflow happening. You can see some longer period in terms of business. Some profit, or at least a break-even." The feeling that one is here to stay.

By year six, Mastek was in *Dataquest* magazine's list of top software companies in the domestic market. The company was ranked #6. "So we said 'Aha! We are not small now!'" The actual turnover of the company at this point was ₹ 46 lakh. The year was 1988.

Where to, from here? Ashank believes there is a difference in the trajectory followed by Mastek, compared to other software companies. Mastek was one of the first companies in India to build 'software products'. It introduced both financial accounting and stock broking packages. The company also signed on with 'Ingres', a database package competing with Oracle.

Selling these packages, as well as custom-made software, made for a sound business. But it was clear that high growth would be possible only through exports. The question was, how does one crack the overseas market?

"The other strategy was to divide the project into many micro steps so that every delivery gets some money. In time some banks started giving credit against invoices."

"The IT industry is like sitting on a tiger. You have to keep reinventing yourself."

The team had no experience in software export. Neither did it have a family or friends' network in the US. "That's the way it started, all exports in India at that time. Some NRI cousin would say, 'Can you do so and so project for my company?'"

So Mastek took much longer to break into the export market. In fact, it took 10 years. Ashank was the first person from Mastek to go abroad. It was a big thing; he recalls, all his colleagues came to drop him at the airport as he boarded the flight to Singapore!

The role models for Mastek were TCS and Tata Burroughs. Yet Mastek stayed true to its roots, which lay in 'solutions'. The bug was to do something different, to build complete solutions for the global markets.

So in 1989-90, the company began working on a product called 'MAMIS' – a manufacturing ERP which was unheard of at the time. The company received venture capital of ₹ 80 lakh for this project from TDICI (an ICICI company). TDICI had burnt its fingers eight times, Mastek was the ninth company it funded. But the faith was well placed this time. Mastek went public in 1992 and TDICI made a 25x return on its investment.

Mastek was the first software company to go public post liberalisation at 'free-pricing'. Its shares were sold at a 60-rupee premium. Incidentally, 80% of Mastek's revenues, at the time of its initial public offering, came from the domestic market. Yet people had faith and invested.

Mastek itself strongly believed in the domestic market. The company's approach was to build products and solutions which were IT based, launch successfully in India and then take them to the world market. It did not quite happen that way, but that was the operating philosophy.

What happened was that the Indian market opened up to foreign software. The entry of SAP effectively killed MAMIS. As one of the founder members of NASSCOM, Ashank was one of the people who pushed for software duty to be reduced to zero per cent. Which was good for Indian industry as a whole but not for domestic software companies like Mastek.

What about the money Mastek took to build MAMIS? Well, that capital was not linked to the development of a particular product so the world did not come crashing down.

Interestingly, in those days, there was no concept of valuation against the future, or 'sweat equity'. To get ₹ 80 lakh, Mastek would have had to give away 80% of the company at book value (net worth at the time being less than a crore). The arrangement thus, was that TDICI gave a loan which was repaid against the royalty. Later, as part of NASSCOM, Ashank was to play a big role in changing all this and bringing in the culture of 'sweat equity'.

There is a point in the life of a company when it just takes off. Pre-IPO, Mastek's revenues stood at ₹ 4 crore. By the end of that year, the company was doing ₹ 9-10 crore. Exports were booming and so was the domestic market. Financially, life became comfortable, there was no everyday struggle or problems in paying the promoters a fair amount.

This comfort is an important turning point in the life of an entrepreneur. Because 'working capital' is the one thing that stresses any and every start up. Ashank still recalls the book he would carry around, with details of how much money was to be collected and from whom. There was no finance available from banks for software, where there are no physical assets to pledge.

The trick was to get 20-30% advance from customers. The other strategy was to divide the project into many micro steps so that every delivery gets some money. In time, some banks started giving credit against invoices.

The next phase from '95 to 2000 was one where the company focused on exports. One of the partners, Sundar, practically settled in the US to make this happen. Ashank was based in India but running around all over the world – Singapore, UK, Germany, Japan. Ketan and Sudhakar were busy building the software, the team and the organisation as a whole.

> **"I don't know whether we made
> sacrifices. Ultimately all of us do
> what we do, because we like it. Yes,
> if you take a normal family life,
> ours was definitely not balanced...
> I took my first holiday 15 years
> after starting Mastek!"**

"So it was a good thing that we started, Narayana Murthy, myself... " muses Ashank. Software exports became a larger cause and that helped the whole industry, including Mastek. Ashank became chairman of NASSCOM in 1996, taking over from FC Kohli. "That gave me some kind of feel of how the world operates, helped us on the strategy front."

The other major milestone was building internal systems and processes, so crucial for any company but especially in software. No outside consultants were involved, it was all done by the founding team.

Ashank was passionate about HR while Sudhakar and Ketan put into place the software development side of it.

Take the appraisal system, for example. It came into being in 1987 when the company was relatively young, with just 35-40 people. Mastek also built a 'balanced score card' system in 1991-92 to make sure that even at the lowest level, people were connected to the company's larger goals and mission. In software development, this manifested in things like ISO 9001.

Then came the very important concept of financial discipline. The idea being that an organisation has to run through systems and processes, in a predictable way, without human interference.

"Remember how I was making phone calls in '88-89 to get money from clients? This showed lack of discipline. My programmer should be the project leader. He should automatically collect money because he is responsible for it. Why should the owner of a company, even in '88-89, start calling? So we built those systems and processes as well as motivation and incentive for everyone to take charge of financing, cost."

The company started measuring gross margin and incentivising people on that. And of course, IT was put to good use to make it easy for all this to happen at the click of a button or two. The top management could keep track of what was happening. At the same time, it was not interfering unless necessary.

Powered by strategy, systems and new markets to conquer, by the year 2000, Mastek achieved a turnover of ₹ 250 crore with 900-1,000 employees on board. The growth rate on the export side was 40-45% year on year. Mastek has consistently ranked among the top 10-15 in the software industry.

Of course, keeping one's place itself is a challenge because in IT, technology is ever changing. However, Mastek was able to keep up with the times and the arrival of the internet, for example, impacted the company positively.

As a solutions company, Mastek had built a lot of work in the internet domain much before any other Indian company, including a tool called JAAL. So the company did a lot of work for dotcom companies but, unfortunately, also lost a fair bit of money when most of these companies went down the tube in 2001.

However, Ashank has no regrets. In fact, he recalls, it was a conscious decision to stay away from Y2K work and focus on the internet and new technologies which were more challenging.

Of course, building websites hardly seems 'challenging' today – 12-year-olds can do it with a variety of free tools available online. But back then, building a complete marketing portal interface for companies with e-commerce capability was a 'high technology challenge.'

"When you are sitting on a small market, you have to be good at many things."

> **"Ultimately, when you are running a company, you have a risk, you have a responsibility to make it successful. So the buck stops at you. So to that extent, there is a difference between an executive and the owner."**

The point is, the bar keeps moving and you have to move with it. Technologies change, customer requirements change and your old software gets obsolete in no time.

The other challenge was handling many different things. As the Indian market for software was relatively small, it made sense for Mastek to keep its fingers in many pies to stay profitable.

However, once you enter the global arena, it's a much bigger market. There you can focus and be number one in a specific area. So, there is less turbulence in what you do.

"The point I am making is stability versus size. When you are small, you have to do 20 different things. Smallness adds to the complexity of operations."

Mastek was doing work across many industries upto the year 2000. The company was trying to figure out what worked best for it. With time there came focus but the question is who decides *what* to focus on?

"There is always debate and discussion. There is sometimes a fight... Sometimes we agree to disagree. All that happens, but if you trust each other, a consensus emerges." Although all partners do not enjoy the same shareholding, in the sense of what say they have, and what they do, they operate as equals.

Of course, Ashank reflects, they may have been lucky. The partners had spent close to four years living together, on campus and sharing a flat, and knew that they would be able to work together. This 'courtship' period built a mutual trust and respect for each other and a sense of common values.

Coming to the most recent phase, post 2000 was the era of 'focus'. Under an initiative dubbed 'MASTEK First', the company decided it made sense to focus on large customers and in particular, the financial space. In insurance, for example, the company has built a package and the Gartner Group has given Mastek a ranking as one of the promising companies in this space.

Further, Mastek's core strength lay in systems integration and large projects, so that was the positioning the company adopted. That was how Mastek bagged the prestigious 'London congestion charge' project. Ashank is especially proud of this project, not only for its size but its impact on the lives of six million people.

"If we had screwed up, India would have screwed up," he says in all seriousness. All went as planned and it was a feather in both Mastek and Brand India's cap.

Of course, all this effort to focus and consolidate involved considerable heartburn. Many projects were scaled down, some were discontinued. Several employees felt disheartened and left the company.

Besides that, 2001 was a rough period due to both the dotcom crash and 9/11. As with all export-oriented companies, growth slowed down. At the same time the company was also re-engineering itself, adding to the complexity.

But there was one silver lining through these clouds. Mastek entered into a joint venture with Deloitte Consulting, which brought some more experience and more focus in the company. A strong management team was in place and CMM assessment also happened in the year 2000.

"We were the first IT company in the world to get 'People CMM' or PCMM. So what I am saying is, more importantly, we had built an institution, an organisation which has vision and values."

The values were articulated way back in the '90s. Although the vision was a little fuzzy, it all worked very fine. In time, focus got clarified, there was a sense of stability, sense of financial discipline came and now, there is financial muscle as well. But that has happened only in the last 8-9 years.

Today, if you look at Mastek, 60% of its balance sheet is liquid, ie cash. And it has not been raised through a public issue or ADR, the company has not gone back to shareholders after 1994. All the money was self-generated.

Another important area where Mastek scores is corporate governance. People do not question integrity, character, trust on the numbers that the company publishes. Investing time and effort in building investor relations is always a good idea. Of course, at every level and every size, requirements change and you do what you need to.

"Corporate governance was not important in '93-94. Because there was no competition for money, our stock markets were not so mature, our analyst community didn't know what it is. That was not the case by '99. So we had to meet the challenge."

It is an ongoing journey and tomorrow may bring something new, who knows?

As of 31st March 2008, Mastek is a $200 million company with a strength of 4,000. It celebrated 25 years in the software business with considerable fanfare last year. No doubt a great achievement but one cannot help comparing it with some other names in the software business!

Ashank admits the Infosys and Wipros of the world have scaled up much faster – but they followed a strategy of size while Mastek focused on 'IT solutions'. Y2K gave these companies a foot in the door of many Fortune 500 companies. Mastek on the other hand did not climb on board the Y2K bandwagon at all.

"There is a DNA for each company. And that DNA has to manifest. So that is why I say again and again, Mastek is a story still unfolding."

And the founders believe in that story and have firmly refused every M&A offer that came its way.

"All these years, there was always a constant pressure, somebody coming and saying, 'Why don't you join us. Together we will be larger.' But we never diluted. We said, 'We want to run this company ourselves. Whatever we want to do, we will do it ourselves.' We had that confidence. And I don't think that was a wrong decision."

Ashank is now vice chairman of SINE (Society for Innovation and Entrepreneurship). This is an organisation set up by IIT Bombay which mentors and incubates young companies.

"I tell young people, we were not as lucky as you guys. You have some support."

But as the Mastek story shows, you don't wait for someone to step forward and 'support' your idea. You simply go out there and make it happen.

<u>ADVICE TO YOUNG</u>
<u>ENTREPRENEURS</u>

Ashank:

You require a team which feels trust for each other. And which is willing to designate one of them as a leader. Not based on shareholding alone but respect, trust and competence because that is self-sustaining.

There is no one formula but I would say yes, get 4-5 years of experience – learn at somebody's cost if I may use the word. Get a bit of a feel, bit of financial stability, some savings. After all, venture capital is there but you need your own money too. But don't wait too long.

Everyone does not need to build a 100 crore or 1,000 crore company. Small vs big vs superbig is a choice that an entrepreneur makes himself or herself depending upon the ambitions, values and what he likes doing.

Sundar:

1. Don't just think about it, don't just wish for it, jump into it and do it, if you are really serious.

2. Once you get into it, go all out, never look at quitting as an option.

3. Remember that if the start-up fails, it is your idea that failed, not you

4. Great companies are created by great people. There is very little any one individual can achieve alone.

Ketan:

- Bringing a right team together (more than synergies of skills, synergies of values and attitudes is more critical).

- Make plans but remain open to all possibilities as events unfold in the marketplace.

- Think big and behave as if you have already accomplished your greatness. We started implementing many practices way ahead of our size.

- Retain work-life balance.

GIVER OF
ALL GOOD THINGS

R Subramanian (PGP '89),
Subhiksha

He quit his job at Citibank 15 days after joining, feeling restless to do something 'more'. That something is today India's largest grocery chain – Subhiksha. Subramanian famously rebuffed offers from Reliance Retail as he believes the best is 'yet to come'.

I am really keen to meet R Subramanian. His stores, Subhiksha, are at every street corner but the man himself is a mystery. One reads his name in the papers every now and then but never have I come across any details. The reports are always about the 100 new Subhiksha stores being opened. Or about a 'buyout' by Reliance Retail.

Which he denies, each time.

Yeh kaun sa banda hai jo hanste hue Reliance ko "No thank you" *kehne ki aukaat rakhta hai?*

Those questions, and more, were answered when I met R Subramanian at his sales office in middle class Matunga. It's a smallish space on the first floor of a residential building, right opposite Ruia College – a functional office, with a lot of people and activity. There is a buzz in the air, a sense of the heat and dust of the marketplace.

Unlike the 'five degrees too cold for comfort' office of any large multinational.

Subramanian, or RS as he prefers to be called, is also warm and expansive. He apologises profusely for being 15 minutes late. We settle into the conference room and begin our chat.

GIVER OF
ALL GOOD THINGS

R Subramanian (PGP '89),
Subhiksha

An entrepreneur is a person who has a mind of his own. And that is clear not just from the act of starting an enterprise, but decisions taken through the course of her or his life.

Like most of the first generation entrepreneurs profiled in this book, Subramanian's family was into 'government service'. The only child of a bank officer, the expected career path for bright young kids in the family was IIT, followed by study abroad.

RS was a bit different. After studying at IIT Madras, he joined IIMA. In the first year of the course he was very clear about wanting to do marketing, and even the company he wanted to join. It was Pond's, based in Chennai – "a nice little, small company then."

As a summer trainee at Pond's he even had a final placement offer in hand. But then, Pond's was acquired by Unilever globally. The offer to join remained but RS realised that HLL was a different ball game altogether. He decided to join Citi Investment Banking instead.

Fifteen days at Citibank, and RS realised that if he stuck on there, he would never be able to do something of his own in life. "I thought, 'This bank will make me too comfortable, give me all sorts of soft loans, make sure that I will be a bird in the golden cage.'" So he put in his papers on the 15th day of work. He had in fact joined early, right after the convocation in April. By the time his batchmates joined in June, RS had left!

The first few days in your job, right out of campus, are always filled with angst. Am I in the right place? Is there anything challenging for me to do here? Will I just be hanging around doing this work far beneath my capabilities... forever?

Of course, most trainees rationalise, "This is life." But to RS, 'this life' was not good enough. The words of IIMA chairman V K Krishnamurty at the post-convocation dinner rang in his ears. He asked, "Why we are you fellows joining banks, Citibank and all that? Why aren't you doing something smarter?"

And at that moment, somewhere deep inside he knew, "I will be better off doing something on my own."

"I had some rebellious streak all through," he recounts. "Rebellious is not in the sense that I was forming a union or something like that, but I did try different things or try to do things differently."

Such as?

While at IIT, in the first year summer break, RS enrolled for an accounting course. Not very typical for a BTech in electronics. Then, he recalls following a lifestyle at IIM campus different from everybody else. "The entire campus lives at night. I used to go off to sleep at 8.30 pm in the first year!"

Early to bed and early to quit the rat race!

So that was the end of the Citibank phase of life. Then RS recalled a discussion with Mr S Viswanathan who used to run Enfield, the motorcycle company, in Chennai. It was a sick unit. RS had met the chairman and owner of the company for a marketing project. At the time he'd said, "Why don't you come and work for me?"

The offer seemed attractive now. But the man could not be reached, he was on holiday. RS decided to go there, meet him, and "see if he takes me."

"I told him, 'I have quit my job and I want to join you.'

So he said, 'What job do you want, what salary?'

I said, 'My salary is some 5,500 rupees, in Bombay.'"

He agreed to match that. RS joined Enfield as a 'special officer' but working directly with the chairman.

It was a large company, a typical consumer products manufacturing company. There was manufacturing, marketing, purchase and loads of people in each department. Four different factories, 5-6,000 employees in all. The company was hugely loss making, a BIFR case. The trouble had started with the entry of Japanese bikes which were lighter, cheaper and fuel-efficient. No one wanted to buy an Enfield anymore.

"I worked with them for a couple of years, got a lot of interesting insights. I learnt everything about life in business working in that company. Basically, I was put in and told, 'Do what you want.'"

So, he did some financial restructuring. Then there was a project which involved planning the entire purchase operations, followed by production planning.

It was basically doing "all kind of things all over the place."

"I got a sense of dealing with people, handling operations, working with institutions to raise money. Macro-level stuff mostly. I don't know how good a job I did, but I learnt a lot."

All these efforts paid off. Eventually, Enfield was taken over by Greaves Eicher. Mr Viswanathan made decent money. "I can't say I was responsible, but I played some role." Vikram Lall of Eicher asked RS to come and work for the company in Delhi. But by this time he knew it was time to move on. To his own thing.

Intellect and ability are important in life. But relationships are even more important. In 1991, when RS told Mr Viswanathan he wished to leave and start something of his own, he asked, "What do you want to do?"

"A financial services company," RS replied

Viswanathan asked, "What do you know about financial services?"

"Nothing," came the reply.

"Do you have money?"

RS admitted he did not.

Mr V said, "How much money do you want?"

"If we had known how difficult retailing is, we would have never got into it. Operationally, it's a very challenging business, the pain factor is very high. But the pain factor is also what we love so much. That's what makes it so difficult for competition to come in very easily."

"The biggest number I could think of at that time was two and a half crore. So I said, 'I want two and a half crore.' He said, 'Okay, I will give you that much over the next two years. I will invest, you run the company. I have no intention of owning this company so whenever you can return the money, buy the shares back.'"

And that's how it happened. No written agreement, just a spoken word. A word of trust. Viswanathan gave ₹ 50 lakh to start off. And thus Viswapriya Financial Services & Securities Ltd was born in 1991.

"Basically, we were the first to do asset securitisation systems in India. In 1992, this was not in the country's financial lexicon. ICICI Securities did the second asset securitisation 30 days after us. Citibank did the third, 60 days after us."

The big break came in 1994 when Viswapriya started 'IPO financing', something which is common today. "The whole concept," RS exclaims, "was the brainchild of Viswapriya. Any bank which does IPO financing today follows the structure that we created in '94."

The product became very big. Viswapriya Finance made a lot of money. The company had struck a pot of oil or gold or whatever and it kept growing. Markets were very good during 1994, right up to '96. Then, the stock market collapsed.

There was a lot of money but no business. No one to lend to. That's when they started looking around. By then, there was a professional management team, 75 people in all. From that initial ₹ 2.5 crore the company had grown its net worth to ₹ 80 crore. Each of those years – '94, '95, '96 – Viswapriya lent around ₹ 1,500 crore.

Each loan was for the period of the IPO, 2-3 months, so there were many lending cycles in a year. The company had a fairly large balance sheet and a lot of bank borrowing at that time. And it was still, notionally, owned by Mr Viswanathan. Sadly, he passed away in 1994, which was a major blow for RS, personally. However, Viswapriya was not affected as Mr V had no operational role. It was completely Subramanian's baby.

So, it's 1996. There is money, there is staff, but not much to do. "The markets were very weak and we were not sure we wanted to do anything else." So Viswapriya decided to put money into property. Funds were getting deployed, fetching returns, yet there was frustration. They were not *doing* anything.

What a wonderful state to be in, many would think. People who work at boring, stressful, highly paid jobs constantly tell themselves, "I'm doing this so I can make enough money to retire peacefully… some day." Well, here was one such golden chance! But all that RS could think of was, "I am not well occupied. My team is not well occupied."

Entrepreneurship is an itch. The only ointment which soothes it is work. Lots and lots of it! And it must be interesting, intensive and audacious.

The team began to look at various businesses, such as software. But they realised it was probably too late to get into that. There were too many players already. Then, they looked at retailing.

"I would like to claim that we are revolutionaries and all that. But broadly we saw two things. From our point of view, it was an under-serviced market. There was hardly any organised retail while the middle class, even then, was reasonably large. Salaries were moving up, we could sense consumption will rise."

Looking at it from the Porter model, exit barriers were low, competition was weak. Unlike the Viswapriya phase, where it was simply 'jump in and start swimming', a lot of study and strategic thinking went into this second foray.

"We tried to understand how the retail business works, how it makes money, accounting practices, understanding what the consumer wants." Based on all this research, Subhiksha went in for a completely unique 'Indian' store. "We took a call that

"People saw that telecom had happened, insurance had happened and financial services had happened. They said maybe retail will happen as well, let's go the retail way. So, we could attract quality manpower. Getting the right people at the right time made a huge difference."

ultimately, the Indian consumer is going to shop in a particular way and Indian consumers look for value. And to deliver value in India, you need to do things differently from what you do in the US."

Retail has two main costs – space and people. In the developed world, retail happens outside cities, where space is very cheap. Everybody has a car, so they drive down and shop. And in most of those parts of the world, people are very expensive. So what they try to do is have 'very low staff, large space' formats.

In places like India, people are much cheaper, but space inside the city is incredibly expensive. And you have to locate in the city because no one will sit in a bus and spend two hours to travel outside the city and reach your store. You need a smaller space but an 'overmanned' kind of format. And to compete with the thousands of local retailers, you have to deliver the best prices and have an amazing supply chain management.

So Subhiksha created a unique 'neighbourhood' store strategy with the promise of best value. In March 1997, the first store came up in Chennai. An investment of ₹ 5 crore was made in the new company.

The first two years were very tough. Because despite all that research they had no clue about what it really took to run a business in retailing. Luckily, neither did anyone else.

But that was not an issue. "We deliberately decided not to hire anybody from the existing retail sector because we didn't want to be stuck with people's dogmas about what will work and what will not work."

In 1999, after much trial and error, Subhiksha got a sense of being stable. It was looking like it would make tiny money. By this time, the company was running 10 stores in Chennai. But the bigger triumph was that the format was working. Customers were buying. And they were coming back for more.

By June 2000, Subhiksha had grown to 50 stores in Chennai. That was a fairly rapid scale up by retail standards of those days. This was the era of dotcoms, and venture capital funds were all over the place. "So we did our bit," says RS and funding of ₹ 15 crore came in from ICICI Venture for a 10% stake.

The money was used to expand all over Tamil Nadu. But there was a lot of mess and confusion. From running a one-city operation, Subhiksha was suddenly running 30 centres across Tamil Nadu. By 2002 June, Subhiksha had 120 stores. "It was a nightmare. The organisation and systems were not keeping pace."

"By 2003 end, we were trying to put all this back in order – streamline operations, improve profitability. But then things stabilized. We got the hang of how to make things work."

A second distribution centre was put up in Trichy. And then in 2004, Subhiksha started working on the expansion outside Tamil Nadu.

"We talked to our sales team and to ICICI and said, 'Let's go for it, let's do a large expansion.' They agreed to finance it."

2005 was a year of gigantic growth. In phase 1, Subhiksha focused on AP, Karnataka and Gujarat. Money was raised for that. Then came phase II – Delhi and Bombay. It was followed by phase III, then IV and now the company is moving towards phase V. At the time of this interview (Nov 2007), Subhiksha had over 1000 stores up and running.

"I don't think I look at myself as the 'owner' of the company. I look at myself as a manager working for the company. I am as amenable to rational logic as I would be if I were an employee."

"The '90s were very kind to us. They gave us very low salaries, so it made us worry very little about taking those sort of jumps. What do you risk? You hardly risk anything... If I am sitting on a one-crore paycheck, obviously I will think twice. It's not the same as leaving a Citibank job of 5,500 rupees."

"1,000 are officially announced. Some more will come up in the next few days. We did 1,000 stores on Diwali day, 2007." Wide smile.

"But you are making it sound very easy," I protest. From one store to 1,000 stores... *Jaise koi badi baat nahin.*

"I think the first 50 stores were more tough than the next 1,000. Because when we were doing our first 50 stores, our own knowledge base of what we wanted to do was zero. We were learning every day. It's not as if we have stopped learning now. But we were learning different things at that time."

"When we were doing 150 stores in Tamil Nadu and 1,000 stores across the country, the challenge was being able to manage in terms of mass scale expansion. And manage a very large team."

Interestingly, Subhiksha is structured and run like telecom companies which have the concept of 'circles'. Certain aspects of Subhiksha's business are centrally controlled, but local teams handle a number of areas independently.

There are budgets and broad principles. The financial aspects are controlled centrally. So is IT, marketing and purchasing (bulk discount deals with large companies in particular!).

Regions have flexibility in deciding where they want to put stores, how many stores they want to put up, what price they want to sell at, what they want to sell. And what consumer marketing initiatives they want to take.

Sounds wonderful but none of it works without an incredibly motivated and talented set of people to manage it.

"One of the biggest challenges is to manage a team of far higher quality than we had ever operated with," admits RS. In Tamil Nadu, it was a gradual ramp up, so the company could manage it with the initial core team who were all very good. Lots of people did join, but in operational roles.

But as Subhiksha expanded, the company brought in very senior people to run the various regions as business heads. "Managing their aspirations, getting the system to respond to them, taking advantage of their experience and market knowledge – these were the new challenges."

The core operation guys think about how to leverage scale. They also play a mentoring, questioning role with local teams. But there is no 'corporate office' as such. The head of finance sits in Bombay, the manpower guy in Delhi. "We sort of run from one place to the other, keep talking to people."

Evidently. Any day of the week you call RS, you'll find him in a different city. He is personally and very integrally involved – kind of like the centre which spins around holding the loose structure together.

"It's not a very hands off style," he grins. "It's a fairly live affair." It is also reasonably unusual.

RS gives much credit to technology. "We could not have done this 10 years back. Today you are so wired that it really doesn't matter."

I don't know how many would subscribe to that view and unbundle their corporate offices but evidently it works for Subhiksha! With 1,381 stores* on ground the company is expecting a turnover of ₹ 2,000 crore in the coming year, and a profit of ₹ 40-45 crore.

"Typically, the margin in this business is two and a half per cent. Which is low… but that, fortunately or unfortunately, is the business However, we say Subhiksha is adding ₹ 240 crore of value. We are able to deliver ₹ 200 crore to the consumer and we say that what we deliver to the consumers is part of our profits."

* As of May 2008

"To drive towards your goal, you are working on a path. But that path is not 100% right. You are correcting yourself by learning, by experience, and making these corrections and moving forward on the system and coming out a winner... The sheer value of learning, every day, is what keeps you going."

The consumer saves money because Subhiksha exists. "So as long as consumers save money and we make money and we don't destroy value for ourselves, it's quite okay," says RS, on a more philosophical note.

Having a philosophy makes sound business sense. The belief that your job is adding to more than the company's bottomline is a tremendous motivator for employees. Incidentally, 'Subhiksha' is a Sanskrit word which means 'the giver of all good things'.

Subramanian's story involves struggle, but not on the financing front. After all, he started out with 2.5 crore (which in 1991 was a lot of money!).

"True, but I have done quite a bit of scouring around for money in the sense that for the IPO finance product we raised those 300 crore of bank loans. But yes, it was not like 'From where am I going to get my salary?' – that was never the case."

Did having access to money make him bolder? Was it all about 'thinking big'?

"No, the basic idea when we did securitisation, for example, was that here is something which has not been done in India. Here is an opportunity. The idea was to do differentiated things. The idea was never necessarily to do large things. Large things happened."

"IPO financing started. It proved to be very successful, it became very large, so we were happy to do it. But did we start Subhiksha with the idea that we wanted to be India's largest retailer? I don't think so. I think we started Subhiksha to prove the point that there could be an Indian format of retailing."

"In 1997, if you had asked me what you want to do next I would have said that the next things we would possibly look at is garments, then stainless steel... eventually we will become Chennai's largest retailer. There was never a logic that we will become a food retailer across the country."

It was only in 2000, when Subhiksha embarked on the Tamil Nadu expansion, that the team actually sat down and thought about its priorities.

"That is when it hit us – we had picked up domain expertise in selling food and groceries. And trying to recreate this domain expertise in consumer durables, in garments is going to be tough. So it's not a geographical market that you are an expert of, but of a domain. And we thought we should sort of keep pushing ourselves on that."

And that's how it happened. Not as per a grand, pre-determined plan but where the currents of life took them. Only there was a vision, a *keeda* so to speak, to 'think big, think scale'.

Expanding a business means what you have done once, you do again and again and again. But the scale-up phase, some entrepreneurs feel, is just not as exciting as the process of starting up.

"It's more repetitive, sure. But if you had asked us 2-3 years ago, 1,000 stores would have been a shock. I would have said how can we think of it? After eight years in business we had just had 140 stores."

So, what is the magic that made it happen?

It lies in three parts, believes RS. The first part is the market itself – the readiness of the market to absorb you and the readiness of the market to finance you.

"And in our case if you look at it, I think even more than the money, the fact that retail became hot and a lot of people who would have never joined retail became willing to join retail. Ultimately, any business is done by manpower. And quality manpower. A lot of senior management talent became available to us. And without that, this never would have been possible."

Then of course, Subhiksha had a track record, a lot of positive vibes from the market, which helped.

"The backgrounds we come from, there is only so much money that you can spend... I don't think money is important in terms of having personal ownership. Enough money available to the company for what it wants to do, is a good thing but even there we have a worry that too much money makes it inefficient and lazy."

"The eight years spent in doing 140 stores was the foundation on which we could build the rest of the pieces slightly better. It's not as if we didn't make any mistakes, but the point is that we could avoid some of the dumber mistakes."

But the most crucial decision was the call on how the organisation wanted to expand. Would it be a central command model or did it make sense to decentralise and run an unconventional kind of structure?

"If we had decided to centralise everything in Chennai and put in place a top-down structure, which is what many retailers were trying to do, we would not have been able to get the expansion speed required. Others did that and failed, and I don't think they have worse people than we have."

The decentralised model, the SBU model was a winning choice. "But fundamentally, it's about having the confidence that you know the business."

And now it's about taking this even further. "If you sit on 1,000 stores, 2,000 looks possible. Now what I am saying sounds a little outlandish, but people are saying why don't you take this model to other parts of the world? Like Africa, or Bangladesh, or Pakistan?"

So there is still that sense of thrill. Of wonder and excitement. How far can we push ourselves?

And that's why buy-out offers hold no interest. "You will sell out if the business is not doing well. Or the business is not likely to be well in future. We are doing well, business is growing, we are making money. So why should we sell? Tomorrow will always be better than today."

Although money *per se*, that has very little attraction. Learning and growing each day is the more valuable paycheque RS earns from his company.

"We believe that we are a work-in-progress company... we constantly work at change and there is always chaos among us. Chaos is nice because that is what challenges you."

"If there is no chaos, and everything is well ordered and you come to work and you sign files and read reports and then go back home, what's the fun? The challenge of wanting to do new things, the challenge of disturbing the status quo externally and internally, is what keeps us happy."

But is 'happiness' wholly and solely tied to one's work? What about life, spouse, family, relationships, relaxation...

Yes, they are affected. "I can blame it on the job. But it's also your personality type. There are people who work at a company and keep a 20-hour work day. There are entrepreneurs with a 20-hour work day." And RS is one of them.

"Obviously, mine is not a very normal kind of personal life. I sort of typically get back home after 10 and leave early at 7-7.30 in the morning. I work six days a week and even on the seventh I am on phone half the day. But I guess you have a sense of priority to the family and you know that when they need you, you are there."

"And if I would put this question to your wife and kids?" I ask.

"They will have a very meaningful smile, I guess. I am sure that there will be gripes but the gripe will also be covered by understanding..."

Will you then slow down, at some point? "I keep promising this to my wife. But she never believes me. She says I will probably find something new to do."

How very true. To succeed at one's first enterprise and then to say "Hey, let's do it all over again!" requires an extraordinary amount of energy. But every now and then it's nice to stop and smell the roses. And take a few home, to that understanding wife.

ADVICE TO YOUNG ENTREPRENEURS

If you want to be in a rarified space, a financial space, then it probably makes sense to join Goldman Sachs. Pick up some threads, some contacts, get a bunch of colleagues who will come with you and begin something.

The way we look at it, there are two worlds – the real world and the virtual world. The virtual world is something which the financial types operate. The real world is where a lot of us slog to physically do work.

If you want to do something in the real world, sell products to people, impact consumers, it makes more sense to work in real life companies, the smaller the better. Don't join a Hindustan Lever or a Coca Cola. Join smaller companies because you will get far more exposure. I can't believe that in two years, in any other company, I could have sat for IR negotiations or financial restructuring negotiations.

The larger the company you work in, the less you are able to get to the nuts and bolts, the less you are able to see the bigger picture. You need to go and challenge yourself, you need to go and fight your way in the market. That experience will make all the difference!

SWEET
SUCCESS

**Narendra Murkumbi (PGP '94),
Shree Renuka Sugars**

He shut down the first company he started after graduating because a ₹ 5 crore turnover was not 'large enough.' His second venture Shree Renuka Sugars, is today a ₹ 1,000 crore company, and has changed the lives of hundreds of sugarcane farmers.

Magazines used to create lists of millionaires. Now the bar has been raised to 'billionaire'. Call it morbid curiosity, or a human interest in the net worth of one's fellow human being, people love to go through such lists. And I am no exception.

So there I was, idly flipping through an issue of *Business World* titled 'India's new billionaires', when suddenly I stop and exclaim, "This guy looks familiar!" The name is Narendra Murkumbi and hey, he was a year junior to me at IIMA.

Of all the chappal wearing, not-washed-jeans-for-a-month, living, breathing, thinking, blinking inmates on that campus, this guy is the first I know to get on the list.

What's more, he's done it by putting up sugar plants. Sugar. Not IT, dotcom, BPO, services, consulting. Sugar. An industry you associate more with politicians than businessmen. Certainly not a magnet for MBAs.

An MBA with 'good job prospects' deciding to become an entrepreneur is crazy enough. An MBA who decides to plunge into an unglamorous, old world industry like this – doubly so.

Management gurus and even entrepreneurs believe it's important to be the pioneer in what you set out to do. Narendra's story, however, is a contrarian one. He wasn't the first to get into sugar by a long shot. But he saw in the industry the potential to do things in a way no one had before. At a scale that had never been done before.

It is one helluva inspiring story.

SWEET
SUCCESS

Narendra Murkumbi (PGP '94),
Shree Renuka Sugars

"I come from a family of traders – the family has been into trading for many, many generations. I did my electronics engineering and I was all set to take over my father's trading business. Then a family friend said: "Why don't you do an MBA?"

So Narendra gave it a try. And got through the CAT at the first attempt. The boy from Belgaum thus landed up at IIMA. But his priorities were clear and different from the very beginning.

"I always wanted to do something on my own."

What he would do crystallised in the second year. Meanwhile, Narendra did his summer training at Sohan Silk. An owner-run, first-generation company which, at the time, was India's largest silk exporter.

'Placement' was a term that had no meaning in the Narendra version of the Oxford English dictionary.

By his second year in the MBA programme, Narendra zeroed in on what he would do after graduating. A family friend had once worked with the Tatas on developing bio-pesticides. The project never got commercialised. Now, the gentleman had retired and wanted to 'do something' about it.

So the young man and the old man joined hands and set up 'Murkumbi BioAgro'. Narendra borrowed ₹ 5 lakh from his father as seed capital. Another ₹ 25 lakh was raised through loans. And in 1994, the company started manufacturing pesticides in a small shed.

Over the next four years, the company built up a national network – 80 sales people, spread across eight states of India. By 1998, Murkumbi BioAgro had achieved a turnover of ₹ 5 crore. The margins were decent and the company was making profits of close to ₹ 40 lakh.

A happy situation, wouldn't you think? Not for Narendra.

"Our main problem with that business was that we couldn't scale it up. We were frustrated with the size of the business. Because after four years, it was at a turnover of five crore. You could not call it a large company."

What prevented the scale-up? "It was a niche product. Bio-pesticides are not very favourably looked at by farmers. Because the products, while they are safe, are slower acting than chemicals. It's 'concept selling'. Always tough."

One of the attractions of bio-pesticides was the huge potential overseas. The idea was to tap the US market. But eventually, Narendra realised that the registration norms in the US were a huge entry barrier. Despite spending quite a bit of money, they could not cross that hurdle.

So, key managers continued to run the bio-pesticide business. Narendra began scouting for other opportunities.

Now sugar may seem a strange choice but for him it was a fairly natural one. "Sugar is THE large industry in my part of the country, in Belgaum. Also, in 1998, it got decontrolled. And therefore, for the first time in Maharashtra and Karnataka, after 30 years, you could actually set up new sugar mills in the private sector. Otherwise, it had been reserved for co-operatives."

It was a new opportunity, it was a large business. Enough to excite a young man for whom small was not beautiful!

Manufacturing is a business which requires physical assets.

Physical assets require money.

Lots of money.

So how was the money for Shree Renuka Sugars raised?

"Well, the initial project was obviously much bigger than what we had been doing. We essentially diverted the capital from the existing business. The rest we borrowed. We borrowed against our existing business, we borrowed on our personal account, we borrowed from relatives."

But the company was still short of capital. So Narendra thought out of the box – he sold shares to the farmers.

There is a culture of co-operative institutions in Maharashtra and Karnataka. Farmers are used to contributing capital for societies – milk societies, sugar co-operatives, cotton co-operatives. So Shree Renuka Sugars employed the same format in a public limited company.

The second interesting thing Shree Renuka Sugars did was to identify old factories. The company bought one such factory through a tender put out by the government of Andhra Pradesh. "Our project cost came down and secondly, we got a soft loan from the government of India. Because this was a sick factory and we were reviving that factory."

The factory was shifted and VRS offered to 500-odd workers. The trouble was that the factory had been put up in a place where there was no raw material, no sugarcane. So it had to be shifted to Belgaum district.

Why take that headache? Because it was much cheaper. A brand new factory would have cost ₹ 100 crore. Done this way, the total project cost was only ₹ 50 crore. Of this, equity capital was ₹ 12 crore.

The factory was relocated, and started operations in 1997. Results were encouraging, and evident immediately.

"In the first three years, we processed more sugarcane than the factory had done in its old operations in 21 years. Then we invested in co-generation, so we were producing power as well."

"You keep thinking about how to grow the business. Of course, you have a lot of ideas, and not everything succeeds. In fact, I think very few stories are written about the failures... But as long as the successes are big enough, I think things take care of themselves."

Co-generation involves burning the sugarcane fibre that is a by-product of the process. The power is distributed by laying lines to the nearest electricity station. Again, not an original idea but one which was identified and applied where the business needed it.

Because sugar alone did not make the project economically viable at the time.

Of course, all these ideas did not just happen. A lot of time and energy was spent on learning the business.

"I visited more than 40 factories in the first two years. And I hired the best consultants in the country to do the technical designing. Because we were shifting the factory and also expanding it. And putting in a co-generation plant required a lot of modifications."

But Narendra did not leave it all to the technical consultant.

"During the initial set-up stage, I stayed for six months at the factory. So even today, I know a lot about the mechanics of manufacturing sugar and manufacturing power and all that."

The company never made a loss, thanks to the co-generation unit. But for the first three years, it did not make any great profits either. By the year 2000, the turnover was ₹ 50 crore. The profits? ₹ 2 crore.

"It was lower margin but it's a great business because it has size. Sugar is a staple – it's a product that does not have a cyclicity of demand. Production fluctuates, but demand keeps growing."

And yet, like any industry, it goes through its ups and downs.

In 2002, sugar prices crashed. Things became really difficult. So the company shifted focus.

"I took to doing a lot of exports trading and all that, in order to survive. That actually increased our size of business. In a year when the whole industry was in losses, we remained profitable because we made money trading sugar overseas."

Others could also have done it. But they saw themselves as manufacturers. They believed that trading "is not our business." This rigid definition of what you will do, and what you won't is sometimes referred to as 'core competence'. Stick to what you know.

But entrepreneurship is about *jugaad*. And a period of struggle is when that quality really comes to the fore. Your core business is not making money. You take a lateral view – are there other opportunities which are slightly out of your direct line of sight?

It all depends on what slot you put yourself in.

Do I see myself as a manufacturer? In that case, I will get into other kinds of manufacturing but not trading.

Do I see myself more narrowly – as an agricultural manufacturer? Then I will see peripheral opportunities in processing other kinds of agricultural produce.

Narendra took a 360 degree view of sugar. "We do anything that is connected to sugar." So he saw any and every opportunity connected with that.

The next Big Idea was to build a refinery. Sugar refining takes low quality raw sugar and processes that into edible sugar. The beauty of it is, you can import the raw sugar from wherever it is competitive in the world.

After sugar prices plunged, the amount of sugar cultivated in India itself went down. There were, therefore, massive imports in 2002-05. In fact, India became the largest importer of sugar in the world. We had the capacity to refine also. So, the government opened up imports of raw sugar and made it duty free. That made the idea of setting up a refinery all the more attractive.

"In every business, the more you know about the grassroots, the better."

The interesting thing is that sugar was a business that had not changed for 40 years. It was licensed, stagnant, run mostly by co-operatives. But like every other sector of the economy it did open up, bit by bit. And it attracted outsiders like Narendra. People who saw its potential with fresh eyes and new energy.

Shree Renuka Sugars is now building a dedicated raw sugar factory in Haldia. There is no sugarcane in West Bengal so this refinery will take only raw sugar and refine it to white sugar. All this raw sugar will be imported, hence the plant is built next to a port – Haldia.

And what of the farmers who subscribed to the initial equity?

"They supplied cane to our first factory. We give priority to their cane over non-shareholders. At that time, this was a big attraction for the farmer. Because this was a licensed industry, there was a shortage of industrial capacity."

"But that is a very small benefit now. We have increased capacity over three times. In fact, we now have six factories."

Of course, when Shree Renuka Sugars listed at ₹ 285 per share, the farmers got their bonanza.

They had bought shares for just 10 rupees.

The interesting thing is that while about 50% have sold all their shares, the rest have held on. They are happy with the 20% annual dividend. "Those who have sold, I think, most of the guys actually bought more land. They have, in fact, become bigger farmers. Because that's the business they understand."

"The other innovation that we did was, we couldn't build new plants fast enough. The country was going into a shortage, sugar prices were going up. So what we did was, there were some sick co-operatives, we went to the management, to the board of directors, which is essentially the local leaders. And we said, we would lease those factories and run them on management contract. So we got the first one for two years. In

2004, we did another one for six years. Today, out of the six factories that we run, three are leased. We are running them, but we don't own the assets."

The advantage? It is much cheaper than putting up a new plant. And faster also. Every factory Shree Renuka took over, it managed to turn around in no time. The first factory for example, was running at 50% per cent of capacity. Last year, Shree Renuka ran it at 115% capacity.

Speaking of innovation, the idea of a young man going into business with his mother is a unique one. But that's the story of Shree Renuka Sugars.

"I think both of us were looking at doing something together. In a sense, she was waiting for me."

I don't know why it isn't more common. After all, so many people go into business with their fathers, brothers, sisters and even wives. But somehow it is unusual. How many sons would believe their mothers have sound business skills? And how many mothers would have that confidence?

In this case, both sides did. From helping her husband with the trading business, 61-year-old Vidya Murkumbi became an equal partner.

So how did they divide responsibilities?

"Fundamentally, we have very different strengths. I am better on finance, the external interface. Whether it is the financial market, export market or world market. She has a very deep strength dealing with farmers, with local people, local administration, local government. And she looks after the internal administration. I am not a good details person."

Mrs Murkumbi is still based in Belgaum – she visits the factories regularly. Narendra is now based in Mumbai and heads south once a month.

"It has been a good partnership... There is obviously that amount of trust when working with someone in the family. And it is always better to have company. You have a lot of peers when you are working, while entrepreneurship is essentially a very lonely occupation."

> **"I am an entrepreneur because I want to create something. It's not the money that motivates but the size of what you build, the scale."**

Shree Renuka Sugars crossed a turnover of ₹ 1,000 crore in September 2007. In the current year, Narendra believes it will achieve ₹ 2,000 crore. The second quarter figures (Jan-March 2008) indicate 95% growth in revenues, meaning he is well on track towards achieving that.

So what keeps him going as an entrepreneur?

"Well, firstly, it is a very large business in scale. So that is exciting. Secondly, it is very fulfilling that you are directly creating value on agricultural turnover. I think the great part of my own satisfaction in this business is that I created wealth not only for us, but 75 employees and 10,000 farmers directly through the stock."

"I have built three new factories, at three new locations. And each of these factories, the minute they start doing well, the economy around you visibly improves. That gives great satisfaction."

But Narendra is barely 38 today. Another 20-30 years of working life ahead of him. Are the challenges he faces ahead, in this company, big enough?

"When we were 50 crore, 100 crore, the growth in this business was limitless. Even today, at 1,000 crore, we have a market share of only 2.5%. The way in which we are growing, we are out-performing the rest of the industry at the moment."

"But 3-4 years down the line, growth will slow down. I never thought I would say this, but now I think that even this business has certain limitations."

Already, things are kind of stable. More and more senior people have been inducted. Soon, there will be a Chief Operating Officer. Once revenues touch ₹ 7,000-8,000 crore (it's just a matter of when, not if!) you can be sure Narendra will have moved on. To something new and even bigger.

"You see, beyond that level, the incremental market share would be very tough to get. It would be very expensive."

Energies would need to be redirected somewhere else.

"I think the drive to start off something on your own, once you have it, you will continue to have it. If something is running well and smoothly, you will look for new challenges. And in India, there are so many new opportunities, that I think it doesn't make sense to stick to one business."

"I think the old philosophy that we all learnt even on the campus, of core competence, of doing one thing world class, it no longer holds in this country. The more successful entrepreneurs at the moment have successfully been able to jump into new opportunities. And also scale up those opportunities."

And each new business is a challenge but it will never be as tough as the very first one.

"Nothing is as formidable as the first four years – when I was in the bio-pesticides business. Running a small business, you have to do a lot of running around yourself, it's very hard. You can't attract talent, you can't pay high salaries."

"For example, when we started, we were a partnership firm. Then we realised that if you want to grow across the country, people won't even *join* a company that is a partnership. So we changed it to a private limited company."

What are the other changes that come with a label like 'success'? How does it feel to have enough money not just for needs but for any conceivable want?

"I don't think my lifestyle has changed that much. I am still in a rented flat. Our own flat is not going to be ready for another year. And I bought that last. I bought this office, before that we built three factories."

In terms of priorities, 'personal' things have always been last.

> **"It is always difficult to switch off. Mentally you are always there and that's hard for the family. Partly maybe personal style. Also because it's your own business, you are that much more connected."**

"I think there is an ambition to grow larger as a corporation, as a business and that is a primary motivation. Personal wealth doesn't really matter. When you are the owner and CEO of a company, most of your expenses are anyway taken care of by the company. Car, travel, holiday once a year, all your medical expenses."

So no 'billionaire' purchases – yacht, jet, Lamborghini? He laughs.

"You know when the *Business World* guys first approached me I talked about the Ambanis. Because they are the real billionaires. If you write about me, then it has to be about how we created this wealth with the help of the farmers. How we shared it with them."

And it's not just for reasons of 'public image'. This new generation of entrepreneurs genuinely feels socially responsible. In a way that extends beyond the idea that "we are providing employment, and that is uplifting people." These entrepreneurs earmark their money and professional expertise to make it happen.

An example – the Shree Renuka Sugars Development Foundation. 5% of the company's stock is in this non-profit trust. The foundation runs schools for the children of contract labourers who harvest the cane. It is now starting health centres and building a hospital in the factory, among other things. The net worth of the foundation is close to 100 crore and it is run by professionals.

For the last two years, Narendra has also been on the board of ICICI Bank. "They were looking for somebody with a mix of experiences," he shrugs with typical modesty. "I think they found a combination of both an entrepreneur and agriculture background in me."

These duties take up 12 days a year, but according to Narendra, the exposure is tremendous.

If there was a moral to the Shree Renuka story it would be summed up like this – there is no old business. There are only old *ways* of doing business.

The first business that Narendra ventured into might be termed as pioneering. After all, 'Bio-pesticides' was a new product idea. But the business was run in a traditional way. Nothing pathbreaking there.

"Then I entered this very old-style business. And I think everything that we do, every day, is innovative. It's not that you have to dream of something that nobody has ever done. All my best ideas have been done by others. We have done only two things."

"One, we have done them better than the guy who got that idea. And second, we have scaled those ideas up. If somebody did something on a very small scale, I said, why can't it be 10 times bigger? When somebody put in a 50-tonne refinery in India to process raw sugar, we said, why not start at 200? When imports started, we said, why not 1,000?"

The limits are in your own thinking. The impossible is what you believe cannot be done.

<u>ADVICE TO YOUNG ENTREPRENEURS</u>

It's tough to start off on your own right away. You learn many things the hard way. But at the same time, I don't think the kind of jobs that come on the campus prepare you for entrepreneurship at all. You are very very segmented. You are in the higher paying and specialised professions like investment banking which are absolutely no background for starting off on your own.

AT YOUR SERVICE

Chender Baljee (PGP '72), Royal Orchid Hotels

His family owns Baljee's, Simla's most famous hotel. Yet as a young management graduate, Chender decided to carve out his own niche. It took him 35 years but today Royal Orchid is a ₹ 150 crore hospitality business.

The word to describe Chender Baljee is stoic. He relates his story almost in third person, like it happened to someone else.

When you've been in business for 35 years and been through every possible up and down I guess that's only natural. Because you can either become bitter and cynical or just shrug and say, "This too shall pass."

Baljee's story demonstrates that there are forces beyond one's control when it comes to 'success' and 'failure.' Zipping ahead versus merely chugging along.

Sometimes you encounter sheer bad luck and not once or twice, but over and over again. Litigation, strikes, debt, 9/11, SARS – all these and more, affected the growth and expansion plans of Baljee's company. An IPO that should have happened in 1985 only became a reality in 2006.

The wait was certainly worth it, I think, as I stand in the tastefully furnished lobby of the Royal Orchid hotel. The question is: how many of us have the patience to stick it out that long?

AT YOUR SERVICE

Chender Baljee (PGP '72), Royal Orchid Hotels

Anyone who has ever been to Simla would have eaten at Baljee's. That is the family Chender Baljee belongs to.

Born and brought up in Simla, Chender completed his BCom in Delhi and then did his MBA from IIMA. He didn't take up a job, instead he joined the family's hotel and restaurant business. But in a few months it felt a little crowded. With his dad and brother already managing the show, Chender didn't have much of a role.

"I started a restaurant called 'Fascination' in Simla, mainly catering to the college crowd. A little upmarket," he recalls. Then, in December 1972 there was an opportunity. A family friend mentioned that there were two hotels available on lease in 'Mysore state' (as Karnataka was then called).

He sent Baljee a tender form for the two hotels – the 'Brindavan Garden' and the 'Metropole'. A bid was put in but the previous lessees went to court, so the matter got stuck. Then the friend suggested another hotel in Bangalore, which was not doing too well.

Baljee decided it was worth a shot and his bid succeeded. The family funded the ₹ 5 lakh required as lease deposit. 'The Stay Longer' hotel was refurbished and renamed 'Harsha'. And that is how Chender Baljee started his very first hotel.

It was January 1973. Bangalore was a pensioner's paradise. The city was home mainly to public sector undertakings – there were very few business travellers. What's more, there was a definite off-season when there were very few visitors.

But as they say, *pyaar kiya to darna kya. Business kiya to ab socho karna kya*. "I tried many things," recalls Baljee. "I opened two restaurants on MG Road by taking over existing ones. I also started a bakery unit to supply bread to the city." Baljee's wife Sunita also pitched in – helping with menus and joining him when the restaurants required putting in late nights.

Business was okay. Not 'hot' or 'great'. With marketing, cost control and sheer hard work, Harsha had been turned around. But by the year 1985, there was the urge to do something more.

"We had a good life – cars, house, everything you needed was there," says Baljee. "But the business could be made bigger and better so I decided to go for an IPO." Unfortunately, just as the company was about to file its prospectus, the market crashed. The IPO, and all the expansion plans, were put into cold storage.

What's more, the restaurants closed down due to some lease issues. And in 1987, the hotel staff went on strike. "It was difficult running the business day to day," he recalls. Facing a cash crunch, the bakery unit was sold off at the time.

But there was more to follow. In 1988 the lease of the 'Harsha' hotel expired and the only option was to buy it. That meant taking a bank loan.

So the situation was pretty tight from 1987 to 1990. But then it slowly improved. In 1992, an opportunity to lease some prime land close to Bangalore airport came up. And Baljee bid for it.

This meant putting money upfront. But once again, things did not work out as planned. Due to litigation, the deal got stuck. The legal wrangling went on till 1998. Construction could start only in 1999.

"It was an ambitious project, built mostly on debt. It was to be a 3-star hotel but we decided *yeh bhi kar lo, woh bhi*. So it became a 5-star." Raising the debt – of ₹ 17-18 crore – was fortunately not difficult. Baljee has always enjoyed a good connect with people in the banking sector.

Was there a definite business plan in place? Yes and no.

"The easiest thing is to make a spreadsheet but assumptions are on paper only," says Baljee. Take something like 'room rate'. One can put down anything but the actual rate is determined by market conditions.

And of course the market goes up, and it goes down. When Bangalore boomed, so did the business. 1994 to 1997, was a relatively good time and there was a surplus. That was to come in handy later, in lean times.

"From '98 onwards, my son went to college in America, so that was an additional expense. I took another loan to fund that. I had no choice but to borrow, borrow and borrow more."

Was all the borrowing ever a source of stress?

Baljee muses, "You see, basically I am an optimist so I said, *chalo* – let's see. When you are in a soup you have to continue to be in a bigger soup, *theek hai*... you can't do anything more."

However faith eventually brought with it good fortune. In 2001, the Royal Orchid hotel was finally launched. And yet, even before one could celebrate, there was the shock of 9/11. It was a disaster. Business travel plummeted and so did occupancy of hotels.

"We had debt to repay, and by then I had two sons studying abroad. So that was a very crucial, tough period."

Still, Baljee never despaired. Careful money management and cost control saw the company through these tough times.

"One thing I have always believed is that whatever you do, you do in a very honest manner... I never ever defaulted on any financial institution payment or salaries to employees."

"When things are tight you monitor every expense. Only when business is doing well inefficiencies creep in."

"We compete with the big names – the Taj and Windsor Manors of the world."

It was this impeccable track record which allowed Baljee to raise so much funding at relatively low rates of interest.

2003 saw a turnaround and since then there has been no looking back. Business started booming and the company also got the chance to lease another hotel on M G Road which was renamed 'Royal Orchid Central'.

Then, in 2004, the Hotel 'Metropole' came up for lease. This was the very same hotel which had drawn Baljee from the hills of Simla to the Deccan plateau in the first place. This time, he was successful in winning the contract.

By 2004, Baljee had four hotel properties and decided it was time to expand to other cities and establish a national presence. The turnover of the company at this point was ₹ 15-16 crore.

Royal Orchid signed new projects in Jaipur, Hyderabad and Pune. All these hotels were on lease, keeping the company asset-light. To fund this expansion Royal Orchid decided it was time to IPO.

Compliances, corporate governance, getting accounts right and putting all the companies under one umbrella took a year. In 2006, Royal Orchid had revenues of ₹ 36 crore. The company raised ₹ 130 crore through its maiden public offering and private placement of equity.

The USP of Royal Orchid is high quality at 'value for money' prices (in the 5-star market). Whereas Royal Orchid Central is a brand of lower priced, 4-star hotels.

"We compete with the big names – the Taj and Windsor Manors of the world. But everyone finds their own niche and develops their own loyal customers," says Baljee.

In March 2007, Royal Orchid's revenues stood at ₹ 125 crore and PAT (profit after tax) at ₹ 35 crore. With various projects close to completion, that is expected to rise substantially. The flagship hotel in Bangalore still contributes over 50% of the turnover but that will change over time. By 2009-10 more hotels of the Bangalore size will be operational.

So how does a localised and family run set-up manage such a rapid scale-up? The company has professionalised and hired people at the corporate level to handle finance, operations and business development.

Both the Baljee sons have also joined the company. 27-year-old Arjun is a hotel management graduate from Cornell while 24-year-old Keshav is a graduate of Wharton and ISB. The question of a 'succession plan' now looms large.

Baljee is practical when he says, "In every family business there is eventually a split. See what happened with the Ambanis." So the challenge is to structure the company in such a way that someday – if required – it can be divided.

As of now Arjun is handling an independent project – setting up a budget hotel chain called 'Peppermint'. While the first property is funded by Royal Orchid, Arjun is also looking for VC funding. Meanwhile, younger son Keshav (who worked with Lehman Bros in New York before returning to India) looks after new projects and sources deals.

"That could be the way," says Baljee. "Leave the main business to be run by professionals and let them manage their own projects." In fact, Baljee muses, ownership and operations are best kept separate. But there's still confusion on this front – it will take some time to become a concrete plan.

At the end of our conversation I can only think, wow! It has taken 35 years to take this company this far, and even up to five years ago things weren't exactly 'stable'.

For the first time since we've been speaking, Baljee smiles. "You have both ups and downs in business... You need to have staying power." So what if the IPO happened 20 years after it was first planned?

"I never felt disheartened... God has been very kind. This is all part of life."

ADVICE TO YOUNG ENTREPRENEURS

Identify what kind of work you want to do. I love the hotel business – food, making menus, everything to do with the business. If you love the business you take up, you will definitely make a success of it.

Learn the business you want to get into for a couple of years. Raising money is not so difficult today. There are VCs, or at least angel investors. There is even lease financing, for example, unlike my time!

Your family life may get affected – for example, you can't take long holidays and when you do take a holiday, phone calls and emails may follow you.

But if you enjoy your work, you won't feel it is an intrusion.

SUCH A LONG
JOURNEY

Madan Mohanka (PGP '67),
Tega Industries

In the 1970s it took Madan seven years to get government approval for a foreign collaboration. But he persevered with his dream of excellence in engineering and today, Tega Industries is the world's third largest company designing solutions in the field of mining equipment.

The first-generation entrepreneur is technically someone who does not come from a 'business family'. But it is often as difficult – or even more difficult – to scale up and professionalise a family-run business. It is a challenge thousands of second and third generation entrepreneurs are facing in India today.

In transforming a small business dealing in electrical installation into a multinational engineering company, Madan Mohanka faced all the hurdles and challenges of starting up from scratch. But then Madan had what you would call – *'junoon'*. A passion, which one is driven to pursue at any cost. That passion is what led to the creation of Tega Industries, and kept it alive through the most trying of times.

It is no coincidence that Madan's home and office are right next to each other, in the peaceful New Alipore area of Kolkata. On a Sunday afternoon, you can catch him having lunch with colleagues in the Tega canteen, overseeing a training programme, instead of enjoying a nap.

I marvel – how do you get a kick out of the company you started after over 30 years? Let's find out!

SUCH A LONG
JOURNEY

Madan Mohanka (PGP '67),
Tega Industries

Madan Mohanka is one of the very early graduates of IIM Ahmedabad. In those days the institute didn't have much of a name. In fact, Madan's was a business family and it seemed rather pointless that he should go and *learn* how to do business.

"I had done my engineering and my family thought it was time that I started *doing* something."

But Madan did join IIMA and it changed his outlook towards business. "In the environment in which I was brought up," reflects Madan, "the only thing that mattered was the rate at which one increased the family fortune." *

Despite these reservations, Madan did eventually join the family business after completing his MBA. The company, Techno Electric Pvt Ltd, was in the business of electric installation. It was fairly traditionally run and this was something which Madan decided to change when he joined.

For example, despite the nature of its business, Techno Electric did not employ any qualified engineers. Madan hired five graduate engineers and added new lines of business involving a higher order of complexity in technology.

Techno Electric started undertaking the design, supply and erection of Fuel Handling systems. Very little investment was

---

* *Some of the information in this chapter is based on a series of cases on Tega written by Prof V L Mote and Prof Jahar Saha.*

required and the profit margins were attractive. But apart from the money, this diversification changed the character of the company. From an outfit which merely supplied materials and labour for electrical installation, Techno Electric was transforming into an engineering company.

Madan was constantly on the lookout for new areas and opportunities for expansion. He used a simple method to spot these opportunities – scanning international trade journals related to mining, coal, steel and power industries. "If any of these products appeared to have market potential in India, I would write to the manufacturers and ask for details." This was a personal passion; other members of the family were busy managing branches of the company in Jamshedpur and Durgapur and showed little interest.

Madan's first successful foreign collaboration was with Bischoff and Hensel, a German company which manufactured motorised cable reeling drums. Techno Electric achieved a near-monopoly position in this business and although the market was small, the annual sales of the company reached ₹ 19 lakh in the first year.

This grew to ₹ 32.5 lakh in 1976, which was a quantum leap for the company. Profitability was high and encouraged by this success, Madan formed two new companies.

The first was Electro Zavod (India), headed by a senior professional from Techno Electric. This company concentrated on project work for steel and power plants. The second – Techno Pipe Works – was formed to take up piping projects.

But even as all this was happening, something bigger was brewing in the background. In June 1971, Madan had come across an ad of Skega AB, Sweden, in a mining journal. Skega specialised in the design, development and manufacture of abrasion resistant rubber products for the mining and cement industry.

"I wrote a letter to Skega saying that I would like to visit Sweden in the first week of July 1971 to meet the Managing Director of the company. They wrote back saying that they were not keen to have an agent for their products in India. But I never received their letter. I sent them a cable and I went to see them."

Naturally, they were surprised but a sales engineer met Madan at the airport. As the MD was not in town, he met with the Technical Manager. The discussions went well and a friendship was established. However, the Technical Manager was doubtful of whether Madan's company had the capability to absorb Skega technology and market its products.

On his return from Sweden, Madan consulted N Guha, the Chief Engineer (maintenance) at the National Mineral Development Corporation (NMDC). On seeing Skega's literature and brochures, Guha urged Madan to definitely go ahead. And thus began a long, arduous and passionate pursuit.

Madan started reminding Skega through letters and cables to send an agency agreement. On August 24, 1971, Skega accepted Techno Electric as their representative for India and Nepal for one year, under certain conditions. In 1972, a representative from Sweden came down to assess the market potential in India. Subsequently, a development engineer from India went to Sweden for training as the product and manufacturing process was a complex one.

In fact, a big change in mindset was required as three different technologies were involved – grinding, mining and mechanical engineering. "We couldn't get an engineer who had knowledge of all three engineering areas, so we had to create our own engineer to absorb the technology and implement it for the customer. And this required a completely different attitude and very strong professionalism."

Meanwhile, between 1972 and 1974, every six months Techno's marketing engineer Mr Manoj Basu travelled extensively to make presentations to potential customers. There seemed to be a good demand. Techno received two orders totalling ₹ 3 lakh and Skega warmed up to a licensing agreement. Madan met Assar Svensen, Skega's Managing Director.

"I was most impressed by this man. Assar was as much at home repairing a machine on the shop floor as he was in the boardroom of a multinational company. Moreover, he was a very warm person."

"When I went into this venture of Skega I didn't realise that this may have a repercussion on the family. Maybe, had I known that the family would break because of this venture, I wouldn't have taken it up at that time. So I don't know whether it was a good or a bad decision. But once I took it up, I never gave it up."

In fact meeting Assar resulted in more self-questioning on the business values of Madan's own company. The Svensen family once owned 100% of the shares in Skega but slowly Assar persuaded the family to disinvest. The reason being that many a time Assar noticed that the interests of the family and of the company were in direct conflict.

Assar and Madan developed a good friendship. Negotiations started but here, there was a problem. Skega wanted a down payment of ₹ 15 lakh plus a minimum guaranteed royalty of ₹ 35 lakh over the next five years. This was not possible under the guidelines laid down by the Government of India for approval of technical collaborations. Secondly, Madan was unsure whether he would be able to achieve enough sales to generate the minimum royalty payment expected by Skega.

A less determined man may have given up at this point. After all, there were other profitable lines of business in the company. And the German collaboration was already in place. But Madan persisted. As expected, the company's first application to the DGTD (Director General of Technical Development) was rejected. The terms DGTD offered were not acceptable to Skega.

The Swedish company sent its representatives to India to meet the officials and explain its rationale for demanding a higher licence fee. After all, Skega's products involved an extensive R&D effort.

Meanwhile, an Indian delegation visiting Europe to purchase mining equipment paid a visit to Skega and came back impressed with the company and its products. In light of this feedback, the government agreed to increase the royalty from 3% to 5% but limited the lump sum fee to ₹ 5 lakh. Skega also had to give a commitment to import material worth ₹ 45 lakh from India over the next five years.

Skega agreed to these terms and signed an agreement on December 10, 1975. The government suggested some modifications to the agreement and a final approval was obtained on February 9, 1977.

So why did Madan fight out this battle? Was there really something so special about Skega?

"What attracted me was they never advertised how much turnover they had. They advertised that we take up *solutions* for the customer. And the customers respected those solutions."

And that in a nutshell captures the allure of Skega for Madan Mohanka. There was already a steady business, profits, good lifestyle. "We were able to live and eat well, no problem on that. It was more the challenge that attracted me to go to Skega."

Of course, the major hurdle in those days was government approval but there was no other way to do business. Yes, many years were lost in the maze of red tape but you had to simply grin and bear it.

However, once approval was out of the way, other issues cropped up at the newly formed Tega Industries. There just weren't enough customers. Before starting, Techno and Skega had undertaken a market survey and most of the customers they met declared the product would definitely sell. But when manufacturing began, orders just did not come in.

Firstly, except for the Tatas, the entire mining industry was under the public sector. "When we went to sell, the first question they asked me is, 'If it does well, I don't get a promotion. If it fails, I lose my job. Why should I stick my neck out for you?'"

Being government employees they had no incentive to improve efficiency, the easiest thing was to maintain the status quo. The only other option to 'motivate' officials was to pay a bribe. But Madan refused to go down that route as a matter of principle.

"If you believe in a product, never give it up. You will succeed. It may take time, it will cost money."

"The irony is, even those fellows who told me that it will sell like 'hot cakes', refused to buy this product!" recalls Madan. Which is a huge lesson for any entrepreneur. Surveys are all very well but the proof of the pudding lies in the customer opening his wallet and handing out cold hard cash.

In reality, Mr S S Nadkarni, then General Manager of ICICI had hinted that such a problem may arise. When Madan presented his business plan to Nadkarni, he had remarked that he was concerned about the acceptance of the product. However, fuelled by the optimism of youth, Madan remained gung-ho.

He later remarked, "Had I stopped in my tracks to think about the comments made by Mr Nadkarni I would either have dropped the project altogether or implemented it in a radically different way."

Madan did get the required funding from ICICI but the next four years were extremely tough. Midway through the project, Madan met with a serious road accident. When he returned to work five months later he discovered there was a significant over-run in the cost of construction. He later discovered that the initial estimate itself was faulty.

Then when the company started executing the few orders it had received, it was found that the moulds it had acquired were not suitable. Additional investments would have to be made. Even after new moulds were made, bookings were poor. In fact, there were virtually no orders from September 1977 to January 1978.

Production was to begin in June 1978 and this was now a full-blown crisis. There was only one avenue – to get a contract from the Kudremukh Iron Ore Co Ltd (KIOCL) to fabricate and rubberline their indigenously procured equipment.

In order to be attractive to KIOCL, Madan devised a pricing where the profit on fabrication was low while the margin on the rubber lining was reasonable. Colleagues at Tega advised that the price he was quoting was too low. Skega also advised against accepting large orders which had a substantial amount of steel fabrication. However Madan went ahead and in June 1978, the company secured the KIOCL contract.

Unfortunately, steel prices started rising. Tega also realised it did not have the capacity to fabricate 800 metric tonnes within the stipulated period. Some of the work had to be subcontracted and given the very low margins, Tega Industries suffered a huge cash loss. In fact, the company's entire capital was almost wiped out.

In April 1979, Tega was unable to pay its employees on the due date. "The memory of that day is still vivid in my mind. I did not go to office," recalls Madan. Noticing his low mood, his wife asked what the matter was. Madan told her about the company's financial difficulty and also that he believed these were of a temporary nature. On hearing this, she offered him her LIC policy and her wedding jewellery.

The world may seem to have ended but if you have the support of your family, you can always make a new beginning. Salaries were paid two days later and an uphill climb to solvency began.

"I learnt a few things during that period in my life," says Madan. "One, if you take a new product, which has not been tried out before, at least plan for 50% or double the investment you envisage. Otherwise you will be in trouble. When your project fails, and you have no money, people treat you like a dog. And you are like a beggar asking for money and help."

(In fact when Tega eventually came out of the red, this case was taught at ICICI training school in Bombay and they took a decision that in future, if there is an entrepreneur with a new technology, they will sanction 50% more money than what he asks for. But they will only disburse it if the project runs into difficulty.)

"Number two, if you believe in the product, and if you believe in the business, don't give it up. Never give it up." When Madan went bankrupt, he mortgaged his wife's jewellery, but did not abandon the dream.

"I have sometimes wondered what is more important to the company as a leader. Till two years ago I heard Muthuraman saying, anybody who became the MD of TISCO must have very good knowledge of marketing and operations. But today he thinks it is more important to have vision and the ability to acquire and merge companies in order to grow."

"Not one man left us. My marketing manager then, an IIT and IIM graduate, an all-rounder, he is now teaching at the University of Pittsburgh. He told me, "Don't worry, we are all with you." Everybody remained with the company throughout the difficult period. Because all felt this was a challenge and we should meet it rather than leave the boat halfway when the boat is sinking."

Thirdly, Madan realised that you need a lot of patience to handle people in the government. "We were very impatient in handling them, so we got frustrated. But it's a matter of experience."

Lastly, integrity matters. In spite of all the difficulties it faced, Techno Electric fulfilled its delivery commitments.

In 1981, Techno Electric went for a sanction for a rights issue but nobody was willing to subscribe for the rights of a company which had become bankrupt. Except Mr Nadkarni of ICICI. "He believed in me, he believed in the product. He took it up as a personal challenge to convince all other institutions like IFCI, IDBI, to sanction the rights issue. If that had not happened, then maybe I would not have seen the light of the day."

From then on, things improved. The company got some orders, started generating cash and eventually broke even. Skega also extended its support. They did not ask for royalty to be paid to them in the difficult period.

At the end of the day business is well and good, but relationships are what really matter. It was Madan's personal equation with his collaborators and bankers which convinced them to keep the faith even when the balance sheet was literally under water.

Of course, it must be added, apart from the business-related problems during this period, Madan also faced another, emotionally draining issue – the break-up of the joint family.

In 1978, Madan's two brothers moved to Kolkata and wished to have a more active role in the business. Their management style did not go well with the professional managers and engineers at Tega and there were numerous conflicts. The entire team at Tega was much younger than at the other group companies, yet they were paid more. Hence, there was simmering tension.

Madan made a difficult choice. Tega was the closest to his heart and so he decided to give up the management of the other three companies. The brothers separated in 1981. Techno Piping was shut down, Techno Electric was sold off while Electro Zavod remained in business. Meanwhile, Madan poured all his energies into Tega.

However, the company continued to grow only slowly. Firstly, the market in India was limited. The mining industry was growing at the rate of half per cent or one per cent. And it was completely handled by the public sector.

In fact, from 1990 to 1998, the steel and mining industry in India was in a very bad shape. When Tega supplied the material, it would get paid in kind and not cash! For example, Hindustan Copper paid in 'tonnes of copper'. This was then sold at a discount to realise the money.

"And that is the time when, seeing the downward trend, we took the decision of getting into export." As per the contract

"We are concerned about Chinese competitors, but we have one advantage – our product requires software and hardware, both. The Chinese can compete with us on the hardware, they will take some time to compete with us on the software. So we think we have a lead on them."

with Skega, Tega could not look at markets outside India. But in 1998, the Skega collaboration ended and Tega was able to start focusing on the world market.

But the company faced two problems. In the developed world, most of the buyers preferred European or American suppliers. Even in African companies, most of the purchasing managers were whites. So for two years, Tega could not sell much.

"It was very difficult for us to convince them that we can supply as good a material as you are buying from Europe or America. Give us a chance! So I had to take a very hard decision. I hired an Englishman and brought him to India to look after the export market for us. His salary was almost equal to the salary of the entire company."

Was it the right thing to bring such an expensive man to work in a small company? Madan reasoned, "There are two ways to look at it. If I don't grow, the company will remain small and die over a period of time. And if I fight and if this man does a good job, the company will fly. So I would rather take a risk and die than not take a risk and die."

"It was the second hard decision in my life – to bring that man. But when he went out for exports, we found nobody asked him any questions – how big the company is, how small the company is, can you supply, not supply? We just started booking orders."

Tega identified pockets where the Europeans were not giving good service to customers. They would supply material at high prices but go there only once a year. Ghana was one such market and Tega was able to acquire a 68% share in that country, over a period of five years.

In the two and a half years the Englishman spent with Tega, the company's fortunes were transformed. The company started growing 50-60% year on year. This was phenomenal because Tega is in a very specialised industry – it only supplies equipment related to mining and mineral processing.

The total market for the products worldwide in the late '90s was ₹ 1,500 crore only, and today Tega is the world's third largest company in this space.

Did Madan realise it was such a small market to begin with?

"No, I didn't realise that. In fact, I never had a vision that the company would become so big. I wanted to change from the electrical business and Tega was a challenging assignment to work and think about."

And what of the other companies Madan set up? How does he manage all the operational complexity?

Getting into some of those businesses was a good decision, others was not. Wherever the customer base was the same, the company started making profits from day one. But in another case a joint venture was set up to fulfill Tega's requirement. 15% of the production was thus consumed in-house, but selling the remaining 85% meant building a whole new network. So this company was sold five years ago.

Eventually all other companies were merged into Tega and only two were kept alive. However, it is Tega which contributes 75% of the group's ₹ 250 crore turnover. MM Aqua Technologies (in collaboration with the German company Munters) contributes ₹ 40 crore while Hosch does ₹ 13-14 crore (but makes an excellent 30% profit margin).

"In the case of Hosch, we don't run the company, it just runs by itself," he explains. "It is very complementary. In the case of MM Aqua, it is a completely different technology, but it deals with water. And water is going to be the business of the future." Madan believes that the market is expanding significantly and future prospects are bright.

The future of Tega also remains bright as, in recent years, there has been an increased demand for metal all over the world. The market has thus expanded to ₹ 3,000 crore. Tega's share currently stands at 10%.

The number one and number two players are both very big. The leader is a $12 billion dollar company for whom this product line is a half a billion dollar business. The number two player is a billion dollar company which does about ₹ 300 crore of business from mining equipment.

"Both are keen on buying us", says Madan. "Every six months they knock my door and they give me a blank cheque. But I am not keen. They give me a blank cheque for two reasons. We have very good R&D facilities and we have very good technologists who can help them to grow. But we are not keen."

In fact, with the new-found cheekiness of the Indian entrepreneur, Madan has dreams of gobbling *them* up some day. "Once we become slightly bigger... then we will knock at their door," he declares.

The interesting part is, much of the R&D which makes Tega attractive today was actually born out of idleness. When the company was going through its crisis period – there were no orders – it was thought one may as well keep people busy in development work.

Speaking of people, Tega has always taken very good care of its employees.

"We were the first company in the country to pay 12% provident fund when the rule was 6% – this was way back in 1976. In spite of that, the labour unions closed our plant for a year. But we resolved the issues and today we are the only company in Bengal to have no union."

Another unique perk of being a senior manager at Tega is 'zero commute'. "Most of my colleagues live within one kilometre of the office. Right in the beginning, we made flats and sold it to people for ₹ 225 per sq ft. So when they retire, they should have their own house."

In the final analysis, reflects Madan, Tega was a product 20 years ahead of its time. And compounding that, the Indian economy was 20 years behind. "Today we bought a company in South Africa (Beruc Equipment Pty Limited), we didn't even have to take the permission from RBI to do so! In my first year when I went to Sweden, even for my travelling expenses I had to take permission from RBI and they sanctioned $25 per day in 1971. So wherever you travelled abroad, whether you were going to meet your customer, or a potential partner, first thing is you looked up to him to pay for your hotel. It used to be very embarrassing and very humiliating for an Indian."

Today, Tega has offices in 12 countries and customers in 43 countries. With the South African acquisition, Tega will start exporting from Africa itself rather than sending goods from

India. "In fact," beams Madan "because the rupee had become stronger, the interest had become zero." The South African company was not doing very well but Tega believed it could be turned around in a year. In reality, the turnaround took only four months.

However, this international diversification was, as always, based on deep personal conviction. And it involved risk. In the year 2000, Tega invested huge amounts of money in opening up subsidiary companies in USA, in Australia and an office in Canada. "In fact all of my personal assets, landed property, this and that. I sold everything to put the money to tap those markets."

So the theme of 'personal sacrifice' remains a recurring one. Besides the monetary hardships and uncertainty, Madan's devotion to Tega has certainly affected his role as a father and husband. He simply did not give the family the time or attention they rightfully deserved. And he is candid enough to admit it.

"When my eldest son was born, it was a caesarean. The operation took place in the morning at 9 am. And five o clock I had to leave to tackle an urgent issue in Dhanbad. When my wife woke up she was expecting I will be holding her hand, standing beside her. She was shocked to know I had left on business. So this kind of a trauma goes on in the family and it's not easy to handle it."

"My children say, their father and mother both, is their mother because their father, I, never gave them time in the early days... Maybe I try to compensate now."

"But you still seem so passionate and excited about Tega after close to 40 years!" I remark.

"I have only two jobs – one, look after the training department and R&D. And when we open a new branch, then I go and see the country, the economics, see what things are." An understatement if ever there was one, as he still works 18 hours a day. Maybe it's just that this isn't *work* for Madan.

It is his life, and he will have it no other way.

ADVICE TO YOUNG ENTREPRENEURS

If you believe in a product, don't give it up halfway through. Be on it. And you will succeed one day. And the results will be good.

Second, have patience during difficult times. Don't lose your balance, and try to carry the team with you.

Third, when you are launching any business, whether it's a new product or an existing product, if it's a new business, plan for 50% more money than what you think you require. At least 50% more to stand by. So in case you have difficulties halfway through, you don't have to close the business or run away. You have some money to put in, to carry on and see the bright side of it.

For a mid-size company, having multi-locations for the plant is not advisable because mid-size companies are owner-driven companies. Multi-locations create problems in terms of management focus.

There is a lot of scope in manufacturing. In India our manufacturing base is only 37%, whereas in all advanced countries, the manufacturing base is 65-75%. If any economy has to become strong in the long term, it can become only with the manufacturing base, not the service base. Service base is only temporary. This will not create long-term employment and if the economy has to become strong, it has to go into manufacturing.

If you are getting into manufacturing a unique product and if you have a passion for the product, venture capitalists will finance it today.

THE ALCHEMIST

Sunil Handa (PGP '79),
Eklavya Education Foundation/ Core Emballage

As the force behind the LEM (Laboratory in Entrepreneurial Motivation) course at IIMA, Sunil Handa has inspired countless students to become entrepreneurs. From a hard-nosed businessman to an educational entrepreneur, his is a fascinating journey.

Sunil Handa has been a teacher, mentor and friend. Not just for me, but for all students of LEM (Laboratory in Entrepreneurial Motivation), a course he has been taking at IIMA since 1992.

That is precisely why it is so difficult to write this chapter. A part of me is worrying about being objective. The other part is wondering, "Will he like it?"

A conversation with Sunil Handa is always fascinating. He is so honest and open about his life. His stories entertain you, they impress you but most of all, they speak to you. And in doing so, reveal a little bit more about who you are.

Sunil Handa's journey is also interesting because it is about change. Not only in business, but at a deeply personal level. Sunil spent 15 years like any entrepreneur – leading a life where the business was the first thing and the only thing that mattered. But an acrimonious split with his brother led him to question the value of leading this completely one-track, build-your-business-at-any-cost kind of life.

Thus was born Eklavya School, and the idea of creating an impact on people's lives rather than a bottomline. The school is as much of a challenge as any business and as with any project Sunil is involved with, it hums with energy and innovation.

And Sunil himself now leads a more balanced life. Or at least tries to.

THE ALCHEMIST

Sunil Handa (PGP '79),
Eklavya Education Foundation/Core Emballage

Sunil Handa's family came to Ahmedabad after partition. And they started life here from scratch.

"My father is a refugee from Pakistan and when he reached Ahmedabad, he lost both his parents. He started his life as a mill *mazdoor* in a textile mill."

Handa Sr worked from 12 midnight till 8 am, living in a chawl next to the mill. In the morning he would go and study while in the afternoon he was a lab assistant in a polytechnic called RC. This is how he completed his matriculation, then BSc and LLB. And although he was always a salaried employee he took up a variety of jobs. These jobs took the family all over India. By the time Sunil completed class 12, he had been at seven schools in all.

"We always lived not in the main city but away from the main city. In Calcutta, we lived in a place called Budge Budge, which is outside Calcutta. In Delhi, we lived in Gurgaon. In Ahmedabad, we were in a small town called Kalol. So we were always in a small place and we didn't have many friends," Sunil recalls.

There was an elder brother and a younger sister, and they were good in studies. But Sunil declares he was 'sleeping in life' until he joined Hyderabad Public School in class XI. "I never read newspapers, I never read books... The best I could get in marks was 45-50%... If I have to say when my intellectual or academic life began, I would say it started in class 11 and 12 in the HPS hostel."

At HPS, Sunil noticed fellow students reading story books. And up to this point in life Sunil had not read *any* books outside his school syllabus. Enid Blyton, Billy Bunter, Noddy – none at all. He went up to the librarian, one Mrs Fatima and told her he had never read a book in his life.

"I cried and asked her, will you help me in reading?" She was quite taken aback.

But once Sunil started he devoured every book he could lay his hands on. He was mad – fourteen years of his life had been wasted and they had to be made up! "Nowadays, I find class 11 and 12 students stop sports, stop reading, stop activities, stop eating outside because of board exams. And all I did in life, I did in class 11 and 12," he muses. This included being on the school hockey team, Hindi debating team, English drama team, winning the President's Scout Award and serving as president of the physics club.

"If you see my two years' biodata, you will say, this is ten active students put together. I tried learning horse riding. I gave up. I joined a poultry farming club, I gave up after ten days because it used to smell a lot. But I read a lot."

There was also a lot of ragging in the school hostel. Sunil was very thin, weighing only around 40 kg at the time. What's more, his English was very poor. "If I opened my mouth in the class and asked a question everyone would laugh at me. Because I had a heavy rural accent."

As a result he was bullied, teased, ragged and hit by fellow students. "I used to come back to my dorm and think, why doesn't the world come to an end. What should I do... How should I get out of this?" One Mr Tiwari, Hindi teacher and hostel warden, changed his life. When Sunil went to him crying that he could not speak English Tiwariji had one simple piece of advice: "Learn it!"

Initially taken aback Sunil took this as a challenge and joined the English Drama club and Public Speaking club where all would laugh at him. But within a year, he was among one of the better speakers in the school.

The second thing which left a lasting impact on Sunil was Tiwari sir relating the story of Japan. After being totally devastated by the Americans, Japan decided to take revenge by becoming better than America in whatever they were good at. In research, in industry, in manufacturing. And how does all of the above tie in with entrepreneurship? Well, the sum of these experiences toughened up Sunil Handa, made him a fighter.

"Like Indira Gandhi used to say, when I am down, and I am pushed against the wall, my best comes out and I don't give up. The fighter in me, the animal in me comes out and says, 'I will do it and show them'. This has come from Tiwariji. So a good teacher at the right time in your life can make a frog into a prince!"

And the frog who got 45% in class 10 graduated from HPS as one of the top ICSE students in India. In some subjects like Physics he was an all-India topper and thus easily got admission in BITS Pilani.

The next five years were wonderful. In the fourth year, Sunil became acquainted with solar energy. In the summer vacation, he stayed back at BITS with a friend. Sunil and Bharat researched a lot of literature and identified one idea called Honeycomb Collectors which the Russians had invented in 1929 but didn't give results. They decided to pick up the idea and work on it.

After two months, it turned out to be a brilliant success. The duo got temperatures on a flat plate collector, which nobody in the world had ever achieved. One afternoon the whole apparatus actually caught fire! In the next semester, in addition to studies, they worked on the idea and wrote a paper on the findings.

The paper was published in an international conference in Italy – at the International Centre for Theoretical Physics, a very reputed institute. Sunil and Bharat were called to Italy to present it. But they would have to bear the travel cost, which was ₹ 8,000.

"But we didn't have eight thousand rupees. I wrote a letter to Kasturbhai Lalbhai. He sent me a cheque of ₹ 250. Then I wrote to Jyoti R&D and Hindustan Brown Boveri, which is now ABB. They said, you come and give a talk on your work in solar energy to our scientists, and we will pay you some honorarium. That was another ₹ 900," recalls Sunil.

> "To take a 23-year-old fresher from IIMA and throw him into Bhavnagar to revive a sick unit, required a lot of guts and the density of learning was very high. If I had spent 19 months in Hindustan Lever as a management trainee, I would not have learnt even one per cent of what I learnt in 19 months as a chief executive of a sick unit."

In this manner they collected ₹ 3,000. By this time, Sunil was studying at IIMA and it was clear that there wasn't enough money for both of them to make the trip. So Bharat cobbled together another ₹ 5,000 and attended the conference.

But the whole effort was all about entrepreneurship. The desire to do something new and pathbreaking. The struggle against the odds to make it to the conference. And even today Sunil is extremely proud of what they achieved.

"If you say Windows is a breakthrough in software, then I can say Honeycomb Collectors is breakthrough work in solar energy. We got job offers from Israel, New Zealand, USA and Australia but we didn't want to make a career in this field. So we left it at that."

But why not a career in research? Why management?

"See, in my final year, I never wanted to do management. My idea of management was they only use jargon, they are superficial and fraud people. I used to have a very poor opinion of MBAs." Sunil had in fact decided to dedicate his life to something in the electrical industry called 'Thyristors'.

"Like your IC chip, you have something called the Thyristor. In my fourth and fifth year, I used to worship Thyristors, I used to write poems on Thyristors, I used to sleep and think that I am a Thyristor. I wanted to do a PhD in Thyristors."

Then Sunil's father took him to Jyoti R&D, a leading company in Baroda at that time. Their personnel manager, Vijay Vannikar, was an MBA from IIMA. He took Sunil to a garden in Baroda called Kamatibaugh near Baroda University.

"We sat for 3-4 hours and he convinced me that I must do an MBA from IIMA. I used to think MBAs are superficial while real people are engineers. He changed that notion. That was a turning point in my life."

Sunil took the CAT exam. 2,200 people wrote the CAT exam in 1977 and Sunil was 13th on the wait list for IIMA. He was also on the wait list at IIM Bangalore, IIM Calcutta, XLRI, Bajaj and Punjab University. "So I was famous in BITS Pilani as 'manager in waiting'!"

Eventually he got into IIMA, but with some inferiority complex. "The first person I met shook my hand and said: "I am an IIT-JEE topper." The next guy I met said, "I am an IIT Delhi, electronics topper." The third introduced himself as a "St Stephen's topper."

At the end of three days, Sunil thought he was in the wrong place.

Then the old habit came back. "One year, I will beat these fellows", he decided. And that year he slogged, staying awake every night till 3-4 am. There used to be seven I-Schols* in those days. Sunil came seventh. But as always he also participated in manyextra-curricular activities.

For summer training, Sunil went to NTPC, which had just started and was putting up a 2,000 MW power plant in Singrauli at a cost of close to ₹ 4,000 crore. The location was in the hills and it was a 'coal pithead power station', i.e. instead of bringing coal to the power stations, you make the power station at the mouth of the cave. It was a complex project and and the daily report used to be one inch thick. The NTPC chairman D V Kapur gave Sunil and his partner an important assignment: "Give me a one-page daily report."

The stipend was ₹ 450 per month but it was a fantastic learning experience. "Somehow money didn't matter. During those days, summer training was true summer training. We were very discerning and gave a lot of thought to what project really excited us."

---

* I-Schols or Industry Scholarships are awarded to the toppers of the class at IIMA and considered extremely prestigious.

"There is potential in every business. Like a school is not profitable in terms of money, but it is profitable in terms of developing character. There, the profit is different, developing human potential. So the word 'profit' I use, but not necessary in terms of rupees."

While Sunil enjoyed all the courses at IIM, ERI (Explorations in Role and Identity) was another turning point. On 2nd October, 1978, Sunil participated in an exercise with Prof Pulin Garg and Indira Parikh. That exercise in front of the group lasted for 2-3 hours. "At the end of the exercise I was a different person. I came out of a tunnel, I saw daylight, I saw my God. My God said take responsibility for your own life."

"I will not blame the situation, I will not blame the weather, I will not blame the government policy. I will not say my parents did this to me. I will say, this has happened, I have to take action, and I have to take responsibility. If something good, I must pat myself, if something bad, I must love myself. I am the reason for my success or my failure, not the environment or anything else."

When Sunil finished IIM, he could have got day zero kind of jobs, but he did not want them. He did not want a tiny role inside a large company but a job where he would get to look after everything. And that is how Sunil joined FAIR – 'Foundation to Aid Industrial Recovery'. At the time FAIR was a hot organisation to join – four seniors and 10 batchmates from IIMA had joined as well. The salary was low – in fact the lowest in the batch at ₹ 1,250 per month (gross). But the idea was exciting.

The concept of FAIR was to take a sick industrial unit from a bank, put a young MBA in charge as the chief executive and turn around the company in two years, retaining all the existing employees. Sunil spent six months going all over India looking at various sick units. Finally, he zeroed in on a company in Bhavnagar and told his boss, "This is the company I want to run... I will revive it, I have a feeling that I will be able to do it."

But in the pre-Bhavnagar months the trainees had to earn their salary. So they did a little bit of consultancy. And this is a digression of sorts but it's important.

One of the projects that came FAIR's way was from the Ford Foundation. They wanted to do for Madhubani paintings, what Kurien did for milk. At that time, Madhubani paintings were sold by extremely artistic women at throw away prices – ₹ 200-500 per piece. The same paintings were eventually sold in Cottage Emporiums for ₹ 10,000. The Ford Foundation mandate was – remove the middlemen, get the artists or producers into a cooperative and do the marketing and selling directly.

So Sunil and his batchmate Sanjeev Phansalkar went to Madhubani and lived there for a month. They organised the women into a 'Master Craftswoman Association of Mithila'. This organisation would market the paintings and fetch the artists almost 80 per cent of the sale price in Delhi. That was a wonderful thing and it exists till today.

But there is an even more wonderful thing the young graduates did which, says Sunil, has become his 'style in life'.

Now the ladies were organised, there was an association. It had a charter, but who would run it after the MBAs left? "I told Phansalkar, this person who is ideally meant to run it, is already there in this world. Let us go through our minds find this person".

He said, "What are you talking about!"

I said, "You tell me, is it a woman or a man?"

"It would be a woman because it's an organisation of craftswomen of Mithila."

"What would be her age?" They argued over this and finally said, "She is between 35 and 45."

Then I asked, "Is she married or unmarried?"

He said, "She is married because a married woman is considered more respectable."

"I have always felt that the way to judge a manager is, after thirty years, judge where his subordinates are. If they are happy in life and successful and doing well, part of the credit goes to that person."

I said, "What is her name?"

Now if you go to Bihar, the Mishras are Brahmins. If you are a non-Mishra, it just won't do. So it has to be a Mishra.

So they started looking for a Mrs Mishra between 35 and 45 years of age. She is not from Madhubani village, she is from the nearby town – Darbhanga.

I said, "Phansalkar, she will be a professor in some college. She will be an assertive personality."

So we went to Darbhanga Girls College. We went to the principal and asked her, "Is there a Mrs Mishra who teaches political science or sociology?"

She said, "Yes."

They went to her and she was exactly what they wanted! She was told, this is a part-time job – 2-3 clerical people will be recruited but you will have to go personally – once or twice a week. And you will be the honorary secretary of the *sanstha*. She was more than happy. In consultation with her, they made a board of governors of some local, prominent people.

"From that day till today, I have a feeling that if I have to start an activity, and I want to recruit a person, I say such a person already exists. I imagine who that person is, where am I likely to find him. And through our Sherlock Holmes type logic, we have to reach the person."

It may sound incredible but it has worked for Sunil time and again.

But getting back to FAIR, Sunil worked with Merchants Steel Industry Pvt Ltd in Bhavnagar. The company had four plants and it made stainless steel utensils, tin containers, drums and rolling mills. After the first one or two months, Sunil shut down the stainless steel utensils because it was loss making. Then, he shut down the rolling mill and concentrated on the remaining two units.

A lot of other work was involved – paying back old loans and back salaries. The old owners were eased out from the board and a new board constituted at Sunil's behest. "I think I did a very decent job of bringing the company back to life."

After 19 months, Sunil realised that this chapter of his life was over. The question was, who would run the show? Even the former owners agreed that the best course of action was to sell the unit. An ad was put in *Mumbai Samachar* and one Kediaji, who owned other steel plants as well, bought the unit. He made an offer to Sunil to join him, but he declined. On 31st December 1981 Sunil left Bhavnagar for good.

Sunil's brother Sushil was running a management consultancy in Ahmedabad. He had made an offer of partnership to a friend who had studied MBA with him. The friend didn't have the faith that this business would run and refused the offer. Sushil had made the same offer to Sunil but he had opted for FAIR. One of the reasons being the feeling, "Let brothers be brothers, if we get into business together, it will affect our relationship."

But when Sushil made the offer again, Sunil joined him. Both became equal partners in a small company called Core Consultancy Services. A couple of months afterwards, it became 'Core Consultants Pvt Ltd'. Along with management consulting, the company started consulting in the area of computers.

"I was personally very good in computers and I made a lot of software for insurance, stock exchange and banking. I should be counted among the pioneers," says Sunil. The company did very well, getting into water management and irrigation engineering as well.

"I think when I was a consultant, I was a very good consultant. I saved my clients a lot of money. I never in my life believed in giving a report. I always thought that my job is to help them in problem solving and why give a report? Is a report going to be implemented?"

"So I would just start. And every day I discussed, every week I discussed. And every week some new ideas will come, we will keep implementing and in six months time, everything will be implemented. Which is how it is in life."

Clients were extremely satisfied. Business was good. The turnover of the company was over ₹ 1 crore a year (which was big money at the time). And consulting is an industry with a fat profit margin, so the profit was at least ₹ 60 lakh. And yet in 1986, they closed it all down and got into the pharmaceutical industry.

Why?

"I wanted an enterprise. There has to be a chimney with smoke coming out of it. There has to be a factory with sounds of something being created, trucks coming in, unloading material, finished goods being taken out... there is a *chowkidar*, workers smoking *beedis* in a corner. You know, a typical factory atmosphere."

Besides, the nature of the business was such that you could not 'scale' beyond a point.

"Frankly, how many ever consultants I appointed I knew nobody could be better than me. But how could I stretch my life?" The solution was to build a factory, build a brand name.

The idea was actually born out of idleness. 1985 saw the second of the infamous Gujarat riots. Hindus and Muslims were killing each other, the whole city was burning. Ahmedabad was closed for a month. Luckily, the Core office was in a place which was not under curfew. However, with most establishments remaining shut, there was no work to do. It was in this period of 'vacuum' that the brothers decided, "Let's start a factory."

Many options were discussed but in 6-8 months they had zeroed in on pharma. The fact that they didn't know anything about pharmaceuticals was not a deterrent. Sunil has always loved the challenge of mastering something new. He will read up, meet people, visit factories or wherever required and figure it out.

"And whatever I have done," he says "there is always innovation."

"People used to laugh at the ideas of a fresh 23-year-old from IIM, but I too was equally stubborn and didn't let up. Today, Saurashtra produces the maximum groundnut oil of India and it is still sold in 15-kilo tins that we used to manufacture. If you go to any *dabbawala* factory in Saurashtra – there are literally hundreds – some of the practices I started are still being implemented by everyone," he says.

"In IV fluids, you go anywhere in India, 95% per cent of what they are doing in the factories are things which we had started. If you ask them what is the batch size, they will say 5,000. If you ask them how many times do you sterilise – they sterilise in two lots of 25 a day. If you say, in one box, how many do you pack, they say 24."

Coming from someone else it might sound bombastic. But from the mouth of Sunil Handa is sounds just this-is-the-way-it-is. Because this is the way I am.

And once again we digress, as Sunil shares his belief in being 'open' and sharing knowledge. "I remember, when I wanted to start an IV fluid factory, I wanted to see some IV fluid factories. I was refused. So I saw two factories stealthily. One by becoming Dr Gadgil from Shardaben Hospital and the second as a 'GIDC inspector'. What could I do? They were not showing legitimately. But when others wanted to see our factory, I showed it to so many people."

Sunil goes on to relate the story of the 'animal house' which is where drugs are tested on animals. It is generally the dirtiest area of a pharma factory. But at Core they took special care to look after the animals well – the house was even air-conditioned. And this small act of 'humaneness' was to benefit the company hugely.

There was a large tender in Sudan – 60 lakh bottles of IV fluid – and only two contenders were left at the very end. Arab Otsuka, a Japanese company based in Egypt and Core from Ahmedabad. A four-member Sudanese team came to Core to inspect the factory, headed by a lady.

"Before they came, we located a mosque and spent 20,000 rupees to clean up the place. We made a lot of other arrangements – we bought some rugs to put on the floor when they did *namaz*. Even in our factory, we created one room, in case they didn't want to visit the mosque, they could do their prayers here. We found out where is north-east and all that."

But the clincher was the animal house – the lady simply fell in love with it and visited it several times during her three-day stay. Core Parenterals got the contract, and later a manager in Sudan learnt that this lady was a PhD in microbiology from Manchester University and had worked in England for 17 years, 11 of which were spent in the animal house.

She said, "Core was the only place where all testing was done on animals with so much of love and compassion." And that is what tipped the scale in the company's favour.

Sunil goes on to reveal the 'secret' of how this house of love was created. "When we started out, we had four rabbits. Then I found out, which rabbits should we keep? People told me, Indian rabbits are very tough. Even if there is an infection in the injection, nothing will happen to them."

So a manager was sent to Belgium, two male and two female rabbits were imported through Haffkine Institute in Bombay. Now, who will be in charge of the animal house? They decided to consult Dr David Reuben, the best zoo keeper in India. Dr Reuben said, "Whoever you select must love animals. That is the most important qualification."

They found such a person – Kanubhai Bhangi from Rajpur village. He had no 'qualifications' but the company recruited him and made him in charge of the animal house.

I could have spent the whole day listening to these stories. But we need to know about the company – Core Parenterals. How did it start, how did it scale-up? Sunil sums up the eight-year journey in a terse two minutes.

The first factory was not IV fluids – it made tablets, capsules and liquids. The name was Core Laboratories Ltd. The company did a public issue which was a flop. The total project, land and machinery, etc was ₹ 60 lakh. 20 lakh rupees was put in by the promoters, the rest came from banks.

One year later, the IV fluid factory Core Parenterals Ltd came into being. The project was ₹ 4.5 crore of which ₹ 1 crore came from equity and the remaining was a loan from IFCI. By

1994, Core Parenterals was a ₹ 600 crore company with five huge factories.

"We used the money very wisely. We put up the project in 8 months and 21 days. We had to unload a six-tonne machine. Getting a crane would have been very expensive. So we found many Indian ways of doing it, such as make a slope and take the machine down, gently rolling it. I used to spend 24 hours there."

He adds: "We did lot on innovations in IV fluids. We have contributed to the international IV fluid industry. We have made design changes in machines, which machine manufacturers have made as a standard part of their machines. I am personally very well-valued anywhere in Europe wherever there are IV fluid machine manufacturers."

There is a lot of pride but it is tinged with pain. The reason Sunil tells so many stories is not just because he is a great storyteller. The stories are a way of remembering the good parts. The bad part was the way in which it all ended. Summing up the Core Parenterals experience he says: "We put up the factory, expanded it. After '94, my brother and I separated. After that I had no interest in doing business."

But he is now the CEO of Core Emballage, a company which manufactures corrugated board.

"Yes. I set it up because I must have some cash cow in some part of the world," he says in a deadpan voice. The corrugated box project was born because of a promise made by brother Sushil. The biggest weakness in the IV plant was that the containers were very bad. "My export boys used to come back from all over the world and show me the kind of packaging that our competitors offered and asked me why we couldn't match up to them. I used to feel very bad."

When the brothers separated one of the deals was Sunil would put up a packaging factory and supply to Core Parenterals. It never materialised. Sunil did put up Core Emballage in 1996 but says he lost a substantial amount of money when Sushil's company didn't pay up.

The factory was set up on a very large scale because the Core Parenteral requirement was very big. Suddenly there was no big customer. A mineral water manufacturer could have been a client but this was a location-sensitive industry, so it did not work out. "This factory is over designed, it is not doing so well as it ought to have done."

"But also because your whole heart is not in it anymore, isn't it?" I ask.

"Forget whole heart, not even one per cent of it is in it. I go to the factory only once a year, for Dassera pooja. I am not interested in doing business anymore. I don't want to earn crore of rupees. I don't want to look at stock prices. If I sell off the company and do nothing, it's still okay with me. But I think it's good to have some activity. And it makes decent profit."

Core Emballage currently has a turnover of ₹ 35 crore. It's in a steady state of sorts. The first couple of years Sunil did pursue innovation, even at this new company. Like producing corrugated folders, 'furniture' just to educate people about what the potential in the product was. But the separation had been traumatic and it changed Sunil's entire outlook to life.

"It was not a happy separation... the trauma went on for many months. And at the end of it, my heart, mind, soul, rejected the concept of making money. And I thought, that cannot be the purpose or end of life. And for the first time in life, I suffered from depression."

"I used to laugh at people. What is depression! It is nonsense. I am a great believer of Vivekananda and Ramkrishna that the basic thing in life is strength. That it's all in the mind, nowhere else." But for once, the mind was not in his control. "For ten months, I nearly killed myself every day," he recalls.

"For ten months, I kept a bottle of potassium cyanide in my cupboard and I would tell myself, 'Tomorrow'!"

A friend from BITS Pilani – Nanda Kumar – heard about this and invited Sunil to stay with him in Bangalore for some days. "He took me to a sadhu who did 'sarpa pooja', gave me three lemons and said you keep it. So I came back and kept them. After some time they dried up so I threw them away. After half an hour, I got them back. I put them in a handkerchief, took my car and went to Sabarmati river, did *Om Bhurbhuvaswaha* thrice and threw it in the river."

Sunil's wife Divya took Sunil to Vishakhapatnam. One 'Pendulum Shastri' came home and tried to treat him with a pendulum. One Muslim man came and tried to treat him with a magnet. And so it went on.

"Those ten months were the most horrible of my life, but I came out of it. Thanks to my wife and my parents. Then I decided I don't want to do this business and corporate thing. That's when the idea of Eklavya school was born."

Actually, before that Sunil considered starting an old age home, but somehow he didn't like the idea of people not looking after their parents. He didn't want to encourage that trend. So he plunged into education and in characteristic style started by hiring the right people – three young IIMA graduates.* They spent about 15 months going all over India and all over the world, to understand what made a great school.

"We went to seven countries and we visited more than 150 schools and colleges including Shanti Niketan, Oxford etc. Basically trying to understand what is a school. One is a philosophical question, *yeh hai kya cheez!* Many small details. We were fairly clear what we wanted our school to be." Eklavya school began functioning in 1998 and today, it is the most admired (and most sought after) school in Ahmedabad. The first batch of class 12 students graduated in March 2006.

"Eklavya is not a profit-making company but it is very entrepreneurial." Running a school has as many challenges as running a regular business.*

Some of the innovations at Eklavya include 'small classrooms' and financial assistance for low-income students to make the school a more inclusive and diverse place. The school has been divided into four different portions – pre-primary, junior, middle and senior school. What is unique is that each portion has its own personality, its own library, resources and even its own principal.

"Our parents' involvement, mothers' workshops and many such ideas are fantastic. It is a very high-quality school. A child

* For more on the challenges faced while setting up Eklavya read Chapter 22 on Venkat Krishnan. He was one of the three IIMA graduates involved at the inception stage of the project.

in Eklavya gets fantastic exposure. In 20-30-40 years, when these children are older, the impact will be felt."

No doubt about that, but this is a paradigm shift from running a business where profit and loss, success and failure is measured year on year, quarter on quarter.

What's more, Eklavya does not believe in results in the conventional sense of the term. Of course, students are evaluated but poor marks would never be the basis for asking a student to leave. "I am sure some of the most successful people from Eklavya are going to be some of the most naughty students whom we did not throw out," says Sunil with a twinkle in his eye.

Eklavya is 'stable' and in a sense self-sustaining but it still thrives on the energy Sunil Handa invests in it. He goes to the school every day and spends a lot of time with teachers and students. "If I don't go there, in five years time, Eklavya will become like any other ordinary school," he adds. "Many times I have thought of succession planning... It's very difficult."

But it does not really matter, he feels. "Why should I bother what happens to it after I go? It will die and some new Eklavya will come. I am doing this as a part of my life and as a part of my spiritual evolution. It's not as if I shouldn't bother at all, but it is not a big deal."

What is a big deal is the impact Sunil has made not only with his school but as a teacher of entrepreneurship at IIM Ahmedabad. He has been taking the LEM (Laboratory in Entrepreneurial Motivation) course on campus since 1992. The course – as you can expect – is different from what is 'taught' anywhere. There are no textbooks, no exams. It's more about sharing of experience, of inspiration and motivation.

Of the 400-500 students who've taken LEM over the years, Sunil estimates 150 have become entrepreneurs. And what is the one 'most valuable' piece of advice he has for these young people? "Be honest with yourself."

"Luck is very important – it is 50%. But that luck will not come unless you put in the effort and in the effort, a very important element according to me is a daily review of what am I doing, where am I going and being ruthlessly honest with yourself. Most people blame the environment... My belief is I CAN CHANGE, and that we must learn to be nakedly honest with ourselves."

And he is nakedly honest with himself when he reflects: "I am a very good logistics manager, technical manager, factory manager, QC manager, personnel and HR manager. But I am not good in finance or PR, and just okay in marketing. Core Parenterals succeeded because my brother is too good in those areas. Between the two of us, we made a 'superfantastic' God-given combination. I would give my brother more than 50% credit. But he could not have done it without a person like me."

And although the partnership soured and he went through hell, today Sunil is a very happy person.

"When I was a successful businessman, I had no family life, I had no other life. I had massive tensions... I don't know when my daughter was born, I don't know when my son was born, I don't know when they started crawling."

"What was the first word they said? What did all that money get?! Nothing at all."

Everyone needs *some* money to be comfortable. Beyond that, it's your choice. You can pursue money or you can set different, higher order goals. And at any point in life you can 'make up' for lost time.

The advice Sunil gives to his LEM students today is very different from what he used to give, to a previous generation.

"I started with the assumption that if I want to be rich and successful, I have to sacrifice family life. You can't get both. Today, I would like to say, that I would like to try to have both."

Trying is what it's all about. Even as you try to grow, and achieve and reach for more, sometimes you need to step back and try, to just *be*.

<u>ADVICE TO YOUNG ENTREPRENEURS</u>

I tell my students, if you want to take up a job, you work for one year, two years, three years, not more, because after three years, a comfort zone may start. But not any type of job. There are three or four types of jobs which are good:

1) You are the chief executive of a closed sick unit. And you have the mandate from the owners and the bankers to be the big boss, take all the necessary ruthless, cruel decisions to revive it. I think there are jobs available in India like this till today, but we have to search. They are not coming for placements but they are there.

2) Executive assistant to the top one or two persons in a medium-sized company.

3) Be a vital part of a project team which is putting up a new project. Suppose there is a factory, say Glaxo, in Nasik. They are putting up a ₹ 50 crore expansion. Or ₹ 100 crore antibiotics project or rabies vaccine. So they have a small nucleus team of 5-6 people, which will slowly grow. Become a part of that team. You brought land for the project, then you applied for pollution board approval. Then you appointed an architect, structural engineer, electrical contractor. By the time you have finished, you have bought a boiler, you have recruited a *chowkidar*, you designed a garden, you thought of what the brand name of the product is going to be. You have appointed an ad agency. The six-man team has become 100. By the time the production starts, about 400 people are working. And you were there from the start. You have walked through the whole panorama.

After 2-3 years in such a job, you can put up a factory easily. May be not a ₹ 50 crore factory, but a ₹ 2 crore one at least.

You can think of more jobs on similar lines. Smaller company, wider job description, and more freedom and power to do whatever you want . But then, there is also a risk factor involved in it because ultimately the onus lies on you.

One of my strengths even in Core was I am able to develop people very nicely. If you are able to do that it gives your company an advantage of not having to recruit expensive people. Recruit raw people, invest in them. Not all will turn out to be gold or diamonds, but over time, you will have a handful. And they will be your biggest assets.

YEH HAI YOUNGISTAN
MERI JAAN

Vardan Kabra (PGP 2004),
Fountainhead School

In 2004, Vardan Kabra turned his back on an offer by multinational P&G to pursue his dream of starting Fountainhead School. He represents a new generation of young MBAs who are giving up seven-figure salaries for the kick of being an entrepreneur.

Sometimes a person acting out of conviction, pursuing a dream, represents the spirit of an entire generation. Vardan Kabra is one such person.

When Vardan turned down a pre-placement offer from P&G in March 2004, in order to set up a school, it made headlines across the nation. It was the irreverence of chucking the job coupled with the idealism of the project itself which captured the imagination.

Since 2004, OOPs (Opting Out of Placements) is a small but significant trend on the IIMA campus. In 2008, the figure reached double digits, with 11 students opting out in order to set up entrepreneurial ventures. Not all the projects are as idealistic as Vardan's but the very act of bowing out of the rat race is one of idealism – the idea that MBAs are meant to do more than sell soaps or manage other people's money, and get paid handsomely for it.

Vardan and Ankita Kabra's story reminds every one of you out there who did opt for a placement – there is more to life than the pursuit of yuppieness.

YEH HAI YOUNGISTAN

MERI JAAN

Vardan Kabra (PGP 2004),
Fountainhead School

Vardan led a nomadic life as a child. His father works with the C K Birla group, and it is a transferable job. This meant living in 10 different places (including Nigeria), studying in nine schools and making friends with people from all over India.

As a child Vardan aspired to join the army. But later he went the JEE way, and joined IIT Bombay where he did both his BTech and MTech. In his 3rd year at IIT, Vardan was the Overall Coordinator of Techfest – the biggest technology festival in India. Around this time (1999-2000), three seniors at IIT started what was probably the first dotcom of India.

"I was quite envious of them – and at that point I decided that I too would do something on my own – that to me was far more glamorous than a hi-fi job."

In fact right after IIT, Vardan tried to start something called a 'Detonation Spray Coating' unit (being a metallurgical and material science engineer). He could not go ahead with the project because of lack of capital and no clue about how to actually run a business. So he decided to do an MBA and joined IIMA.

"During the first year I did get into the rat race for a little while – but soon I realized what I really wanted. The two-month internship at P&G in Mumbai made me sure that a job is not for me. I am too lazy to work well under a boss", he adds with a grin.

In the second year, Vardan took LEM (Laboratory in Entrepreneurial Motivation taken by Sunil Handa). "It was a major factor in keeping the motivation going – and more importantly for showing a direction as to how actually to go about doing things. External factors who tried to dissuade included my parents, relatives, some friends (not too many though as most knew me quite well not to argue with me)."

In his second year at IIMA Vardan visited Eklavya School in Ahmedabad and realised that he too wanted to start a school. It was time to start exploring options. "We formed a team of 11 people with interest in entrepreneurship – then we started working on various ideas. We formed sub-teams with interests in specific areas – education being one of them. Then our team started working on schools. Four of us visited schools across India (Jaipur, Ahmedabad, Baroda, Surat, Mumbai, Delhi). The idea was to get some good points from all the places and understand what's missing."

The team disbanded after graduating with everyone taking up jobs except for one other person, who decided to get into a venture other than education. Vardan shifted to Surat, a city which lacks good schools but where there is a growing demand for quality education. And paying capacity is not an issue.

However, the first six months were a major low period. "I had no clue as to what I was doing and where I was heading." In this period he briefly considered setting up a bookshop but then dropped the idea. In the end, Vardan realised that the first step for someone with no money has to be to start off with a preschool and then grow into a full-fledged school.

Take the baby steps and you will eventually learn how to run the full marathon!

Luckily he was not 'alone'. Batchmate Ankita Diwekar was attracted towards the school project while at IIMA and was quite serious – but she was unsure whether leaving a job and getting started straightaway was the answer or not. So she took up a placement with P&G.

"But even while she was on the job she was still helping me out all the time. She visited Surat 2-3 times and then once we knew that we were getting married, Fountainhead Preschool also took off and she joined full-time two months before marriage."

Funded by Ankita and Vardan's family, as well as Sunil Handa, the initial investment was about ₹ 13 lakh. Fountainhead Preschool started with six kids in April 2005. The 50th child joined nine months later and by January 2007 that number stood at 140+. Even as enrolments were growing (purely on word of mouth) Fountainhead was also becoming known as a 'brand' of high-quality meaningful education in Surat.

While Ankita was fully involved in managing the preschool, in January 2007 Vardan also started a training centre called 'Life Skills' for students and working professionals. Life Skills imparts short-term, job-oriented courses and was set up in partnership with two local businessman. The plan being to set up the centre and get it going over the next one year after which Vardan was clear he would head back to schooling full-time.

But the concept has relevance even there. "What's needed is for schools to teach Life Skills – so that kids can be independent, thinking, empathetic, enterprising individuals."

"People are starting to recognise that marks alone do not mean education and nor do they mean success in life," says Vardan. Still, changing the mindsets of parents and teachers does take time.

The other major hurdle Fountainhead faced was land. You need at least 4-5 acres to set up a good school and how can one afford to buy land at today's exorbitant rates? When Fountainhead applied for government land in Surat in January 2005 everyone said it would take a maximum of 18 months, but even two years on, there was no sanction. Plus, there was no clarity on the concessions being offered over the market rate.

So Vardan also started talking to some private players as it was a ₹ 4-5 crore project. "Getting funds for land and infrastructure has been our biggest hurdle."

The reason is that education is supposed to be a 'non-profit' activity. Hence, you can't attract money in the way you would for a regular company – by making a sensible business plan. Of course everyone knows schools do make money but it is a fact never advertised.

Even as a preschool Fountainhead was able to charge annual fees of ₹ 21,600 (all inclusive). The scope for higher classes would, of course, be more. "At the same time, 8-9 kids at the preschool have been subsidised; children of maids, clerks and workers' kids are paying ₹ 100-200 per month," he adds.

"Education, as a business model is feasible, no doubt about it. Except for the capital expenditure which makes life very difficult. For a preschool there's no problem."

Wages and salaries form 40-45% of the total cost of running a school and even then, finding good teachers is an issue. Eklavya School has provided non-financial support such as curriculum design, teacher training, processes, legal help and so on, making life a little easier.

But it's been a steep learning curve.

All the hard work is now bearing fruit as Fountainhead starts its first full-fledged school from June 2008. In partnership with a local businessman, the school is coming up on a 10-acre campus and will admit approximately 200 students from nursery up to class 5. The preschool will also continue to function from rented premises for the time being.

"The infrastructure is of very high quality," says Vardan with pride. "We are going in for the International Baccalaureate's Primary Years Programme (the affiliation is a 3.5 year process which started six months ago)."

Adds Ankita, "We are very excited with the programme as we believe it has all the right elements and emphasis as far as education is concerned and their philosophy strongly matches ours."

The aim is to make this a model school in the next 4-5 years and then expand rapidly in the schooling segment. In the preschooling segment, Fountainhead is looking to start another branch by November 2008.

If the experiment goes well then the stage will be set to expand into more full-fledged schools.

More schools mean more teachers. Fountainhead's total staff will cross 75 this year and to keep them up-to-date the school arranged for a 9-week training programme through the summer vacation. This included self-development exercises, field trips, educational videos and of course, everything about PYP.

It has taken four years but the vision of a school is now a concrete reality. "We have our fair share of crises and issues, but we are very satisfied with what we are doing. Of course there's so much yet to be done!"

On a reflective note, Vardan adds, "Because I got media coverage at the very beginning, I thought that my dreams would come true immediately. That did not happen – it takes times for big dreams to materialise. So basically more down-to-earth thinking would have been better."

Maybe. But you have to start with your head in the clouds. That's what gives you the courage to take the foolish decision instead of the safe one!

And you can think all you want, but life has its own flow. And you just go with it. In the midst of giving birth to Fountainhead School, Ankita and Vardan also became proud parents. Baby Sunay was not really planned and his arrival changed life in many ways.

Says Vardan, "Sunay's arrival has changed the way we work (or rather how Ankita works – I am being more of a typical father than I thought I would be). Ankita has a lot of stress as a result of being a mother as well as the key person for the school."

For example, Ankita was working till the second last day before delivery and she returned to working for 5-6 hours just 40 days after her delivery. "We actually had a dip in quality while Ankita was away but she was committed enough to come back and ensure that work did not suffer."

There is really no 'correct time' to have a baby, because there is always something more to achieve as far as work goes. But work is not everything – that's why babies come into this world.

And there is no 'correct time' to start a company, because there is always some risk involved. But security is not everything – that's why books like this are written. To drive that point home.

ADVICE TO YOUNG ENTREPRENEURS

Getting the direction is probably a matter of time, and working hard – when you keep working you realise what makes more sense. There were no specific attempts at creative problem-solving, but when the problems did get solved, typically that happened when the atmosphere was conducive to out-of-the-box thinking. So yes, some attempt at creative thinking would be useful.

Know what you want – I take my time when it comes to important decisions, but once made, I almost never give up. I do take the opinion of other people, but when the decision affects me directly, then I alone make the decision (e.g. deciding not to take up a job was against the wishes of almost everyone around).

In my undecided phase I happened to meet a serial entrepreneur from IIT. I told him I wanted to start off on my own but was not sure whether I should take up a job or not as back-up. He said if you are sure that you want to start up then taking a job should be the least of your concerns. Start off, that's it! That's when I realised that there's only one way of jumping off the cliff – you just have to jump off it!

THE OPPORTUNISTS

These entrepreneurs did not plan to take this path but when opportunity knocked they seized it. Their stories go to show that you don't have to be 'born with it', you can develop an entrepreneurial bent of mind at any age.

TRIPPING
ALONG

**Deep Kalra (PGP '92),
makemytrip.com**

Deep went into business the way every entrepreneur dreams it will happen: a venture capitalist offered him $2 million to start up. But with the dotcom bust he had to invest his life savings and buy back his own company. Makemytrip.com is today India's leading travel portal.

Deep Kalra is the kind of chap advertising agencies pick to star in airline commercials. You know the suave-banker-who-travels-the-world-yet-cares-about-family type.

I am not surprised then, when he calls to postpone our interview. Because he is shooting an ad campaign!

"Basically HP is doing this worldwide thing called 'Achievers campaign'. So I said, okay, that's interesting, it's a good brand."

"But more than a personal ego trip it's good for the company," he stresses.

"There is a stream of stories coming out of a printer, and we have shots on that with lots of branding. Secondly, we negotiated lots of printers. They offered us four, finally we got 20."

"I said would you like it if we didn't have an HP printer in some of our offices? You should at least give a discount on others! So it worked out well… it is no fun being in a professional shoot though. We started at some unearthly 7.30 am and it went on all day."

When the thrill of every small saving equals the achievement of every big milestone, you know you have on your hands, a true-blue entrepreneur.

TRIPPING ALONG

Deep Kalra (PGP '92),
makemytrip.com

Deep Kalra is your average Delhi dude.

"My grandfather had a business of dry fruit in Chandni Chowk but there was never any question of joining it. My father opted out of that long ago."

Deep grew up in a typical private sector home; very comfortable. But it was very clear from the beginning – *agar kuch banana hai to khud hi banana hai.* BA from St Stephen's college, and then an MBA from IIM Ahmedabad. He does not sound very ambitious or driven – "Kind of tumbled into it," is how he describes it.

Out of campus, Deep joined ABN Amro. After a year or so he realised '*Banking nahin karnee!*' There was the seed of a thought – it would be fun to do something of your own. But it remained a thought. After three years in banking and exploring various options in marketing (Arvind Mills and Pizza Hut among them), Deep chose to do something 'crazy'. He joined AMF Bowling, which pioneered the concept of bowling alleys in India.

AMF had no operations here, so the job was in essence entrepreneurial.

"India knew billiards, India didn't know pool. And India didn't know ten pin bowling, at all. The more I studied it, I said, 'It's a no-brainer, it's got to do well here!'"

AMF did set up a couple of hundred bowling alleys but

bowling never quite became the 'storm of the moment' that Deep wanted it to be. And there was a reason for it. The cost of real estate in India (even in 1995!) was just too high. Plus, the idea was probably ahead of its time as there were no malls and multiplexes.

Deep spent four years with AMF, and "Really, really tried very hard to make it happen."

"We had three offices, a small team out here. We were pushing it, trying to create bowling as a sport, getting accreditations, sending teams to the Commonwealth, trying to get it done as an exhibition sport in the the Olympics – various things. We also did a lot of tournaments for school kids."

Although Deep worked for AMF as an employee, it was entrepreneurial for two reasons. The fixed salary component was low, it was based around bonuses and how much equipment you sold.

Second, there was very loose support from the US office. Apart from equipment support and service support, you pretty much did your own thing. The disadvantage was that there was nothing new to learn beyond a point.

So Deep began exploring options once again, and decided it was time to go back and work for a big company. An exciting opportunity came up from GE Countrywide – the consumer finance business. Although it was back to financial services, the job was to look at new avenues for distribution. And a man called Nitin Gupta, then President of GE Countrywide, completely inspired him.

Nitin said, "Everyone has been selling consumer finance in the same old way, through the dealerships and DSA network. We want to make a quantum leap, we want to do it differently. The internet is happening, various new things are happening. That's your charter. You have to revolutionise the way we sell consumer finance."

Around the same time Deep came across people like Ajit Balakrishnan at rediff.com, Sanjeev Bikhchandani at naukri.com and the folks behind sify.com. That's when the turning point happened.

"I realised internet is going to change our life fundamentally. And I always wanted to do my own thing. I was 30 years old and said to myself, 'Abhi nahin kiya to kabhi nahin karenge.'"

And so, he took the plunge. Completing his notice period on 31st March 2000, Deep set up shop on the 1st of April. Very aptly – All Fools Day. Because entrepreneurs are fools in the eyes of the world, aren't they?

The years 1999-2000 were a great time for start-ups. You could run a dotcom business with a small amount of capital. And even that could be raised fairly easily from VCs.

"My wife was working, so it made the decision easier. Ironically by the time I set it up, she had stopped working, we had our first baby, a lot of things had changed. I am clearly a risk taker at heart. I won't gamble too much in cards, but I just had an inner confidence that things are never going to get so bad that you won't have a job even if this thing does not work out."

So even as he continued with the day job at GE, the nights were spent planning his own venture. Two models came to mind – one was online stock broking. It made perfect sense, given his training and work experience. But Deep's heart was in travel and that's what he ultimately chose to do – an online travel portal.

And heart should rule over mind when it comes to such a decision. Because that's the only way you'll put not just your body but your soul into what you do. The math you can learn for any business.

Of course it can't be purely love. The market size and opportunity as a whole must make sense. Deep recalls a third idea. His first child had just been born, and he thought, "Why not a kids portal?" Thankfully, better sense prevailed and the idea remained stillborn. Online travel made better business sense – 50% of all e-commerce in the US was around travel.

However, Deep actually made two plans. One was for online stock broking. "What put me off was that this is going to be a big financial institutions play. It will always be their thing and I will be the minor partner. ICICI Direct had proven me right. IndiaBulls has proven me wrong. They have managed to do it as entrepreneurs. But no regrets – travel has been much more fun. I think this is where I truly belong."

Besides being an avid traveller, Deep had another connection with the industry. His wife was making travel shows like *Namaste India* and *Indian Holiday* for a production house. So travel it was!

> ### "The MBA is a wonderful degree. You can either use it as a noose, or you can use it as insurance. I would always tend to use it as insurance".

The venture started out as 'India Ahoy' – a site which is still used to attract high-leisure travellers from overseas. But the main brand and site were later rechristened makemytrip.com – a name more suited for the Indian market.

"I look back at my first business plan and it always makes me laugh."

What was funny about it?

"What was funny was the amount of expectation I had from things like video streaming. I thought that eventually people might even pay to watch videos on travel, which today sounds quite bizarre! The numbers worked out in some strange way... but where the revenues came from were quite different."

Then, the way VC money came in. That was also quite amazing.

"The first guy I met gave me the money. He was Neeraj Bhargava, Managing Partner of eVentures. We actually closed the deal sitting in a café in the Crossroads Mall on a paper napkin! *Hum baithe the chhote se restaurant mein, Food court tha, shaam ka time,* and he was saying '*Chalo yaar* we will give you x million dollars and we will take so much percentage.'"

And Deep rues how ill-informed he was. After consulting a couple of friends he agreed to give away 70% of the company for two million dollars funding.

Luckily, he got a second chance to get it back. When the dotcom bubble burst, eVentures packed up from India and made a distress sale. Deep bought out his own company with his life savings. And that's when he believes he *really* became an entrepreneur.

"The belief in the business was so strong that I went on, without drawing a salary, for 18 months. And whatever I was not taking as a salary, was converted into equity. I also encouraged two senior colleagues to do the same and they were elevated to co-founder status. Of course many others said 'We can't handle this thing *yaar*,' and left."

This was June 2001. The irony was that now, a majority stake was with the management, and the minority was with some angel investors. Some of these angels were individuals in eVentures. So even as the VC firm bailed out, they really believed in the idea and put in their own money.

Salary payments became difficult. The company shrank from 40 employees to around 20.

"We moved from a smart 3,000 sq ft office in Okhla into the mezzanine of the same building which was 1,000 sq ft. We had a running desk around all the walls and just swung our chairs to huddle now and again. *Aur itni jagah mein bhi ek 14" ka TV kone mein laga diya tha jahan par cricket dekhte the*. So it was a lot of fun. Those were the real days I think…"

"The good part," Deep says wistfully "is that of those 20+ people, 15 are still with the company." Two of the senior folks (both VPs) became co-founders because of the sacrifices they made at that time.

"We had two and half to three months salaries to pay. Bills to take care of and no more money. We came *that* close to shutting down. And I told these guys, we can pack up, everyone can get their dues and go back to your comfortable jobs, or we can make a fight of it. We were seeing the metrics, we were going up on every one of them. And improving."

So they decided, "We are going to fight it out boss."

Deep's story tells you that the path of entrepreneurship is a crooked one. You never know what lies around the next corner. But the brave keep hope in their hearts, believe in what they cannot yet see – and keep going.

Talking about business, when makemytrip set out, it said, "We will be the defining travel portal for travel to India, from India and within India." So it was domestic travel, outbound travel, Indians going overseas, NRIs coming to India, foreigners coming to India. Everything!

Within two to three months, it was apparent that, in the India of 2001, no one was buying online. Lots of lookers, very few bookers. Everyone was coming to the site and saying "Wow, this is cool." But that was it.

These were the days when there was TravelGenie funded by ICICI Venture, Net2Travel from Star TV, as well as Travelanza,

> **"You expect people to give you capital for 20 pages of a business plan and confidence that you will be able to pull it off. In travel, where I had no experience whatsoever, the weird thing is that it happened".**

TravelMart India (Citibank funded), and so on and so forth.

The advantage makemytrip had was pure MBA style, cold, hard number analysis. The company realised where traffic was coming from, who was buying, who was not.

"The first metric that I learnt to measure in this business was the cost of customer acquisition. And we now do it as a crazy science. We monitor it by the hour. Our web analytics, the real core of MIS, is the DSS of this business, ie, the Decision Support System. It's amazing what you can get."

It became clear that 'India focus' was pointless. So makemytrip simply stopped marketing in India. All energies were focused on US-based NRIs. And that saved the company.

"This strategy saved us through 9/11, it saved us through SARS, it saved us through the attack on Parliament, it saved us through the dotcom bust... Because that market was a very developed one. NRIs were used to buying online. Also they had a natural reason to come to India year after year. Kids were being born, marriages were happening, so on and so forth."

You didn't have to sell the idea of India itself. Just the convenience of booking online, at good prices.

The US focus continued right up to 2005. Makemytrip became a nice, robust and profitable business. But it wasn't huge – about $15 million in gross billings, $2 million in commissions or 'revenues'. Trouble was, this market was not tremendously scalable.

The same model did not work in the UK or Australia for various reasons. The question was, now what?

Then, fundamentally two or three things changed in India. New domestic airlines were launched. Complete and utter chaos ensued in the market. Every day there were ads in the newspapers offering fares of 99 rupees, 7 rupees and even zero rupees! So it was the perfect time for a portal like makemytrip to come in. With the help of technology, the site gave all the choices at one go. And people could make their own decision.

Power shifted from the travel agent to the customer.

The second big trend which gave Deep a lot of courage was a meeting with the folks at Indian Railways.

"I sat with Amitabh Pandey who is actually an alumni from St Stephens. Senior guy. And he candidly shared with me their numbers. At that point of time, they were doing 5,000 tickets per day.

I said, "Wow! That's impressive."

And he said, "Guess what? They all pay by credit card."

So people had started paying on the net, and using their cards was not a big concern.

However the real clincher for Deep was the fact that 65% of all tickets bought were for non-AC trains. So the common man was buying online. He was paying online, and thanks to Indian Railways, they had instilled this trust in the internet *buyer ki aap ki ticket aap ko kal mil jayegee.*

"We actually made several test transactions on irctc.com. In each of those ten cases, *meri ticket mujhe agle din gyara baje se pehle pohonchee.* It never failed! So I said, 'This is a great model!' Refunds are tough and all, but these two factors convinced me that the markets are ready."

Of course there were also some numbers put out by NASSCOM which said the internet user base would soon be 30 million. But that is more a statistic to take note of, not bet the company's future on.

Ultimately many think tanks churn out reports, with all kinds of projections. Some estimate correctly, others are way off the mark. However real change can be sensed when people start behaving differently... and that's what was happening here.

"Air Deccan did a lot for us... They managed to bring the cheap ticket buyer to the net by screaming and giving these crazy prices. The buyer said, '*Yaar, cheap deal chahiye toh net pe jaana hai.*' So makemytrip did not have to do that evangelisation."

"My motto for my team is borrowed from Jeff Bezos – work hard, have fun, create history. But two out of three is not an option!"

Now the company was faced with another decision point – should it launch a real quick with a rough and dirty site or build the coolest site in the world and take 6-9 months to launch?

"I am glad we chose the first. Because we launched in September 2005, when nobody else was in the market. That made us synonymous with the term 'online travel'. And we still occupy that space. Even though other portals have gone crazy advertising."

The current challenge is to make the India business profitable. Deep expects that to happen in the current fiscal year. But the growth story has been astounding. By March 2008, makemytrip achieved $250 million in sales, ie, approximately ₹ 1,000 crore. That translates into $20 million in commissions or ₹ 80-90 crore.

70% of the business is now from India, with close to 10,000 tickets being sold online each day.

Within 11 months of its launch, makemytrip became the highest issuer of air tickets for any single travel agency location, including the traditional players.

The big challenge now is to sell other products online. With hotels, makemytrip is beginning to see a breakthrough. Still, a big change of habit is required. Then there is the sale of holiday packages. Mostly people collect information online but purchase offline, from a real human being.

Which is why makemytrip now has an 'army' of people selling packages over the phone. The company has set up 20 'travel stores' across the country to be able to sell holiday packages to the various regional markets.

The thinking was – even if people don't buy from these outlets in large numbers, when they see an offline presence, they trust the brand name more. But surprisingly, sales have been excellent offline as well.

"Ahmedabad, last month, one crore in sales. Out of nowhere! They are six months old! Bangalore is going to cross one crore next month. So these are the times you kick yourself and say, 'My God! Why didn't you do it earlier?' You know, in hindsight everything is 20-20 kind of vision. But you have to learn. You can never say *'Hum toh online hai, kabhi offline nahin jaayenge.' That's bullshit! Dhandaa karna hai hamein.*"

You don't define your business too narrowly. Travel means travel means travel – on land, on sea, on air, offline, online, under the line, whatever. You start with an innovation, but then you extend tentacles into the regular side of the business as well.

Growth is a hydra-headed monster with an endless appetite!

Of course all this growth did not just happen. Cash had to be burnt to build a national brand, so investors once again came into the picture. SoftBank Asia Infrastructure Fund was the first to invest. In subsequent rounds, Deep took money from three other funds – Helion Partners, Sierra Ventures and Tiger Global.

But why take money from so many different people? Because different guys bring different things to the table. They also help to manage competitive pressures. Of course, managing so many investors is definitely a challenge in itself!

Deep's investor philosophy is simple, "I have only taken in capital from guys who I think can add value to us. My litmus test is, would I take this guy on my board if he wasn't giving me money? As an independent member? And in every case it has been a YES. We have refused money from bigger 'brands' where I don't think the partner in question would add value to my board."

You have to be hard-headed. When it comes to investors, and even when it comes to your own people, loyalty is important but competence matters more.

"You are hurting the business if you keep giving bigger jobs to the original team when you know there is someone else who can do it better. As fresh blood comes in it is only natural that some of the older folks who don't scale up their skills get left behind."

We leave the bright and buzzing makemytrip office in Gurgaon's Udyog Vihar and head into Delhi. Deep has a

"When it comes to investors, and even when it comes to your own people, loyalty is important but competence matters more."

meeting with IRCTC officials. He hopes to convince them to let him sell railway tickets through makemytrip. As they say, "Try, try and try until they give in!"

By now I've learnt a lot about the business. But what about the journey as an entrepreneur? It certainly does not sound easy. From downsizing the business to then massively scaling it. From 20 to 750 people.

"You are right. We've had quite a roller-coaster ride. It was well funded when it started. A second round of capital of one million was promised to us – it never came. I still like Neeraj because he was honest enough to tell us, 'Deep, I frankly can't do anything, as they (the Limited Partners) are wrapping up the India fund.'"

The understanding was that if the company met certain metrics, it would get a follow-on round at a pre-agreed valuation. However, this was never put in writing. "Rather naïve," he now admits.

"The turning point was when the rubber hits the road and you say, 'Are you really willing to stake everything?' I mean if you start up, you write a business plan, you get funded. Yes, you take a modest salary but you never go salaryless. Fundamentally things don't change. My whole thing was I don't want to impact the quality of life for my family."

"Then you put in your life's savings, you don't draw a salary. *Tab, bahut jack lagti hai.* Because then you are eating into your princely 30-odd lakh of net worth… You are saying, 'This better pay off because it really took a long time to build.' So I think that's the moment of reckoning clearly."

"It comes down to confidence, it comes down to a leap of faith. And, you know I am not saying this to sound politically correct but I think you really need support from home. Especially from your wife. Because you can't be doing this 24 by 7, including working all-nighters if she's unhappy about it."

Luckily Deep got that support. His wife always said, "You have got to do what you love." And that was how he left ABN with no regrets.

During the makemytrip crisis she said, "You have put in so much, you are seeing promise in it. I don't understand business the way you do, but if you think it's getting better month on month, and at some point it's going to be a good thing, then let's just go ahead and do it and make it happen." She even offered to go back to working full-time. The one thing she never said was, "Listen, let's just play safe!"

But it never crossed his mind to give up?

"At one time we came very close..." he admits. So what kept him going?

"Once you have tasted blood, working on your own, I just didn't want to work for anyone. For me that would be the hardest thing to do. That is why if we get a good option to sell out, maybe I'll take it. But that will be time to exit. *Ek do saal kaam kar ke* I would be thinking of the next baby..."

However, the future Deep would much rather carve out for his company is an IPO. To provide liquidity to all stakeholders, make the company even bigger and most importantly, to remain in control.

And then, what happens? The entrepreneur usually remains the single largest shareholder, although small in terms of percentage, and stays at the top to run it. Because he is the best person to run it. Or he moves on to a less hands-on, more evangelist-chairman kind of role.

"One of my VC friends insists that I am going to join his tribe one day... which is an interesting option. The guys who turn VC, it's not just about the money, but the thrill of being able to learn a lot of businesses and vicariously enjoying being involved in them."

At the end of the day, Deep knows he was lucky to get a second life as an entrepreneur. And he is enjoying every single moment of it.

ADVICE TO YOUNG ENTREPRENEURS

1. Choose your field very carefully – there must be a 'huge' (large is not good enough) market and potential. If you don't have personal expertise in this field, get a team of domain experts locked-in, preferably as partners or co-founders.

2. Plan your funding very carefully – ideally raise as little cash as possible in the pre-revenue stage as you end up diluting too much equity. Try raising the first round from angel investors as it is most time-efficient and typically you will get the best terms. However, for later rounds, never risk starving your company of cash; this has killed many good companies!

3. It's all about people – hire the best folks in the business. Don't hesitate to hire people better than yourself in that specific area. Colleagues who challenge and make you feel uncomfortable are your best friends and the 'yes men' are your worst enemies!

4. Make friends at work and promote an honest and open working atmosphere. Ensure everyone has fun at work. People tend to give their best when they are enjoying their work.

5. Don't focus too much on exits (especially not too early in the game). Concentrate on building a solid business, the rest will take care of itself!

BLOOM
AND GROW

Rashesh Shah (PGP '89),
Edelweiss Capital

In a world dominated by the likes of J P Morgan and Merrill Lynch, Rashesh Shah set up a large and successful homegrown investment bank in a single decade. But it wasn't a straight path to success – there were many bumps and detours.

"Grubby." That's the term Rashesh Shah associated with 'business'. And that's why he strived to join IIM Ahmedabad, and become a 'respected professional'.

But the wheel has turned full circle. Rashesh chucked the professional path and went into business. And grubby is the last word that comes to mind as I wait for Rashesh in the super-cool, super-quiet office of Edelweiss Capital. Beyond the expansive glass windows lies the Arabian Sea – what a fantastic view!

And what a fantastic name – Edelweiss. Not the name of the founder, not a pretentious adjective. Just a simple flower which everyone knows from the *Sound of Music*. Very international, very unfinancial, very understated – just like Rashesh.

Investment bankers are usually flamboyant. Rashesh is soft spoken, and stammers slightly. But he has a quiet strength which is very evident and what impressed me most was that he spent two whole hours, as requested, for the interview. No interruptions or distractions.

He makes me feel important. He makes my job easy. That's what leaders do.

BLOOM
AND GROW

Rashesh Shah (PGP '89),
Edelweiss Capital

Rashesh Shah came from a purely commercial, business family. Everybody in the family had always been into business and ironically that was the reason why he decided to break the mould.

"Running a business did not have the same status or market value as a professional," he felt. That too a business dealing in exercise books and stationery items.

After graduating from KC college with a BSc in statistics, Rashesh did an IIFT course and was working with an export company. But he realised that a one-year course was not an 'MBA' So he sat for the CAT exam. The first time he tried very hard, but got into one of the other IIMs. His heart was set on Ahmedabad. So he gave it a second shot and this time, got through.

Rashesh had always been keen on finance and joined ICICI from the campus. This was the time that liberalisation was happening. Rashesh was with the 'export group' of ICICI which handles companies like Infosys, Mastek, United Phosphorus – high growth, entrepreneurial companies. Infosys was, of course, a very small company at that time but it was exciting to see so much entrepreneurial activity. Because until then, big business was basically the turf of the old, established groups.

Rashesh realised that this new set of entrepreneurs would need capital. Up until then, all the capital needs of the industry came through ICICI, IDBI and state banks. But if we look at the US, the investment banks and the capital markets are very important. The market for those services was poised to take off in India. Rashesh thought it was a good idea to start an investment bank in India focused on high-growth companies and capital markets. Friends working at Goldman Sachs thought it was a good idea as well.

This was around '93-94. "The decision to quit was relatively easy," he says because wife Vidya was working with ITC Classic. She then shifted to Peregrine, which was an MNC and paid well. Vidya encouraged Rashesh to take the risk "Why don't you try it," she said. "What is there to lose?"

And so Rashesh took the plunge in May 1995. He estimated it would take 5-6 months to go into business but it took much longer. The phone line took its time coming. So did the people.

When Rashesh announced that he was leaving to start his own company, his head of back office and secretary both came up and said, "We want to go with you, wherever you go." But when he offered them, and two others, appointment letters, they all found reasons to back out.

"I realised that when you want to hire people, having an office with a computer, fax machine and receptionist matters a lot. People want to work for what looks like a *real* company. They don't want to work for ideas."

The idea became Edelweiss Capital in February 1996 with one partner on board – Venkat Ramaswamy, a colleague at ICICI. Pooling in their savings and some borrowing they raised ₹ 1 crore, bought a Category I licence and went into business.

Every entrepreneur hopes to latch onto a trend early on. It's called the 'first mover advantage'. Edelweiss spotted a trend – which was great. What it hadn't reckoned with was how long it would take for the trend to bear fruit.

"What one had not expected was that after liberalisation, India would go through 8-10 years of a very hard time – from 1995 to 2002. If you remember, in '94, the index was at 4,500. In 2003, the index was at 3,000. Adjusted against the inflation, the market had lost almost 80% of its value."

Unfortunately or fortunately, Edelweiss came into existence just as this down-cycle started. The idea was that the economy will grow and hence there will be a need for investment banking but it took several years before there was any real growth. The first couple of years were very hard – the economy had slowed down, interest rates were very high. There wasn't enough business for Edelweiss.

By this time, Rashesh had realised that unlike what they teach you in Bschool, life rarely goes according to plan. The initial plan was to have a revenue of ₹ 30 lakh in the first year, ₹ 50 lakh in the second, ₹ 1 crore in the third, ₹ 1.5 crore in the fourth and ₹ 2 crore in the fifth year. The company actually ended up doing 28 lakh in the first year, 35 lakh in the second and 21 lakh in the third year – which was the worst year in its history.

Fortunately, they were always able to make ends meet and stay 'profitable'. Of course, the partners paid themselves very little for the first five years – about ₹ 3 lakh a year + a bonus. A far cry from the ₹ 30 lakh p.a. earned in the last job!

"Being very enterprising, we always made sure that we had some advisory assignments, and we kept our capital costs low. So we were able to keep our heads above water." Keep afloat and eventually you manage to flag a passing vessel. An opportunity of some kind which takes you places.

For Edelweiss, this opportunity was the dotcom boom. "In mid-'98, things started moving. The internet, IT sector and private equity boom first started and we capitalised on that."

Thus, it happened that in the fourth year, Edelweiss did close to one and a half crore and in the fifth, ₹ 11 crore. Far more than the promoters had expected or anticipated. Of course, these boom years were followed by a slump in 2001. But Edelweiss had liquid capital and with all the internal accruals, decided to go out and expand the business. In what was to be a crucial strategic decision, the company acquired a small brokerage. The idea was to not just be a corporate finance advisory house, but to broadbase the business.

The interesting thing is that in 2001, almost everybody was getting out of the broking business. But Edelweiss was clear that if the capital market is going to be important, then the broking platform has to be important. The company took a contrarian view and went ahead, spending a fair amount of capital on the acquisition.

**"Very few people speak about it but there
is a clear change in the social status.
Entrepreneurship is messy compared to
what things would be if you were
working for an MNC bank."**

Which goes to show that if you fundamentally believe in your
business, you aren't guided by 'popular opinion'. You go by your
own gut feel and put your money where your mouth is.

Of course, the bet took a while to pay off. In 2000, Edelweiss
had just 10 employees. By '03 this number was up to 35. But
2002 and 2003 were once again very tough years, in India and
globally. The internet boom was over, no capital was available
and the market was down. Forward trading had been banned
and there was the Ketan Parekh scam as well.

So how did Edelweiss manage this period?

"See, we were well capitalised for the size that we were at that
time. Some amount of capital always helps you in the lean
days. Secondly, being a very entrepreneurial organisation, we
always kept looking for opportunities and thinking out of the
box. Thirdly, our costs were very structured. We had given
options to a lot of employees."

In fact, when Edelweiss started, it had the Infosys model in
mind. Before starting, Rashesh had gone to Narayana Murthy
for advice.

"When we started, we had an offer from an industrial group for
a 15-20% JV. It was a very attractive offer, this extra capital. After
all we were ex-employees of ICICI and our salaries had been
low. But one valuable advice from Murthy was: 'Give capital to
people who add value, or to strategic partners. Don't go for
capital for the sake of capital'. We followed that and it has been
very useful for us."

The company did take in capital in the year 2000, and
delivered an 8x return to its investors in five years. "By now the
same investment would be 70-80x," Rashesh adds.

Speaking of patience, the people who did believe in the

company and stuck by it did well when Edelweiss went public in November 2007. And we're not talking about a handful of employees but 550 of the 1,100 on the rolls. Close to 25% of the company is in fact held under ESOPs.

As a result, fixed compensation at Edelweiss has been more reasonable though the variable compensation is aggressive. This helped keep costs under control. "It's an 'owner' mindset rather than 'employee' mindset. So if your quarter is bad or year is bad, people are still thinking like owners and that helped a lot in the tough years," says Rashesh.

"We were clear that these were business cycles and each organisation is known by how well it encounters these cycles. We thought, if you survived between 2001 and 2003, you could survive almost anything!"

From October 2003, Edelweiss started expanding once again. By then the company had 3-4 businesses – private equity, arbitrage, investment banking, insurance and brokerage. But what about 'core competency'? Is that another irrelevant Bschool concept?

"There is something known as an intensive and extensive approach to a thing. Should we go more deep into one area or should we be more broadbased? Historically, India has been a very large market, but more broad than deep," says Rashesh. And hence, it makes sense to drop many different anchors to keep your company in place.

There is the example of Reliance which started with petrochemicals, then got into trading yarn, fibre manufacturing, refining, exploration and now, even retail. This is what you call growth through 'adjacent markets'. Rashesh also recalls the case of Nike, which has footwear, apparel and equipment. When they started, Nike was into shoes. Then they got into apparel for tennis, then golf shoes, golf apparel and equipment.

"You go on changing only one parameter, either the product or the client parameter and you keep on growing in the adjacent market," says Rashesh.

But does every small company have the bandwidth to juggle multiple balls? After all, entrepreneurs are never short on ideas, where they often fail is properly *executing* those ideas.

"When you are the CEO and shareholder, you want to avoid raising money because your equity goes down. When you wear only the CEO's hat, all you want is to grow as fast as possible."

Well, before expanding, Rashesh believes one needs to look at 3-4 things. Firstly, have you successfully entrenched yourself in that space? "Very often, you will try something and find it difficult, *competition hai*, and you go to the adjacent market. But going to the adjacent market because of that is not a good reason."

In the case of Edelweiss, the company started with investment banking but in the year 2000, the size of that market was about ₹ 150 crore. Of this, Edelweiss was handling business worth ₹ 5-6 crore, which was 3-4% of the market.

In investment banking, any one player getting more than a 5% share is extremely rare. So clearly, growth had to come from elsewhere. That is why the company turned to brokerage. The brokerage market then was ₹ 500 crore – a bigger space than i-banking. And that's how Edelweiss made every decision about its growth – looking at the market size and the opportunity in that.

Secondly, it's very important to have enough management bandwidth or ownership bandwidth. So when you go into 'B', 'A' is still entrenched. At Edelweiss, senior people were owners, and so the company did not lose any key people through the expansion process. For example, Venkat continued to run investment banking, but somebody else started running brokerage.

The third important thing is that it has to be a compatible adjacent market. Which means an IT software company getting into hardware, or vice versa. Not IT branching into real estate! But the real problem is not choosing how and where to expand but the entrepreneur realising he cannot be Mr Know-it-All.

"One of the first things that I did was, I stepped back. I decided that I will not have a centre of gravity or bias towards any one business, individual partners will handle that." Broking is a very different business from investment banking. Institutional broking and individual client broking are also very different. You have to let each develop, create its own unique culture. Like kids in a family – no one like the other, but all feeling well-loved.

Another strong support came in the form of Vidya Shah coming on board. It happened like this. In the year 2000, Vidya and Rashesh had their second child. Vidya decided to bow out of investment banking which is client-facing work and involves extensive travelling.

This was also the time when Edelweiss was looking to scale up. So Rashesh asked her to handle all the backend work. This turned out to be a blessing in disguise.

In smaller firms, it's hard to get a senior person handling areas like HR, finance and admin. So the CEO often has to get personally involved in these aspects, eating into crucial management time and bandwidth. In that sense, Rashesh feels, he was very fortunate to get Vidya's expertise, on a part-time basis.

The idea was that she would help out for a year or two. But by 2003, when she was originally planning to exit, Edelweiss had started growing at breakneck speed. The company went from 35 people to 100 people, then 200. 200 became 350, and then swelled to 600. Vidya finally quit in August 2007, but continues to head the Edelweiss Foundation.

"Working with Vidya was easy and hard and normally I don't recommend that to most people because there are stresses when your spouse is the CFO and reporting to you." Separating the personal and professional roles becomes an issue.

"Secondly, the internal perception – you don't want anybody else to have extra authority because she happens to be your spouse. Thirdly, how do you interact with each other in the public arena? So we acknowledged these issues and set certain ground rules."

> ## "We always differentiate between a plan and an aspiration. There is always a short-term plan, but there are always long-term aspirations."

For example, Rashesh and Vidya never ate lunch together. They carried separate *dabbas*. But there was one area which they were never quite able to resolve – "We did end up carrying work home."

The positive side of working together was having someone you could completely trust handling two crucial bits of your business – people and capital. However, Rashesh is clear about what is most valuable. "I believe that entrepreneurship is not all about assets, it is about emotional energy as aspirations."

Rashesh is a strong believer in the '18-month plan' and long-term aspirations.

"We always differentiate between a plan and an aspiration. There is always a short-term plan, but there are always long-term aspirations." When Edelweiss was a tiny financial services company, working on a ₹ 1 crore business plan, it had aspirations of some day becoming the Indian answer to global giant Goldman Sachs.

"What happens is that we as human beings, as entrepreneurs, all of us overestimate the short-term and grossly underestimate the long-term. And this is what takes away the emotional energy because in the short-term there are setbacks. The short-term keeps trying you."

So how do you keep your energy up? This is where aspirations come in. The dream is about more than financial and quantitative targets. The 'bigness' of the dream is what keeps you going, and yet keeps you anchored.

And yet, scaling a business can be unglamorous – execution is kind of boring. It means doing a lot more of the indirect work, spending a third of your time in hiring and people-related issues. "On a Friday afternoon, somebody is crying, somebody is cribbing, somebody is not happy. It is very tiring!"

And more so because entrepreneurs are addicted to excitement.

Scaling up meant giving up the part of investment banking Rashesh enjoyed the most, clinching deals. "When you start off, you are worried about *how* to do things. Then, you get other people for that, and you worry about, *what* to do. Then after some time, even that is taken care of and you only try to figure out *who* will do it. The more indirect it becomes, the more unglamorous it becomes."

You sacrifice glamour and build an institution. Edelweiss Capital listed on the Bombay Stock Exchange on December 12, 2007. The IPO was over subscribed 119 times and raised over ₹ 700 crore for further expansion Edelweiss clocked revenues of ₹ 1,088.86 crore in FY08 vs ₹ 371.76 crore in FY07.* Now that's what you call explosive growth!

When you think of great companies, large companies built from scratch, you assume they are built on blood, toil, sweat and family time. Dogged perseverance. 24x7 effort.

"This 24x7, 365 days a year is something that I have not seen with many CEOs. If you do that, it means your organisation is weak, you are not scaled up. You have not prioritised, you have not institutionalised.

"I think there are phases. Many a times there are a couple of months in a year that are very tiring because some business is having a problem. There is restructuring, there are long meetings. So then you end up working even on Sundays. The rest of the time it is fairly okay. But it's not any harder than when I was working for ICICI. In Bombay, 10-11 hours is normal!"

Rashesh goes to the gym thrice a week and also spends many weekends at his farmhouse in Alibaug. He reads a lot, loves to catch movies on Friday nights and also takes two holidays a year.

Which means on the work-life balance front, there's hope yet for us all!

---

* *Edelweiss saw Profit After Tax of INR 273.24 cr in FY08 vs INR 109.89 cr in FY07 (growth of 149%).*

<u>ADVICE TO YOUNG ENTREPRENEURS</u>

Cash flow is underestimated by most people – the amount of cash flow. If it is possible, be a little overcapitalised. There are lot of CEOs who are good product guys, they are great operations guys. But they don't know finance at all. In times of adversities, these are the people who suffer the most. I think being financially savvy is a required part of the business.

Never have equal partners. You start off as equals, but then one does more, one does less, one is the public face, the other is not, and then slowly the whole thing disintegrates. I have witnessed it happen in my family between my father and uncles, and with many other partnerships as well.

So there should be a 'first among equals', who has a slightly higher equity share. That's what Mr Narayana Murthy advised us and that's what I advise my clients now. Also, there shouldn't be too many partners. When we started off, we were supposed to be five people in the company – Venkat, I and three others. But the other three did not join and I think that was a good thing to happen because five people would have been difficult to manage if the environment became hostile. These days I advise people – two or four partners is okay, but ideally not more than four.

The only other thing that I would like to add is that have the staying power, the emotional staying power. Business will not be as per what you had planned, there are going to be hardships. I have seen a lot of businesses close up because after a lot of hardships, at that key point (like the third year which was the worst year), we never thought, "Oh, is it worth it?" We just kept going on.

But if you are working at Hindustan Lever or any such organisation, worried about status, worried about the house in south Bombay and all that, the choice is then very tough. I think the loss of status is what really hurts.

IT'S ALL ABOUT
THE HONEY

Nirmal Jain (PGP '89),
India Infoline

Nirmal shut down his information services business in 1999 and put all his eggs in the internet basket. His gamble paid off and today India Infoline is one of the country's biggest online trading platforms.

Everyone knows entrepreneurship is about risk. But how much risk are you willing to take? This is a question Nirmal Jain had to answer in the year 2000. He was willing to risk everything he owned to save his company – India Infoline.

It was only a few months after the Gujarat earthquake, when one evening Nirmal and his partner Venkat thought out aloud, "Even if we lose everything, we should walk out of this and start something else or take a job. And we should think we survived an earthquake. At least we saved our lives!"

As it turned out, India Infoline survived and prospered. And how!

I arrive at the NSE complex in Goregaon for our interview, only to find I am at the 'wrong office'. There are several India Infoline offices in the same location. "Yeah, it's confusing at times. You see, at one point we used to operate out of one small office. But now we've outgrown even the two larger offices we have here..." grins Harshad Apte, Nirmal's close associate.

Being in the right place at the right time is a crucial ingredient for success in any enterprise. I am in the right place but it's not the right time for an in-depth interview as Nirmal needs to attend an AGM in less than 45 minutes! But life is about making the best of any and every situation so without further ado, we plunge right in.

IT'S ALL ABOUT THE HONEY

Nirmal Jain (PGP '89),
India Infoline

Nirmal Jain is a matter-of-fact guy. The story of his life, or at least the way he relates it, is precise and logical. And yet nobody's path in life is exactly straight and completely planned.

An MBA from IIM Ahmedabad who's completed his CA and Cost Accountancy would naturally take a job in finance, right? And yet, the first job Nirmal took from campus was with Hindustan Lever. He worked there for five years, 1989 to 1994.

"At HLL, I was handling commodities like peanuts and oil. That gave me a good training of trading," he recalls.

Opportunity is about putting two and two together. Around 1991, with liberalisation, the Indian financial services sector started attracting foreign capital. It was clear that the sector was poised for exponential growth.

"Having a strong academic background as well as a mindset for financial services I thought I'll get into this." But he was clear that he eventually wanted to be an entrepreneur. So instead of joining a foreign bank or FII he joined hands with two brokers, Motilal Oswal and Ramdev Agrawal, and set up an equity research outfit called Inquire in March 1994.

After a year and a half Nirmal decided he was ready to start something on his own. That something was 'Probity Research and Services Pvt Ltd'.

"Probity literally means integrity or honesty or independence. And is also an acronym for probe in equity which was our business – analysis, investment analysis." The company's star product was 'Probity 200' which tracked the top 200 listed companies.

This made sense because these 200 companies account for about 90% of volumes and portfolio holdings. So there was a ready market for the information, not only with brokers but corporate, banks and FIIs. Probity also started doing sector reports. At around the same time, a company started by two IIM seniors, INFAC, was already doing industry research but they had left out a few sectors like oil and gas, FMCG, IT and pharma. Probity filled this gap and its reports got well-accepted.

Right from 1995 (when Probity was set up) till 1999, stock markets were not doing too well. "The business could have done much better in a good economic environment," muses Nirmal. "But in a way it was good also because we learnt how to manage the bad time and go through the down-cycle which probably helped us later."

The year 1999 was a turning point. In fact, turning point is too mild a word for the direction Probity would take. It was a complete change of direction. A wild gamble: all or nothing.

"The internet was becoming very popular, US media was talking of internet all the time. Someone came up with the crazy idea that if we put up all our research free on the web, instead of 250 clients we will have half a million clients. We literally implemented that idea and killed our earlier business model. We put up all our research free on our website."

In 1999, India Infoline had about a crore of revenue, ₹ 10-20 lakh profit. A call was made to give it all up. Forgoing revenue is fine, but what about costs? Those remain, and in fact, one had to invest in technology as well. So money had to be raised from friends and an angel investor.

R Venkataraman, an IIM Bangalore graduate with experience at ICICI, Barclays and GE private equity also joined the company as a co-promoter.

Despite early technical glitches the India Infoline website became popular. The content it served was unique and otherwise not available. Soon enough, the company attracted the attention of VCs. CDC Ventures (now known as Actis) invested $1 million.

Around this time the team reached one important conclusion.

"We realised that media selling and information services is not a business model which is scalable beyond a point. It won't be able to generate revenues despite the hype being created in those days about Yahoo! etc."

India Infoline therefore decided to forward integrate into transaction services. The company began working on an internet-based trading model. The idea was to develop something pioneering in-house but that actually took three years to happen. In the meanwhile, they decided to buy technology off the shelf.

In March 2000, India Infoline raised another $5 million from Intel capital and some other investors. Soon after that stock markets and NASDAQ in particular crashed. The dotcom bubble had burst and the company found itself in a crisis.

"We had set up many business lines, employed people, but there was no capital. VCs and PEs kept saying they would give us money but it took 16 months to get a small amount of additional capital."

Both Nirmal and Venkat pooled in everything they owned, ₹ 3 crore in order to keep going. "We had to scale back and shift from 'growth' to 'survival' mode from 2001 to 2003-04."

"We did everything possible… cut down on every penny of cost. Shifted from high cost offices to low cost. We got out of a few unviable businesses such as personal loans and mortgages. We had planned to get into a TV channel, a business news channel. We scrapped that."

India Infoline started focusing only on investment-linked business where the retail customer would invest and it could facilitate or advise. This included distribution of mutual funds and life insurance, and e-broking. Everything else was shut down.

> **"If you are an artist like MF Husain or a player like Tiger Woods your individual skills only matter, and not how good a team player you are or how good a team you can build. The analogy applies to business as well. Do you want to be Tiger Woods, the golfer, or captain of Team India?"**

"It was a challenge because it was very difficult to attract people and retain people also. Dotcom became a stigma – nobody wanted to work at a dotcom."

The company had money which was hardly sufficient for three months. The strategy was to keep generating some revenue and keep going. And many a time there were delays in payment of vendors, delays in payment of salaries. Very stressful and painful times for sure.

In October 2001, India Infoline finally raised another ₹ 6 crore ($1.2 million) from its existing investors. This money came 16 months after it was needed and it was a tiny amount for a company which had already raised $5 million and had planned to raise $50 million.

"Those days the name of the game was to scale up fast. We had filed for an ADR issue and we were confident we'll be able to raise $50-60 million. That's what most bankers had told us. We thought, in the worst case scenario we'll be able to raise $15-20 million."

Ah, investment bankers and venture capitalists! Both believe they are the experts on the subject of spotting opportunity and covering risk. The truth is most of them are happy to invest when a trend is 'hot' and the going is good. They invest in the hope of quickly and easily multiplying their money.

The moment it comes to taking a *real* risk, they have no capital to 'venture'. It is like the entrepreneur is standing underneath the shower, all soaped up, when all of a sudden *'paani chala gaya'.*

You have no idea when the situation will change, become normal.

"Passing through the down-cycle, one of the worst things is the waiting. You don't know when the up-cycle will start. So it's not that you are planning for two years and two months of struggle after which you know *sab theek ho jaayega*. No, you have to struggle and you don't know when it will end."

For India Infoline the 'end' or rather the new beginning came in May 2003 when its trading platform stabilised and the stock markets started looking up.

In 2003-04, the company made its first profit of around ₹ 7.5 crore. Operating leverage is high in a business driven by the internet. So the next year India Infoline multiplied its profits two and a half times. And revenues continued to gallop.

The turnover of India Infoline when this interview took place in October 2007 stood at ₹ 400 crore. As this book goes to print in May 2008, that figure has jumped to over ₹ 1,000 crore.*

So what kept Nirmal going through those difficult days? It all seems obvious in hindsight that despite the dotcom bust, sound internet-based business models would succeed. But it wasn't really that simple.

"You have to have hope, you have to have faith and you have to persevere, and that's what we did. Also a core team of people, 8-10 key people. They are still with us. You have to retain them, they are the pillars of the business. You know you can't do it all alone."

Of course a few people did quit, but many others decided to hang on. What kept these people with the company even when there was uncertainty about their salaries, their future?

"There was always a clarity and honesty of purpose. We were very transparent. Everyone knew I had put in my own money,

---

For the FY08, the India Infoline group posted a 2.11 times surge in consolidated net profit over FY07 to INR 159.88 crore. Consolidated total income in the year jumped 2.40 times over last year to INR 1023.59 crore.

"You always run a risk, it's a game of probabilities. You have to be sporting... however good you are, you may get out for a duck."

everything I had. So they could see my conviction and my commitment."

"Secondly, I shared my thoughts on why I am sticking it out. Even I could have quit, with my academic background and professional track record, a good job was not at all difficult to come by…"

But the core group could clearly see that the internet was here to stay. And on the net, a financial business is the best business to have.

A TV or a fridge or grocery is a 'touch and feel' product. With banking and stock transactions, you really don't need to see what you are doing. Especially now that everything is 'demat'. And once you have a good offering which adds value to customers, the money which can be made on this is also very good.

"We could see the success of some business models in the US, also like E*TRADE. And with common sense you can understand that if the internet is going to change the world it will change quite a few business models, especially financial services."

India Infoline had the technology, the platform, some understanding of the business. "We realised, if we give up now we will lose a huge opportunity, someone else will do it."

"So we thought we'll keep fighting until we have the last penny, or you know, the last drop of blood and see how long we can last it out. If we can get into a positive cycle where we break even and start making money then obviously we can scale up very fast. That's precisely what happened if you really look back."

People start companies. Courage and enthusiasm keeps them going in the initial years. Then one day they realise, this is not scaling up.

What did India Infoline do right? From 15 people in 1999, the company now employs 15,000.

"Consulting and research is an individual-centric business. I discovered that if clients have to talk to me or 3-4 key people, it is almost impossible to scale-up beyond a certain size." Hence the leap into transactions, where individual skills become irrelevant.

Nirmal had the ambition to 'make it big'.

"I knew I had to scale up and in that gamble even if it completely falls flat, it's ok, but you have to take that risk. One of the things I cannot imagine is an entrepreneur who does not take any risk and yet becomes successful."

Then there is competition. No doubt many other companies also saw the scope in internet trading including the likes of ICICI Bank, HDFC Bank and a number of foreign players.

But Nirmal believes India Infoline survived because of its "entrepreneurial way of doing things." And putting in a lot of hard work in technology and research.

The USP of India Infoline is quality research and advice. Nirmal also believes his technology offering is superior in terms of speed, flexibility and ease of use. "It's like a retail customer's Bloomberg – you get stock prices, charts, information, streaming quotes. It's very addictive."

There's also more personalised service since the organisation has grown in an entrepreneurial manner. "There were 50 people I knew who were very close, like a family. Now they know another 1,500 people and the tree grows like that."

The 'ownership' or family feeling continues, feels Nirmal. "If you meet with our branch managers, relationship managers, they are much more empowered and give far better service than their counterparts employed by our competitors."

The lesson is that you don't have to shy away from taking on the 'big boys'. The mouse is always more agile than the elephant. The start up can have a significant advantage, if he has strong domain expertise.

The other important aspect is managing growth at different levels.

"When companies are 10-15 people, that is one size. Another size is 50-100 people, then 500-1,000 people. At every size you have to change in terms of how you look at the business, look at the systems processes, audits, specialities for various functions. Otherwise it is impossible to scale up."

Nirmal's five year stint with HLL – a company known for its systems and processes – was invaluable. "I also have a small family business which my father runs and I used to think here (at HLL) the owners or bosses are in London and yet we work till 10 o'clock, and at times past midnight. How do they motivate as well as monitor us?"

What may have been just another job at a large multinational was actually a five year on-the-job immersion for Nirmal in 'What Large Companies do Right'. And what to get right when he started his own.

Yet, Nirmal remains philosophical. "You always have to take a risk. Then work hard. Luck must be on your side and the timing has to be right as well!"

All four factors may not come together for every entrepreneur. "Everyone is not going to survive no matter how talented you are. If 10 equally talented people start ventures, it's not that all 10 have equal chances or probabilities of success. Ames and Wal-Mart started around the same time, in the same industry. While Ames is no more, Wal-Mart tops the Forbes 500."

So you can't enter into entrepreneurship with an 'end result' in the mind alone. You have to enjoy the journey, every step of the way.

"In the last three years we have become very successful in terms of public image, market cap, getting listed but even before that I was quite satisfied. It's not that money and wealth alone make you happy; if you have created something which is different, good and creates employment, that is a source of satisfaction."

'It's all the about the money, honey' may be the tagline of India Infoline, but obviously that is not the line Nirmal lives by as an entrepreneur.

<u>ADVICE TO YOUNG ENTREPRENEURS</u>

You have to build a core team, delegate and empower your people. When you have done something on your own for 5-6 years you can obviously do it better than anyone else who joins you. So there is always a frustration over why this person I have recruited is not doing it the way I would have thought or done. But you have to get over that, train your team and let them make things happen. Of course you can't go hands off very soon or things will go out of control. It's a delicate balance.

Entrepreneurship is risky. So you should have a mindset, should be prepared to fail. If you are not prepared to fail and can't handle failure then this is not your cup of tea. As late as 2003, we were prepared to lose everything and give up and start once again on our own.

You should have the ability to build a team of the right people and not people you like. Many times you have grown with certain people and become very friendly with them. It is difficult to give a negative feedback or get performance out of them and this is a human problem. But you can't get emotionally attached to people and base business decisions on that.

Ideally, you should work in a large or good medium-size organisation before starting on your own. That always helps.

Whatever the number of partners, there has to be one leader. If there are 3-4 people at the same level and you try to arrive at a consensus, that is the worst of all. Whether it's an army or a country or a company there has to be one person, one leader in charge.

IT'S NEVER TOO
LATE

Vikram Talwar (PGP '70), EXL Service

After a long and distinguished career with Bank of America, Vikram Talwar could have spent the rest of his years playing golf. Instead he chose to set up a company which today is one of India's largest BPOs.

What's the right time in life to become an entrepreneur? Should you start fresh out of college or wait till you have a few years of experience? And what about starting out after a long and successful corporate career?

I meet Vikram Talwar, CEO of EXL Service, in search of some answers. After spending 26 years with Bank of America, he had become a 'classic corporate citizen'. And logically, should have gone on to become a consultant, or a man of leisure. But Vikram chose a more risky path. The path of building his own company.

He may be heading a new-age industry, but Vikram Talwar belongs to the old school. He's got this distinguished, 'man about the world' air. Vikram speaks in precise, clipped English which you don't hear too often these days. And he is slightly distant, and formal.

Just like his company.

Getting inside EXL Services' Noida headquarters is an experience. You have to declare every piece of equipment you carry – laptop, digicam, voice recorder, cellphone. As you'd expect, there is the metal detector routine. And then, the guard points to a box filled with coloured balls.

"Ek utha lo".

If you draw red, like I did, you are taken into the security cabin and frisked once again. By hand.

Finally, I am waved inside. I wait in the boardroom for Vikram a good 45 minutes. At last, he strides in and we begin.

IT'S NEVER TOO

LATE

Vikram Talwar (PGP '70),
EXL Service

Vikram did his schooling from Lucknow's *La Martiniere* College and graduated from St Stephen's College. He joined IIM Ahmedabad directly after that, with no work experience.

"In those days, work experience was not important, though I do believe it is essential today. But in those days MBAs were unheard of anyway in our country."

The year was 1968.

"In terms of my family background, my father worked in the civil services, my mother worked with the government. Both of them came out of the army. So I come from a non-entrepreneurial background. Everybody in my family, at least for a couple of generations, had worked with the government, the army, the civil services."

So how come Vikram didn't go that way? He didn't find it exciting enough and wanted to do 'something different'. His father wasn't overly pleased, which goes to show that fathers will never be pleased with their kids' choices and often don't really 'know best'. In the decades to follow, a corporate career has become far more sought after than working for the government!

After graduation, Vikram was offered a job by Bank of America, which involved going to the US. That was the 'singularly most interesting thing about the job'. He took it and stayed with the Bank for 26 years, working in 9 different countries and enjoying it thoroughly.

"A classic corporate citizen that one finds in such jobs."

In 1996 Vikram quit Bank of America, and 'did nothing' for six months. Something many of us secretly fantasise about. But soon enough he realised that taking it easy wasn't as much fun as he thought it would be. At 48, it didn't make sense to 'retire'. And he certainly didn't want to do anything in the corporate world.

Having said that, Vikram went right back to the corporate world. He worked for a year and a half in New York with Ernst & Young Consulting, setting up their technology practice in India. E & Y wanted to get into the outsourcing space, but eventually shelved its plans. And so Vikram, a firm believer in India's skilled manpower story, decided to do it on his own.

"I was 51. Not the age when people get into entrepreneurship, generally speaking. Not this type of entrepreneurship. You can become a consultant. To take on this, I thought, was pretty challenging. Of course I didn't actually realise the kind of effort required. It was also leading edge because there were no third party BPO services in those days."

The year was 1999 and even technology hadn't truly taken off.

"Y2K was on the horizon and so the technology companies were coming to the forefront. But that was it. None of the companies were listed or anything. It was a very difficult time to start something new in a field that was untested. No financing was available. And I was at that stage in my life when I didn't really need to be an entrepreneur."

Financially comfortable, nothing more to 'prove'. So why not join the board of a few companies and play golf most afternoons?

"It was the fun of the whole thing, more than anything else that drove me. It was the creative aspect of my nature – I love to cook, for example. I find that creative. Corporate life isn't creative – it was more mundane, routine..."

And at the very heart of it all, there was the challenge of trying to find out, can I do it on my own? Can I survive and thrive outside the comfort of the corporate world?? It's a question few well-heeled multinational types dare to answer.

Today EXL is a ₹ 720 crore* company and 'BPO' is a huge industry. But back in 1999, did Vikram actually see the potential in the business? Did he realise it would one day be so big?

Not really. The opportunity was there, the size of it became apparent only along the way. What was clear, however, was that this was an extremely capital-intensive business that required tons of money. Raising funding was therefore crucial. A business plan was created but it was not an easy sell.

EXL finally got money through a gentleman called Gary Wendt, the former chairman of GE Capital. He was a personal contact. But he was also one of the few who knew the industry and wanted to be in it.

"So quite honestly, that's really the first stepping stone to getting into this. Not realising exactly what the future held. Normally entrepreneurs get into a field which is proven, especially people who don't have experience in that field. With us, there was absolutely nothing. There was nothing that one could fall back on."

EXL actually started with three partners. Like many such ventures, things unravelled at some stage and one partner made an early exit. And that's just one side of the ups and downs EXL faced in its early years.

"One of the company's first clients was Conseco, a large insurance company. There was a slight conflict of interest as Gary Wendt became the Chairman and CEO of Conseco and then decided it would be best if he bought our company and created a GECIS type of model (GE's captive internet offshoring centre in India)."

So EXL was sold. But soon after, Conseco ran into serious problems – in fact it went bankrupt. So Vikram and his partner Rohit bought it back.

---

* Revenues for the year 2007 were $179.9 million, an increase of 47.7% over the prior year.

"It was the fun of the whole thing, more than anything else that drove me. It was the creative aspect of my nature – I love to cook, for example. I find that creative. Corporate life isn't creative – it was more mundane, routine ..."

"We really restarted the company from scratch in 2002 with no clients. Because our only client was Conseco. And they ran into trouble, so we had no work from them. We had some buildings, some infrastructure and some 1200 employees. But no business and only a limited amount of money. Enough to survive for 6 months."

New investors were brought in but they did not put up big money. They provided a lifeline of sorts but beyond that it was up to the management to keep its head above the water. And somehow, it did.

To cut a long story short, EXL managed to get new clients, and in a matter of 5 years starting January 2003, it has grown to be a 'fairly decent-sized company'. EXL listed on the NASDAQ in 2006 and its current market cap exceeds $750 million. The company now has close to 10,000 employees and revenues of $180 million. So everything did work out.

"Having said that, it's not something that happens very often. It's not something that is easy to do. Luck is as important in this as hard work. What people don't realise is what happens to your life in the period when you are doing it and what sacrifice is required. It is genuine risk. It is purely risk."

Meaning, no family life. No time for anything but your work. And in the case of EXL it was a little worse because it was a round-the-clock operation. You are on call literally 24 hours a day.

"You need to be able to say I am singularly committed. You need the support of your family, your spouse."

Again, the question arises 'why'. You tried, you sold out, now why go through a second round of trials and tribulations by buying it all back?

"It was a challenge. The challenge was that you cannot fail. We could have walked away, we had already made money out of it."

It was also a responsibility.

"You started something, you had 1,200 employees to worry about. At the end of the day, I had given my personal word to a lot of people who had come along with me. People had left good jobs to come work with us. You can't just walk away... And of course, there was the desire to leave behind a legacy. You put all that together, and you charge on."

So how did this turnaround actually happen?

"It's a little bit of luck and little bit of extra effort. The little bit of luck is that we were servicing an insurance client and one of the people who was looking to come to India to get services was a large insurance company. And we were able to say that we can be operational for you very quickly. Because anybody else will have to learn, we don't have to learn."

In life, timing is the single most important thing.

In this business you grow rapidly. The first year was spent in raising money, the second in putting up a building. Sitting in the sun literally.

"You really get your hands dirty. And specially for people who come from the corporate world, where you have a large infrastructure, you have a good position – it's hard. All of a sudden you are out there typing your own letters. You are sitting outside government offices, trying to get approvals. Some *babu* makes you wait for six hours... it's a totally different ball game."

It means stepping down, getting rid of your ego. And it's a single motivation that makes it work. A motivation that is beyond money alone.

"At the end of the day, I had given my personal word to a lot of people who had come along with me. People had left good jobs to come work with us. You can't just walk away... And of course, there was the desire to leave behind a legacy."

"It has to be an inner drive to succeed in what your objective is. And it cannot be money in my mind. If you want to get into entrepreneurship to make money, I don't think you will be as successful..."

"It has to be an inner drive to succeed in what your objective is.   And it cannot be money in my mind. If you want to get into entrepreneurship to make money, I don't think you will be as successful. Because ultimately there is only one thing that drives this: passion. I will quit the day I don't have any more passion for this job. I am very certain."

And you need an ability to share or you can never build a company of size and scale.

Today, Vikram owns 6% of EXL. And he never owned more than 12%. The rest was with investors, shareholders and employees.

How about an Azim Premji then, who owns 80 per cent of Wipro?

"Yes, but it was a family business much before they got into IT. There is very big difference between rich young men going to become entrepreneurs and middle class, non-moneyed individuals becoming entrepreneurs. Would I call Mukesh Ambani an entrepreneur? The answer is absolutely no. He is a good businessman, not an entrepreneur. Sunil Mittal is an entrepreneur. That's the difference."

Point taken. But Sunil Mittal started out on the entrepreneurial path early in life, whereas Vikram chose to do so decades later.

"Well, you could get into entrepreneurship on a whim or a fancy like I did. But if you want to plan how to be an entrepreneur, get some solid experience – how companies work, how people are managed, what finance is all about."

And if you do start a business, select your partner very carefully. At EXL, as with many start-ups, the three founding partners had worked together in the past. One dropped out, early on.

"It's tricky. Working with a partner requires a huge amount of sacrifice, understanding and tolerance. It's like a marriage at the end of the day. I mean, worse than a marriage."

"First you got to have a common objective. There has to be a vested interest on both the sides for it to work. Two is, you got to have equivalence – not saying 'I am the boss and you work for me', it doesn't work."

In the case of EXL, Vikram and Rohit Kapoor are IIMA grads but Rohit was 16 years younger, and brought in a very different perspective.

"Rohit is left-brained – I am the opposite. We recognised each other's strengths and we optimised each other's strengths. It's that recognition and ability to say 'I don't know this, why don't you do it', that's the trick. You take your ego out of the equation, let me put it that way."

Yet, one partner is often better known or is the public face of the company – as Vikram is with EXL.

"Okay, so what! It sort of funnels its way out. The point is, the chemistry between the two partners should be perfect."

However, life is never perfect. You make plans, they have to be changed. But you keep moving, keep flowing along. You simply keep taking decisions, on the fly.

"The toughest thing in life a human being has to do is make a decision. Whether you are an entrepreneur, or a husband, or a wife, or a company. Decision-making is tough because human nature is such that I hate to be wrong and I hate to take the blame. And that's why companies are run by committees."

Vikram admits EXL is now a 'normal corporate entity' as with any company of its size.

"...Working with a partner requires a huge amount of sacrifice, understanding and tolerance. It's like a marriage at the end of the day. I mean, worse than a marriage."

"A public company can no longer be entrepreneurial. Because the rules are set for you, you've got to follow. And yet, he says, it remains exciting."

I want to know more, but it's as difficult to penetrate the mind of Vikram Talwar as it was to get inside the EXL premises.

What can be said, however, is that you are never too old to embark on a new adventure in life. You can retire, or reinvent yourself. The hair may be white but the heart can be as young as you want it to be!

<u>ADVICE TO YOUNG ENTREPRENEURS</u>

I would say, never start straight out of college. Work for about 6-7 years, get some experience in the world of business. How and what happens there. Become extremely conversant with finance, especially if you are going to into some form of a fairly complex, large type of operation. You can't get that knowledge in textbooks.

Don't be an entrepreneur without very good financial knowledge. Or have a trusted partner who knows all about this.

Being an investment banker doesn't necessarily train you to be an entrepreneur. So don't go for that. Go hard-core, bottom of the barrel. Join a company which does not pay you that much but where you have the opportunity to learn.

DRUG BARON

K Raghavendra Rao (PGP '79), Orchid Pharma

Raghavendra Rao has built up a 300-million-dollar pharma company in 13 short years. The son of a working-class Railways employee, he now dreams of making Orchid India's first $1 billion pharma company.

K Raghavendra Rao could probably sell ice to an Eskimo, *garam chai* to a Bedouin and plastic bags to Greenpeace. He has that kind of charisma.

The impressive thing about Orchid Pharma is how grand a plan and vision it was from the very beginning. While most entrepreneurs start small and mature into large entities, Orchid was big from day one. The project Rao conceived required ₹ 11.95 crore of capital and scaling it down was not an option.

So first of all, he put in everything he had. And then, he raised the rest of it. From institutions, from the general public, from friends and even strangers. Like colleagues of his brother, who was a doctor at Apollo Hospital.

Orchid Pharmaceuticals stands testimony to the fact that where there is a will there is more than one way. And if it means tagging along with him on the way to the airport to hear more of this fascinating story, so be it.

DRUG BARON

K Raghavendra Rao (PGP '79),
Orchid Pharma

K Raghavendra Rao came from a working-class background. His father was an employee of the South Central Railway. "We don't have any liquid assets or ancestral property. Nobody from our family was in business basically. And we don't have any lands or roots in any particular place."

Rao grew up in the town of Tenali with his parents and grandmother. That's where he did all his schooling and college. After BCom he went on to IIMA and then took up a job in Kwality Ice Cream in Bombay. Rao put in two and a half years with Kwality and was part of the team that helped turn around the brand in Ahmedabad, where it had not been doing too well.

But there was nothing more to learn there beyond a point. So Rao moved on to Ashok Leyland in Chennai, the makers of buses and trucks. He was one of the few people who was rotated in different departments – budgeting, accounting, costing and development. During that period he also did his Cost Accountancy and Company Secretaryship because there was nothing much to do after office hours.

There was this urge to constantly 'do more' and Ashok Leyland wasn't proving to be enough of a challenge. So in 1986, Rao joined the Standard Organics group in Hyderabad. The group had many activities like medical diagnostic centres, leasing, hire purchase and bulk drug manufacturing. "That is where my exposure to the pharmaceutical business started."

What's more, the chairman of the company, Mr Chandrashekhar Reddy, gave the young man a free hand. Rao joined as a project manager, quickly became vice president (finance and projects), and then vice president (operations). "Right from making applications to ICICI to getting loan sanctions, to recruitment of people, purchase of equipment and coordination with marketing, I was *de facto* in charge of everything. I got a lot of exposure."

Among other things, Rao helped set up diagnostic centres in different locations in India and was one of the key members of the team which expanded the bulk active plant near Hyderabad.

Standard Organics was one of the first companies to get US FDA approval for its sulphamethoxazole antibacterial product and Rao was closely involved in that effort.

The two and a half years he spent there were enthralling. The company grew five times, from ₹ 5 crore to ₹ 25 crore. More importantly, the seed of an idea was planted in Rao's brain. "I realised I have it in me to develop and successfully manage enterprises. And if I can make other companies bigger, why not start something on my own?"

By that time, Rao was married and had a daughter. His wife was a homemaker and his bank balance was a princely ₹ 11,200. That was after working for almost nine years!

"As a salaried employee in India, being able to start something of your own is very difficult. I didn't want to start a small-scale unit. They fail because of lack of economies of scale and market reach. And to start a medium-sized industry, you need capital."

So Rao made a conscious decision to go abroad. The idea was to earn a tax-free income, save most of it and then come back to India to do something in the pharmaceutical field. With that intention, Rao went to Oman. But it was not a typical accounting or management job. Rao joined a group called 'Al Buraimi' which wanted a financially oriented professional to take its hotel business forward. AF Ferguson had put out the ad and the interview was held at Mumbai's Oberoi hotel.

"When I landed in Oman, it was a kind of rude shock for me because there was a small 16-room hotel (three-star type) and a few pieces of land but the owner had all kinds of ambitions.

And there were only 20-30 employees, the highest qualified was only 12th standard pass."

But Rao decided to take this as an opportunity and try to grow the place. In three-and-a-half-years, between end-'88 and mid-'92, there was a complete transformation. "I was the *de facto* chief executive, the director and the top person. I assembled the team to make that kind of a thing happen. From less than two million dollars annual revenue from a 16-room hotel, we made that group into 80 million dollars in about four years time."

Based on the Standard Organics experience, Rao helped Al Buraimi put up a pharmaceutical factory called Oman Chemicals and Pharmaceuticals in 1990. It is the first and only bulk active plant in the entire Arab world even today. And it was done with Indian equipment, Indian manpower and Indian technology. In this period, the company also put up a readymade garment unit, the biggest in the Gulf called Al Buraimi Garments. Rao also put up a steel plant called Middle East Metal Industries and a five-star hotel. Employees grew from less than 20 to 2,000. A small-scale business was now a conglomerate.

There was no question of shareholding, as only locals can be owners in the Gulf, but Rao was "taken care of very well." From a $2,000 p.m. salary, he was soon earning $10,000. The Buick car was upgraded to a BMW. Having made enough capital, he decided it was time to return to India to start his own company. The year was 1992.

"Of all my experiences I chose pharma for two reasons. One is that this has been my first love in terms of my entrepreneurial spirit blossoming. I came to know of my own potential in Standard Organics. And secondly, this is one industry which can never go out of fashion. As long as people are there, medicine will be required."

Rao had savings of about half a million dollars and he invested all of it in the company. "I took a two-bedroom rented flat in Madras and started Orchid Pharmaceuticals. For the balance amount, I went to private equity people, IDBI and also to the public. We started as a public limited company right from day

> ## "We started as a public limited company right from day one of the organisation. Because I went and told them, I am committed to this, this is my plan and this is what I have."

one of the organisation. Because I went and told them, I am committed to this, this is my plan and this is what I have. I have put everything I own into the company."

The total project conceived initially was ₹ 11.95 crore. ₹ 15 lakh was the state subsidy as the plant was located in a developing zone. The balance ₹ 11.8 crore was to be funded thus – ₹ 6 crore as capital, ₹ 5.8 crore as loan.

Rao went to IDBI and met the General Manager, Mr Maitra. "I always believed in directly going to the top people in the institution. And going and making a pitch in an open manner. Lot of people say you need to lobby, and use your contacts. I never did any of those things in any of the departments, any of the institutions, any bank whatsoever. I have always met with only appropriate responses from the right people when I take things head on and talk passionately about what I believe. That's what I have done."

IDBI agreed to provide the ₹ 5.8 crore as loan. Rao then told them that ₹ 6 crore was the equity but he had only ₹ 1.5 crore in cash. That's what he had managed to save in Oman. IDBI agreed to put in another ₹ 50 lakh as capital, one of the very few and first instances of IDBI participating in equity capital of a first-generation enterprise.

But Rao was still ₹ 4 crore short. IDBI suggested the company should float a public issue and agreed to lead manage and underwrite the issue. This would raise another ₹ 2.5 crore. But still, there was a shortfall. The only option was private equity people or venture capital. So Rao went and knocked at a few doors. It took a bit of perseverance but he managed to get ANZ Grindlays – 3i, PLC to invest ₹ 50 lakh. The balance came from friends, both in India and abroad.

Pitching your idea to investors is something every entrepreneur is prepared to do. But it's one thing to make a PowerPoint presentation to a venture capitalist and quite another to speak to people you know, people like yourself, and sell them your dream. Rao's brother, a medical doctor working in Apollo Hospital introduced him to many of his colleagues. Rao went and talked to them, individually, and several put in their money.

It takes a really strong belief in yourself and what you're doing to raise capital like this. But it can be done – Orchid is testimony to that!

But why was it so important to raise exactly ₹ 11.8 crore? If capital was hard to come by, could he not have downsized the project?

"It is not a question of cutting the cloth to suit your size. Without that kind of a minimum critical mass, that project would not be viable. We didn't create or invent any new niche there, we needed to set up a 100-tonne antibiotic plant. The cost and technology were not in favour of downsizing the project."

MBAs who take up entrepreneurship are generally attracted to knowledge-based industries, or services. Few venture into large, manufacturing projects.

Rao reflects, "With due respect to the service industry and trading and things like that, I feel that here you create something. By adding different types of chemicals, we can come up with something which is not there. It is always a fascinating experience for me, rather than taking from X and selling it to Y or just converting knowledge into money. These are also good businesses but I was always fascinated by manufacturing."

By this time Rao had of course set up several projects – for Standard Organics and Al Buraimi. Was it any different now that he had invested his own money?

"Wherever I worked, even when I held zero shares, my attitude towards the work and the project has been absolutely the same. If anything, now there is a bit of additional responsibility

"Wherever I worked, even when I held zero shares, my attitude towards the work and the project has been absolutely the same."

when you take money from other stakeholders. So many people have trusted me and looked at me and given their money, so I must repay the faith that they have reposed in me."

That faith was well placed, everything went as per plan. In fact, better than expected. On 1 July 1992, the company was incorporated. On 24 November 1992, Orchid received the sanction letter from IDBI. Exactly one year later, 24 November 1993, the project was inaugurated by former President of India, Mr R Venkatraman. Trial production started immediately. Commercial production began on 1 February 1994.

On 6 September 1993, Orchid also had its maiden public issue. As per the prospectus issued then, the company was supposed to complete the project by 31 March 1994. That deadline was actually achieved five months ahead of schedule. In fact Orchid had two months of commercial production from 1 February to 31 March and thus managed a turnover of ₹ 5 crore and a profit of ₹ 43 lakh in its very first financial year. And this over-achieving streak was to continue.

In 1994-95, the company had projected ₹ 27 crore of turnover but actually did ₹ 43 crore. In 1995-96, the revenue figure mentioned in the prospectus was ₹ 32 crore but actual turnover was ₹ 111 crore. The following year's figures were even more spectacular – ₹ 192 crore, as against the projection of ₹ 37 crore.

"There wasn't an enterprise in manufacturing that did a turnover of ₹ 192 crore in three years flat, starting from scratch. I was voted as the best young entrepreneur of the country and represented India in Canada for the finals. And I got a gold commendation there also. That was in 1997."

So what was the secret of this success?

Rao says it boils down to three things. One is an excellent

team -very, very good people. Rao had taken some of his colleagues at Standard Organics with him to Oman. And subsequently the same people came and joined him when Orchid was set up.

"These five are professionally qualified, experienced people in their own functions and they used to gel as a good team. I am not against family-owned organisations or anything like that but somehow I feel very comfortable to deal with a co-professional finance chief rather than my brother-in-law, or father-in-law or whatever. So that way I have been fortunate to have a technician, a commercial person, a strategist, an engineering person, and a finance expert – a chartered accountant."

The commitment of the team was such that for the first five months, until the IDBI sanction letter came, no one took any salary. Whatever common expenditure was required, that was incurred. Of course, all these individuals had a shareholding in the company as well.

The second thing was, smartness in terms of identifying the product group or some therapeutic area that Orchid should be in. Because the pharmaceutical industry is very vast. There are companies that have succeeded doing a bit of many different things. However, Rao had a different approach.

"I have always felt that you should take a niche segment, go deeper and broader into that, create a nucleus and reach a critical mass so that you become one of the low-cost producers. And add value. You then replicate that in other therapeutic areas. So by design, you will limit competition. Even if others try to replicate it later they will be less efficient because they will be trying to catch up with you."

So how did Orchid identify the right niche? There are two main kind of microbial drugs – antibiotics and antibacterials. The subtle difference between the two is that one kills the bacteria, while the other maims the reproductive ability of the bacteria. In antibiotics, the most well known is penicillin which was invented in the 1920s. But penicillin kills indiscriminately, destroying even the good bacteria which is required by the body.

**"I used to market to them my 'five-year plan'.
In fact I always carried the five-year plan
book with me and I would say, with or
without you, I plan to do these things."**

Then came semi-synthetic penicillins with lesser side effects, but the spectrum they cover is also narrow, i.e., the drug is not as effective against a variety of diseases.

Then came cephalosporins which act on the cell walls of the bacteria so that the immunity or the resistance system is not damaged. And its spectrum is also broad which means they can selectively kill different types of bacteria rather than a narrow range. So without going into too much of technical detail let us just say that Orchid chose to focus on a cephalosporin range, where by definition, competition is limited.

"That is something which has got a bright future because it is only the third generation of antibiotics ever invented in 75 years," adds Rao.

Within the cephalosporin group, Orchid manufactures many products, from orals to injectables. At the time, there was no company which specialised in cephalosporin in this manner. And even today there are only five companies in the world who have attempted to do it.

And the third reason Rao offers is that Orchid was one of the first companies born out of liberalisation with a global view. "We were the first company incorporated as EOU, ie, 100% export-oriented company in the pharmaceutical space. People used to say, 'Oh! India contributes only one per cent of the total requirement of the world in pharma.' So I said, 'Great, that means there is 99% of the world available for us to look at.' Even though we are basing ourselves in India we can conquer world markets."

Were there any problems in convincing foreign buyers to import drugs manufactured in India? After all, this was the early '90s, when India was not exactly known for its high quality in anything. However, this was not an issue for Orchid.

"In pharmaceutical language, to keep things simple, the basic ingredient which cures the disease is called the bulk drug. It is made in a large quantity and cannot be eaten by or injected into people. It has to be given in a 'formulation', i.e., made into a tablet, capsule or injection. So formulation is the front end, and bulk active or basic active is the back end."

Orchid entered the bulk drug segment first because even if it was a nameless, faceless operation to begin with, it would help the company build the business, achieve turnover and reach more people faster.

"It is like selling picture tubes. Who knows what is there in Sony or Panasonic. They are competing at the brand level, but the input can be from any vendor." Similarly, other companies used Orchid's bulk drug to create a formulation and sell it under their own brand name.

Orchid started exporting only to three countries – Singapore, Hong Kong and China. In the second year, this was expanded to 12 countries. By year three, Orchid was exporting to 30 countries. Now the company has clients in 75 countries. America and Europe were tough markets to crack but today, one third of Orchid's revenues comes from the US (if you take the value of Orchid products eaten by or injected into US customers or US patients).

Few companies grow so big, so fast. And yet, it is never easy or painless. The initial challenge was attracting talent apart from the core group. Pharma is a highly technology-oriented, process-oriented and hazard-oriented industry, so you can't just go and pick up anyone out there. It has to be people who have experience in this field and convincing them to join a new company was no child's play. As always, Rao sold them a dream.

"I used to market to them my 'five-year plan'. In fact I always carried the five-year plan book with me and I would say, with or without you, I plan to do these things. But if you join me, you can contribute in this way." It wasn't merely higher salary or

> **"There is no point in merely saying we are all a family. We have to believe it, we have to show it, we have to behave, we have to walk the talk."**

designation that Rao used to lure these people. He told them "this is your chance to *make a difference*."

"If you want to believe and join us, you are most welcome. If you don't believe, see me after 2-3 years, judge what has happened. Join me at that time, so that we can make the next step happen." And once again, some bought his argument and joined Orchid. They have grown with the company, manifold. And of course, they have an ownership stake.

In fact, a large number of people at Orchid hold shares in the company. Right from the boy who brings tea to the Deputy Managing Director. "And I did that even with my own money, even before we went public," says Rao. "So those employees who were there at that time, 135 of them, all have shares. We didn't know the price or the value that will come out of the shares later. It is the gesture that you do and your intent that speaks." In fact, other than IT companies, Orchid was the first company in India to give ESOPS, in 1999.

Little wonder that the attrition rate in Orchid is quite low. "One reason is the rapid growth of the company and the variety of opportunities that we give to people. From scratch we have built up a 300-million-dollar company, in about 13 years, I don't think any other pharma company has done it at that pace."

Early on, Orchid invested in R&D and gave its scientists a free hand to convert their ideas into reality. When the centre first came up in 1997 people remarked that it looks like a hotel, and was so much expenditure really necessary? Rao emphasises, "Without that R&D centre, none of the processes that we boast of now would have been possible."

The second challenge was growing beyond the initial model, i.e., moving from bulk active to the active dosage form. The company would need to expand beyond cephalosporin to diversify its risks and also invent new molecules. To do all this, Orchid needed about $100 million dollars.

"As a five-year-old company, organically built up, you don't have 100 million dollars of cash, however successful you might have been. So I said, 'Okay, I will make another five-year plan from 2000 to 2005. I will go to international investors and private equity guys and market this story. You want to believe in it, participate in this, and together we will execute the plan. And don't look every day, every quarter at *Economic Times* and see what is Orchid's share price.'"

What Rao promised was that in four years time, Orchid would do all four things – build up FDA-approved manufacturing plants, build dosage forms and go to regulated markets, develop R&D, and patent its own processes. The idea was to have international marketing tie-ups in place and sell these products as soon as 'product patents' expired in 2005. Schroders put in $40 million and IFC provided $20 million and the balance $40 million was borrowed from the banking system.

This time it was far easier raising money. "But the first time we had more vigour, more youth, more passion and drive, comparatively speaking," recalls Rao. "We were rejected then by four different agencies yet did not take 'no' for an answer." It is one of the ironies of life that money chases track records, but few fund the entrepreneur seeking to lay down that track.

Orchid's plans went exactly as projected. 2005 saw a massive ramp up in operations – the company found success in regulated markets and tripled its profits. Profits have again doubled for the year ending 31 March 2008.* "It is an innovation-led, formulation-oriented, international market penetration story."

---

* Orchid achieved ₹1,301 crore of revenues and a net profit of ₹175 crore for the 12-month period ended March 2008. Revenues for the year ending 31 March 2007 were ₹985 crore against the profit of ₹78.5 crore.

"...the bus service to this area dropped the workers 5 km away. When Rao noticed it, he decided to buy a bus. There was no food facility in the area, so Orchid opened a canteen."

Half the company's revenue is coming from the dosage form, one third of the revenue is coming from the US market, and the activities and product range of the company have been successfully diversified.

Execution was, of course, a huge challenge. "International marketing of formulations is a different ball game, intellectual property or looking at the patents situation is a totally different story. And making bulk active of carbapenems is quite different from making cephalosporin injectable. They are like chalk and cheese."

Different lines of business require different sets of people. "Only corporate planning, philosophy, motivation and finance departments, you could say, remained the same."

This time, getting the people was not difficult but executing different pieces and integrating them into the culture of the organisation was the key issue. "Because an R&D scientist will be in his own world whereas a formulation or a sales guy for the local market, wearing a tie and going to meet a doctor, will have an entirely different mindset. To make both of them think that this is one Orchid, was a big challenge."

One of the unifying factors is Rao himself. The company now has 3,700 employees and 10 locations but he makes it a point to visit, interact with the staff, share his thoughts with small groups and encourage them to speak to co-workers. Rao ensures his presence and participation in annual days and sports events. Even his fluency in 4-5 different languages, especially South Indian languages, has helped in building that personal connect.

At the policy level also, there is a 'company as family' approach. "There is no point in merely saying we are all a family. We have to believe it, we have to show it, we have to behave, we have to walk the talk."

For example, the very first factory Orchid put up was the 24th one to come up in that location. And the bus service to this area dropped the workers 5 km away. When Rao noticed it, he decided to buy a bus. There was no food facility in the area, so Orchid opened a canteen. And of course, workers got shares.

The company also funds the further education of employees without taking any bond. "I said let us help someone become a post-graduate by attending evening classes or whatever. If we are not able to give him a better opening and he gets a chance elsewhere, he becomes a better person. So be it. I can always recruit another graduate." Higher education of children of employees, paternity leave, birthday gifts are all par for the course and it is equal for all employees. Irrespective of the level or the cadre.

So what lies ahead? Rao has a 'specific plan' to take the company to one billion by 2011. It is a very ambitious kind of target and this time it is not so much about raising money but differentiation in terms of identifying niche products, where the competition will be limited. "Development based on knowledge and innovation are going to be the keys to take us from 300 million to one billion."

The idea is to be the early bird in some segments instead of jostling around with many other players in the large and obvious market opportunities. The secret is that niche products always command higher margins.

"What I mean is we will focus on a couple of niche products each year. Once we do that, others will notice and try to catch up. Prices come down, and by that time I move on. I have 'new hills' to climb in the form of another 10 products that are lined up for launch in the next four years." Smart choice of products and proper timing is what Rao is banking on.

Everything is planned in advance. But does life really work out that way? In the pharma industry, perhaps.

"It is different in the electronics or fashion industry, where obsolescence is high. In pharma, it is a patented regime – what is happening is all documented and is in the public domain." So one can use that information and plan accordingly.

Of course, the same information is available to all other pharma companies as well. You still need to put the pieces of the puzzle together. And there is also a risk you take in terms of investing a lot of money to make it all happen.

"When you create this kind of excellence where you are able to create such 'hills' in the sub-specialisation of antibiotics, you need to make separate dedicated investments in those products and wait for 3-4 years to reap the benefits."

Pharmaceutical exports need to abide by FDA regulations. Due to issues like cross-contamination, you are not allowed to make cephalosporin in a penicillin plant and so on. A patient may have an allergic reaction and even die due to a microgram of the other drug being present.

"Right from canteen to godown, everything has to be different. So how many companies will be discerning enough to make those kind of niche investments silos, wait for the product patent expiry to take place, then launch a product? We have done that and we will keep doing it..."

The price of ambition is a tremendous strain on the balance sheet. "We are quite leveraged, we have borrowed, we have invested, we are waiting. But the hills are beginning to unfold now..."

And more are waiting to be climbed, ahead!

Epilogue

On Monday, 17 March 2008, the stock price of Orchid Chemicals & Pharmaceuticals Ltd fell by 39.09% to end at ₹ 127.05.

Commenting on this, an Orchid spokesperson stated that a combination of macro factors and market rumours contributed to the sudden negative sentiment on the stock.

The trigger was the sale of a stake held by a major institution (Bear Stearns) liquidating its position in many companies. This was coupled with the margin call on a particular portion of the promoters' stock which was funded. As a result, the promoters' holding fell by 7.9%, creating further pressures on the stock price.

In the process, K Raghavendra Rao is estimated to have lost close to ₹ 75 crore in what can only be called a 'Black Swan' or unforeseen event. What's more, Solrex, a Ranbaxy-owned company, used this as an opportunity to snap up close to 15% of the company by buying shares from the open market.

Following speculation about a hostile takeover, the two companies formally announced a 'business' alliance on 22 April 2008.

Speaking on the development, Mr Malvinder Mohan Singh, CEO & MD, Ranbaxy,* said, "Orchid is a niche player in the global pharmaceutical industry with an impressive track record, particularly in sterile products. We are pleased to enter into this long-term strategic alliance with Orchid. The agreement will be mutually beneficial and synergistic, allowing both organisations to leverage each other's inherent strengths."

Commenting on the alliance, Mr K Raghavendra Rao, Managing Director, Orchid Chemicals & Pharmaceuticals Ltd said, "We are happy to join hands with Ranbaxy, India's largest pharmaceutical company. Ranbaxy's global scale and market reach and Orchid's state-of-the-art development and manufacturing capabilities would expand the business of both companies. We believe that this will be a win-win arrangement for both companies."

As they say, always expect the unexpected and then make the best of whatever hand life deals... And who knows what the next round holds.

---

* Ranbaxy was acquired by Japanese pharmaceutical giant Daichi for $4.6 billion in June 2008.

ADVICE TO YOUNG ENTREPRENEURS

Choose a goal and focus on it. It can be in the area of product, service or knowledge. Longevity of the field is important. Combine reason and intuition. If there's a tie, go with intuition. Think either big or niche. Doing what many others do won't take you anywhere. Build teams. Believe in dignity of labour. Be passionate and direct about your ambition. There is no dearth of capital to back right ideas and entrepreneurs. Aim to create lasting value. The country will remember you for that.

THE BANKER WHO
BLINKED

Jerry Rao (PGP '73),
Mphasis

A career Citibanker, Jaitirth (Jerry) Rao was bitten by the entrepreneurial bug in his late 40s. He built up a large and profitable company (Mphasis) but recently sold out to EDS because business is about passion as well as knowing when to let go.

He built a corporate career.

Then he built a company.

Now he's sold it and moved on.

Jaitirth Rao, or Jerry as he is better known, does not mix emotions with entrepreneurship. Being attached to the company you create, is '*moha*,' he says. You have to do what's best for the business and if that means selling out, so be it. There are absolutely no regrets.

We meet at his Alexandra Road residence on a weekday afternoon. It's a fancy address but not one of those new-fangled skyscrapers. The house is modern, comfortable but rather spartan for someone who's done really well for himself. No *moha* in that area of life either.

Jerry is lingering over his lunch. Perhaps that is what you call true luxury – to have time on your hands. Books occupy the entire room, from floor to ceiling. But not for effect alone, Jerry has read most of them. He is now writing a book and there are other 'plans' but he will share them when the time is right.

Right now, it's time to look back and reflect on the journey so far...

THE BANKER WHO
BLINKED

Jerry Rao (PGP '73),
Mphasis

"I was doing my BSc Chemistry and of course my dad worked with the government so he was keen that I should go into the IAS. But one had heard vaguely about IIMs. This is in the early '70s. And so one applied."

Evidently, the MBA was a pretty unknown commodity in 1971. In fact, Jaitirth Rao landed up at IIM Ahmedabad because of a technical problem. At age 19 he was too young to sit for the IAS exam. "When I am 21 I will definitely write the entrance," he assured his dad and packed his bags for IIM.

Two years later, Jerry joined First National Citibank (later known as Citibank) through campus placement. He went to Beirut for training and even sent for the forms for the IAS but eventually decided to stay on in a corporate career. Because Citibank was a good company. It was a heady place in those days, it had great ambitions.

Citibank was then the second largest bank in the world and it was internationalising its management staff. From a purely 'American' bank it was becoming more multi-cultural. So it was a good time to be there.

"I came back from Beirut, worked for 2-3 years in India, then went to the Middle East. Then I wanted to quit corporate life altogether and decided to go into academics."

In 1979 Jerry enrolled in the University of Chicago to do a PhD

Two years later he realised he wasn't cut out for that kind of life and abandoned the PhD halfway.

He rejoined Citibank, but this time in New York, and then South America. In 1984, good friend Rana Talwar persuaded Jerry to come back to India and set up Citibank's retail and consumer business.

"It was within the umbrella of a large corporation but it was very entrepreneurial. Very unusual. We were writing on a blank canvas so it was quite an interesting time. There was no consumerism, no retail at the time. We introduced ATMs, for example. Even though the technology was 20 years old, it was revolutionary for India back then."

Nine years later Jerry moved to Europe, and then he was asked to head the technology development division of Citibank, kind of like an R&D unit. He was reluctant – after all wasn't this the job of a techie? "But there was a kind of feeling that in Citibank, technology was getting separated from business. It was felt that someone with a business background would be better to run that division."

It was a very exciting time because the internet was taking off – this was 1995. Jerry redirected a lot of R&D expenditure into the internet. In those days everybody in California was starting a new company and every day Citibank was giving business to different vendors – many of them in India. That's when it struck Jerry, "Why shouldn't I be on the other side of the table?"

"Financially I was relatively secure so it wasn't a high risk kind of thing for me. And if it hadn't worked I could have always got back into a corporate career. Also my career in Citibank was plateauing. I was in the top 50, but it was clear to me that they were not going to promote me to the top 10 or 15. And I was not excited about pushing my way through corporate politics in New York."

Everything came together. Along with a colleague, Jeroen Tas, Jaithirth quit Citibank and started Mphasis. The year was 1998.

"I went to my boss and said, 'Look, I don't want people to say that you fired me so I want you to be the chairman on my advisory board. I am not going to give you any money, just lend me your name for exactly one year.'"

He agreed, and Citibank gave Mphasis its first small business. Very soon there were other, bigger clients. People often ask whether MBAs have any advantage in doing business? Jerry's experience clearly shows how the IIMA network can help.

"Early on we acquired a small division of an Indian company called Byzan Systems. Byzan Systems was run by IIMA alumnus Mohan Krishnan. So he became a third founder of Mphasis along with me and Jeroen. Then, when we were looking for money, Citibank Venture Capital was very interested in investing with us and I was negotiating with Latika Monga, an IIMA alumnus also."

The Citicorp venture capital investment didn't come through. But the next investor who came to invest was from Barings Private Equity headed by Rahul Bhasin and Subbu Subramaniam, both IIMA alumni. When it came to recruitment, again there were IIMA connections. "Among our early employees were Radhika Rajan, Vikram Jaipuria and Preeti Shenoy."

The Citibank and University of Chicago networks also helped. The first investor in Mphasis was Rick Braddock. "Braddock used to be the President of Citicorp and he liked me very much," muses Jerry.

1999 was a very heady year. Mphasis was growing 100% quarter to quarter. Of course, it was the dotcom boom and everything was growing crazily at that time. And Mphasis positioned itself as a company which did internet-based technology solutions for legacy companies – an area where Jerry had been on the other side and knew exactly what a client would want.

Besides, he'd been an early believer in the technology itself.

"I had started internet banking, internet brokerage and I was chairman of the internet steering committee in Citigroup. So I was very much a part of the internet movement and was one of the founders of something called the Online Banking

"I should have started it 3-4 years earlier. If you think about it, it could have been much bigger if we had started in '95. But that's life. You start when you get your break."

Association. I had gone to Washington DC and testified before the US Congress about internet financial services."

Meanwhile, Barings had invested in a company called BFL whose CEO had quit the year before. Barings had a 25% stake in Mphasis and a 52% stake in BFL. Mphasis and BFL were merged and Jerry became the CEO of the joint company.

Actually, it was a reverse merger. BFL was already listed in India. Mphasis changed its name to Mphasis-BFL Ltd and got listed. The valuation was excellent, in fact, the combined stock price went 'through the roof.' Mphasis and BFL combined, the fiscal year ended March 2000, had done $34 million top line and had broken even on the bottom line.

For the fiscal year ended March 2001, the company did $64 million in revenues. Almost a 100% growth and a 10% bottomline ($6 million). So basically the merger seemed to have worked.

But there was a problem. Starting January 2001, as dotcoms crashed, the business also ran into trouble. Luckily in 1999, almost by accident, Mphasis had started a small call centre operation. In 2001, when the IT business slowed down, that took off. And today, of course, Mphasis is a major player in the BPO segment. 33% of its revenues come from BPO operations.

So you can plan and plot but who can actually see the future? Putting your eggs in multiple baskets makes a lot of sense.

"In 2001, among the Indian public companies in the IT space, we would have been number 25 or 26. By 2006, we were in the top 10, basically because we continued to grow as others faltered. But also, it was becoming clear that this call centre business is capital intensive."

Mphasis raised capital from ChrysCapital. "They were very bold investors. Because they invested with us at a premium over the prevailing prices. But you know, nevertheless they did quite well with their investment. I am quite grateful to them."

Actually the company never used their money – the 10 million dollars was simply put away. "It helped us to sleep better."

However by 2004-05 it became clear that something peculiar was happening. The top six players in IT and the top two in the BPO industry were growing faster than the industry average. Usually smaller companies grow faster than the bigger companies. Jerry and his team realised that the consolidation phase had set in. Also IBM, Accenture, all the global players were becoming big in India.

It was time to look at a different strategy.

"We could have continued as an independent business – it was nicely profitable. But we said 'No, then we will be marginalised.' So we initiated discussions with EDS and finally we became an EDS subsidiary."

This made sense because now Mphasis had a great marketing engine. And the EDS brand to get business. Post merger the company once again started growing faster than the industry average, proving Jerry's point. But of course it meant selling out.

"I think one reason why we were able to sell out is, we were not that emotionally attached. Many entrepreneurs who start off in their 20s and have never worked in a corporation... for them it can be gut-wrenching."

"In America, if you look at it, people are much more cold-blooded about their companies. At the right time, the CEOs resign, retire, sell out. India I think, the first-generation entrepreneurs get very, very attached to their companies. Not in rational market-related terms but in very irrational emotional terms. We didn't have that. That is what made the EDS transaction possible."

> "Many companies over-invest.
> Especially these days they get plenty of
> private equity money so they get
> fantastic offices, this and that and that's
> a big mistake. You have to invest in pace
> with your revenues. But you must be
> aware of your inflection points."

It's a cold-blooded, clinical assessment. Actually the entire story has been related with a kind of detachment. "This happened. Yes, it happened to me but I can see it completely objectively. Very different from the other, younger entrepreneurs."

I don't see any personal anecdotes coming. So I decide to ask for some *gyaan*.

"What do I take away from all this? I think timing is very critical. In 1973, even if I had wanted to start a company, there was no private equity, nobody would have invested. Whereas in the 1990s, and today of course, there is capital available for people with ideas, people with intelligence and risk-taking ability."

"Second thing is, networks are very important. Because networks give you credibility, they give you access. It still means you have to do your job, but at least it opens the doors."

"The third thing that I could say I take away from all this is you need some luck. In fact the call centre decision was luck. Originally our board was against it. They said: 'Oh my God! You are such a high-end IT, internet systems architecture company. Why do you want to do this low-cost call centre work?'"

"In fact they forced me to put it in a separate subsidiary with a different brand name so that it wouldn't confuse with the high-end brand name. But it was a lucky and a good decision."

"A couple of other lessons that I have is that particularly in the initial days, you have to be focused on two things. You, the founder, have to spend a lot of time with customers. It cannot be delegated to junior salespeople. You have the passion, you have the conviction, nobody else can replicate that."

"And if you are a small company, you have to be extremely transparent and honest. Big companies can afford to cover their tracks, but in small companies, you have to say, 'We did a bad job, sorry, here is a refund'. So you establish a reputation of being reliable, of high integrity."

"Reputation is very important for attracting talent. Because when you are a small company, nobody has heard of your brand, you are not important. Why should anybody join you! One reason why many people joined me was that I had a very good track record at Citibank as a manager. People knew I always took good care of the folks who worked for me. I was fair to them."

Now research has shown that transparent companies have a lower cost of capital. But purely from experience Jerry believes that the more transparent you are, the more people are willing to invest in you. So from day one, Mphasis hired KPMG for audit. The company kept very strong, very high standards.

The other thing you have to do in business is take some very tough decisions. There were two senior co-founders. "We had to part ways. It's tough when you have to sit down in the same room with a co-founder and say goodbye to him. But you need to look ahead, not look back as you grow."

Another lesson was that a company which is growing had to keep improving systems and processes. "We had absolute pain when we grew from $100 to $200 million. We suffered every day because our systems were all cottage industry systems."

"You must not lose focus on cash... If you don't have cash, you are up against a wall. You end up raising money at the wrong time or walking away from the business."

> **"Plans are all okay, but if you don't have the courage to make mid-course corrections and changes, particularly in highly changing environments like the technology space, you will get into trouble."**

Take a recruitment system, for example. The company would make an offer to somebody it had rejected six months ago! There was no recruitment database that kept track of that. Customer systems were weak. If an individual in a client firm shifted to another division he or she was lost and along with the person went the business.

And of course one has to plan to set up these systems some time before they are actually required. The trick is when. Not too much in advance because no small company can afford to over invest.

Focus on cash is very important. "We had even taken a small loan which we didn't use. But that didn't matter. We were always sure that we would have cash. In some of the early months, I had to write personal cheques to meet our payrolls. Because cash is what can get you into trouble."

Mphasis, in the initial days, was very cost-focused. The founders used their frequent flier miles for travelling. They lived in a friend's home in New York, never in a hotel. The idea was – don't create overheads you can't sustain.

The use of PR is also crucial for small companies which cannot afford to advertise. For instance, Mphasis had a small PR agency in New York who managed to get Jerry a front page article with his photograph in the 'American Banker'. "By God! That did so much for us. We were able to go to so many banks with that article. And it gave you immediate credibility. 'Ex-banker has started an IT company'. It was a great piece. I think investment in PR is very very important. It pays off disproportionately compared to advertising or general marketing."

Recruiting senior people is a major problem. It is as much a headache as buying a company. "Integrating a senior person who doesn't know your culture and who is not part of your original founder group, is very very difficult. We made at least two-three mistakes with that and it's very expensive."

Not only do you have to pay salary, which is expensive, but headhunters' fees also. The person will bring in his/her own people, bring his/her own systems.

"When in doubt frankly, if the person on the inside is only 80% suitable, I would say promote that person. Because when you are in a growth phase, it is better to take that gamble than try and recruit senior people. Try and recruit people at the middle level, and grow them. Do not try and get the senior salesperson who is going to solve all your problems. Usually that doesn't work. It didn't work for us."

There are no shortcuts!

Lastly, you have to offer a clear and definite advantage. If you are coming into a business where there are already existing players and you are 10% cheaper, don't even bother. You have to come into a business where you are 50-60% cheaper, by doing something different.

Mphasis also recruited some unusual talent. The company was very flexible with location, working from home and so on. And of course, like all new economy companies Mphasis-BFL shared a large chunk of equity with employees – 15-20%.

There is also a sense of pride in the fact that Mphasis contributed to the larger scheme of things. "We are doing to

> "I always feel very sorry for people who worked in the Indian corporate sector from 1956 to 1991. They could have been such bright fellows but they were stifled. What could they do? We are lucky and we have to ride that crest of the wave."

"You are a vendor sitting somewhere. You call a secretary, she says, 'Who are you, which company, why should my boss see you?!' As a big corporate guy you got so much red carpet treatment."

the service industry what Henry Ford and Frederick Taylor did to manufacturing and we are doing it globally... We also created 12,000 jobs in seven years. And each of them probably created four or five indirect jobs."

We are nearing the end and he hasn't yet mentioned the 'P' word. Passion. Is that part of the whole 'let's not get emotional' approach to running a company?

"I talk about passion, not emotion. The two are different words. Emotion is what you feel for your children. Even when they do something wrong, you are willing to overlook it. But passion is different. I did believe and I still believe in the liberating and productivity-giving power of internet technologies. I do believe and still believe in the Indian talent story."

"Emotional, one shouldn't be, that is my personal view. Some people are. Because emotion, translated in Sanskrit is *moha*. *Moha* is this kind of false attachment you feel that this is my company, I have built it, I don't want to leave it."

"I think that is stupid. I think you have to know when it is the right time to detach yourself and change your role. And maybe eventually leave it; at least be willing to change it from executive to non-executive. From leader to mentor. All these things, you have to be willing to do."

Even if it means 'Mphasis' slowly dies. There is no legacy.

"Well if you think about it, many great names disappear. When I joined banking, Manufacturers Hanover was a big bank. Irving Trust was a big bank. Chemical was a big bank. All those names have gone. Those were very big, multi-billion dollar banks."

Currently Jerry is on the Asia Pacific Advisory Board of EDS VP – a non-executive role.* Clearly, he has scaled down his involvement even as the company is going from strength to strength.**

So what does it feel like to semi-retire after working 20 years and a 7-8-year stint as entrepreneur? Is it that stage of life now where you feel "Ah, I can now spend the next 20-30 years doing 'whatever I want'?"

"But why do you think I haven't been spending the last 20-30 years doing what I want? That too was what I wanted. I enjoyed every minute of working in Citibank. And in the last few months when I didn't enjoy, I made my plans to quit."

"You can't postpone your whole life to the future. People who are endlessly planning for their retirement are stupid. You could die tomorrow. There is no point in planning for retirement and saying 'When I retire, I will do something.'"

In short, anyone who thinks, "I am doing this business so I can sell out and then enjoy my life" is an idiot. But there are many idiots out there. I sincerely hope you aren't one of them!

---

* *EDS was bought by HP in May 2008.*

** *Mphasis revenues for the year ended 31 March 2008 were ₹ 2,423 crore, a 38% jump over the previous year. Profits stood at ₹ 255 crore.*

ADVICE TO YOUNG ENTREPRENEURS

Today, virtually nobody I know will work for 20 years for any one company. That is over. However, I think there are some companies, and Citi is a good example of them, where a 4-5-year stint can be extremely helpful because you pick up discipline, networking skills, navigational skills, cost disciplines, audit disciplines. All of which are invaluable.

I think people who, immediately after graduation, start their own companies tend to be naïve about cash, bank loans, negotiations, about networks. Unless you have a truly fantastic product idea I would not advise you to take the plunge at age 24.

And in your sales pitch, the first point should be about your weaknesses, not your strengths. You should tell people what you are not – you are not large, you are not this, you are not that. Okay, people think – there is some honesty, these people are speaking the truth.

And when you try and showcase stuff you have done, customer references are very important. Sometimes people are unwilling to give written references, persuade them to give telephonic references. But there is nothing like a customer reference for a small company. Nobody trusts what you say in your PowerPoint.

ITCH BIN EIN

ENTREPRENEUR

**Shivraman Dugal (PGP '76),
Institute for Clinical Research in India (ICRI)**

Shivraman is someone who is always looking for the Next Big Thing. After a string of interesting jobs he set up one of India's first private colleges with a foreign tie-up (Wigan and Leigh) and is now pioneering clinical research education in India.

Shivraman Dugal is a man with the Itch. From high-end fashion to fans to computer hardware, he'd seen it and sold it all. And then he became an entrepreneur.

In the 15 years since, Shivraman has set up a software company, a slew of colleges and now a clinical research institute. In each case he was a pioneer of sorts but he hasn't built any one company to fantastic proportions. Because size and scale is not his trip.

Shivraman is a serial entrepreneur. He would rather scale the next uncharted peak than set up camp at any one place and enjoy the view. Boredom is what motivates him to keep moving forward. And I can't help thinking, "It's all about the journey, not the destination." And about feeling alive, every minute of it.

ITCH BIN EIN
ENTREPRENEUR

Shivraman Dugal (PGP '76),
Institute for Clinical Research in India (ICRI)

Shivraman Dugal was an army child. After a degree in economics from Delhi University, he chose to do an MBA. Although government service was the more popular career path back then.

"It all kind of happened by accident. I applied for the MBA, got through the examination and got into IIMA. I wanted to do something non-military and this sounded like a good option."

At the end of the course Shivraman joined an Anglo-French company called 'Tutal'. He worked for them for 7 years – 4 years in London, 3 years in New York and a year out of Beirut, before Beirut became a bad place to be in. The company was in the high fashion garments area. Shivraman's job was merchandising and marketing of topnotch brands like Louis Vuitton and Armani.

An unusual job – and it wasn't through campus, strictly speaking. Shivraman actually joined Mettur Beardsell from IIMA, a Chennai-based outfit which was the holding company for a large number of multinationals which functioned in India. This was an area office reporting to Hong Kong.

"In 1976, when I graduated, there was no FERA. And India was a very liberalised economy. We have come full circle, but we have not gone back to what India was in 1976, let me assure you."

Then Indira Gandhi passed FERA in the fag-end of 1976,

along with textile control orders. Shivraman was responsible for selling the very famous brand of textiles called Mettur 'mals' and Mettur 'long cloth' in the southern region. After FERA, Mettur Beardsell decided that it didn't wish to expand anymore. The company exited India over the next 4-5 years, selling off all its textile mills And today Mettur 'mal' and Mettur long cloth don't exist.

So what happened to employees like Shivraman? Were they absorbed by the head office? Well, not officially.

(Grins) "I was sent for training those days to Manchester... So they forgot about me. Someone said, 'What will you do back in India, why don't you look after YSL?' So that is how it started."

Shivraman agreed and went on to work with brands like DKNY and Laura Ashley in the US. He also did cold storage in the Middle East (a different division within the same company). Then he came back to India on a holiday for ten days. But never went back.

"I didn't understand what I was doing in USA, I felt I was wasting my time. I thought I could have a very good lifestyle in India. I didn't see what I was gaining out of being in the US. And my father was very unwell. That was I think a part of the question. He died a year later. It was a part of the pressure on me to stay back."

Again, no great 'life plan' – it was just about listening to one's heart.

The year was 1983. Shivraman joined a company called Intercraft and set up what is possibly India's first modern retail chain: Intershoppe.

"I brought in the concept of fashion retailing. Large format outlets with neon signs, different way of stacking goods, things like jeans with studs. Today it has become standard. When I brought it in India, that was the first time anyone had done anything like that in this country."

Shivraman also brought in a foreign denim brand – FU's – owned by his former employer. He launched 23 shops in one year and it was a truly entrepreneurial exercise. Not just the job content but the fact that he was paid a rather low salary plus a percentage of profits.

"We were extremely successful in one year's time. At the end of the year, my future father-in-law told me that I couldn't be selling clothes. He was an ex-ICS officer. So... I had to find myself a 'respectable' job."

It wasn't about money – Shivraman made a 'hell of a lot'. But Intercraft wasn't a large, well-known company.

"You have to go back to a context 26 years ago. It wasn't considered very respectable working for a small-time organisation wherein you have a small-time stake. In any case, being a businessman was not considered great." So Shivraman joined Usha International, owned by Lala Sriram, and got pa-in-law's blessings. He became a divisional manager and stuck on for about six years.

It was completely different from anything he'd done before.

"My job was to sell their products which were largely consumer durables, things like fans and diesel engines. I did it in Uttar Pradesh, then Assam, then Orissa, then Gujarat. Each territory was bigger than the last. And they used to pay me phenomenally. Didn't have any complaints about that. But I still consider those six years as a 'desert'. If I look back, I don't remember a single great achievement... Those six years are blank."

There was money, there was responsibility and enough spare time for a decent family life. But Shivraman was thoroughly bored!

One fine day, he decided, I've had enough. Arjun Malhotra used to own HCL. He was one of the directors and Shivraman met him by chance when he was walking around Nehru Place, pretty dissatisfied with life. "We met purely by accident. We had a chat in the middle of the corridor and he said, come up for an interview. So I went up and he offered me a job in HCL."

And it was once again a move into a completely new kind of job, role and company. A recurring theme in his life: to boldly go where few have gone before. To never get too comfortable and move on to the next adventure.

"Professionals are better than entrepreneurs for running the running business. Because an entrepreneur is too much in love with his creation. When you love something, you are blind to everything which is wrong in it."

The other important thing for Shivraman was making a mark, wherever he went. Leaving behind something which lived on.

Even in that boring stint with Usha International, he recalls *one* major legacy: the coloured fan. "If you see fans in brown, black and what not today, that's courtesy me. Nobody had thought of a fan other than white back then.. there was a lot of resistance," he grins.

And in his very first job, Shivraman had impacted the town of Balakole in Andhra Pradesh. The town thrives on the production of lace. "Have you seen lace bedcovers? It's a whole industry and I kickstarted it when I was working for Tutal. Because I discovered that there was a huge demand for English lace doilies."

The doilies used to be very expensive. Shivraman realised they could be made a lot cheaper as a cottage industry. So he trained people, brought in raw material, got someone to set up the thread unit. Now that industry employs 45-50,000 people.

Whenever there was an opportunity, Shivraman could simply not sit still. He had to do something about it. So it was with HCL – something new and exciting. Never mind if it meant working on a lower salary and higher commissions again.

"In HCL, I started the reprographic division i.e. photocopiers. It was more or less unheard of in India. And I brought the fax machine into the country and sold huge quantities of it at prices which were crazy."

It was that revolutionary a product back then!

"When I saw the first fax machine in Japan I didn't think it was real. It was transferring paper via telephone line. I brought that fax machine, and gave a demonstration in MTNL, in Delhi."

The MTNL guy said, "*Theek hai,* you transmit this paper to China and ask them to transmit it back to me." When they saw the paper coming out of the machine they couldn't believe it. HCL sold its first fax machines for ₹ 2 lakh each.

"You can imagine the kind of profits that we made," he says with a straight face.

Of course all was not completely hunky-dory. This was 1987. There was nothing at that time called 'software'. Everyone was selling hardware, and HCL was the single biggest company in that domain. But its second biggest division was Office Automation (OA), and that was dying. Which was why Shivraman had been brought in.

"I more or less revamped the whole photocopier division. I brought in a whole set of new products from Japan. Certain machines which were brand new, which had never been seen before. I did not sack even one person. A division which used to sell 10 machines a month started selling 500 machines a month, in 12-18 months' time." HCL competed very strongly with Modi Xerox and had almost an equal market share in those days.

And then, Shivraman became an entrepreneur. Another leap taken by what he calls 'pure accident'. The year was 1989.

"My wife had an exhibition, it was on the ground floor of my house. She used to design jewellery. My kids were very small, so that day my job was to look after them while she went about her work."

Shivraman thought to himself, "She is having some fun, nothing much is going to come out of the whole exercise. But doesn't matter, why should I discourage anybody... " That evening he casually asked her how much money she had made.

"I still remember.. it was some ₹ 45,000. That's when it hit me. ₹ 45,000 is my salary for an entire month and here she's made it in one day! What am I doing?!"

Shivraman decided to test out if her jewellery would sell abroad. Carrying samples at that time was very dangerous.

> "Working at other companies in my early career helped me.. to understand how an employee thinks. It also taught me the value of systems and how important it is to employ people who are better than yourself. Or your organisation will never go anywhere."

Any samples you carried had to be sold, you could not bring them back. But ever the optimist, Shivraman went ahead.

"I had more or less my full life's earnings in a little bag... a suitcase... I went to Japan and then Hong Kong but I couldn't sell anything. Not a thing. It was one of my most unsuccessful sales trips."

It was his last day in Hong Kong and Shivraman was at a place called Ocean Terminal. He didn't know what he was going to do with the jewellery, "I thought I would have to chuck it in the sea because you are not allowed to carry it back."

Suddenly, the suitcase slipped out of his hand and all the jewellery fell out. A lady came and started helping him to put it back in the case.

"My flight was at 4:30, this was at about 12 in the afternoon."

Then the lady asked, "Are you going to sell this?" And that's how Shivraman found a buyer for the entire lot, at a little over the cost price. The lady happened to be one of the top 50 importers in Hong Kong and meeting her was just a stroke of luck. "She is still my wife's agent in Hong Kong. But I realised this business was not for me and I went back to my job."

Shivraman did start a company of his own but far removed from jewellery. He decided to get into software. It was 1992 when he resigned from HCL. "I had two schoolgoing kids to support and not enough income," he recalls. But *dekha jaeyega*, and he went ahead and set up Orange Technologies, which specialised in ERP solutions.

There were four partners – Vijay Moza (a regional manager in HCL), Naval Bansal (a sales executive in HCL) and Vinay Pasricha, who was a friend. All four had an equal stake in the company. Vijay Moza never joined the company, citing a family commitment. Naval Bansal joined but 9-10 months later, got a green card and disappeared. So it was Shivraman and Vinay who took it forward.

"My total PF was ₹ 1,20,000 for all the years I had worked... Out of that, I had put ₹ 30,000 into the company. This company, I took to a turnover of ₹ 3.8 crore in 2 years' time."

Shivraman had no technical background and no clue about programming. He simply hired programmers. "We set up a software company and we sort of learnt it all. From one person, we jumped to 45-50 people in about two years." Shivraman did the selling while Pasricha handled the operations. The company was doing very well in its niche but it was extremely exhausting because of cashflow issues.

"Nobody would extend us any credit. We bought every computer cash down. We bought everything cash down. There was no such concept of venture capital. We were in quite a bad shape."

The company ran on a system of advances from clients. Plus it was in an area which was technologically new, so there was no competition in the real sense of the word.

"Our profit margins were crazy. To give you an idea, if I was selling for 100 rupees, my cost was 20. First year we made good money, second year we made good money. Third year, I decided that this business will never grow very big."

This was 1995, and the software business had still not taken off. Orange Technologies was as big as Infosys at that time. "Infosys must have been ₹ 7-8 crore, we were at ₹ 4.5-5 crore. Infosys had a public issue by then and it was making some money, but nothing great. They became a very big company later, around 1999-2000."

Orange too was making good money – the partners had no cause to complain. But Shivraman admits he did not have the money to expand the business. And he did not know how to raise it.

Or maybe it was just that eternal itch to do something new. "I decided we should get into education."

Education was attractive for one simple reason: it was a self-financing system. People always pay fees in advance, so no cash flow problem!

Shivraman also realised that British education did not exist in India. And he thought that it was a nice niche to get into. Secondly, barring the IIMs, there was no decent management education. So there seemed to be an opportunity.

The idea was to set up a proper college, not a coaching institute. Shivraman secured the all-India rights to set up 'Wigan and Leigh' in India. "We brought foreign education into India for the first time." The year was 1996.

It all started when Shivraman met the Wigan and Leigh representatives at an exhibition. They were looking for a partner and things fell into place, despite the fact that he had no previous experience, investment capacity or real estate.

"My business model is what everyone uses today. Firstly we always rented buildings. The second part was that I advertised. I brought advertising to education."

Strange as it might sound today, the *Times of India* rang up when Wigan and Leigh booked a front page ad for the first time, to confirm the booking. They said, "Are you sure? We don't think education is done like this". Today, of course, education is one of the largest advertisers in print and the *Times of India* brings out full-fledged supplements such as 'Education Times'.

But there was more to come. AICTE went after Wigan and Leigh. The Government of India raised questions. Everybody said, 'How can they teach like this?' Higher education was firmly associated with being 'public sector' or *sarkaari*.

"For a change, someone was doing a decent job. Government institutions *mein to teaching hoti nahin thi...*" Shivraman laughs.

So there were problems with the Establishment but absolutely no problem attracting students, or faculty. Teaching staff received training from their UK counterparts.

Once Wigan and Leigh took off Shivraman set up various other colleges in collaboration with institutions in the UK. These included an MBA programme with Herriot-Watt University, a BBA with London School of Economics (external programme) and Huddersfield University. A publishing unit was also set up catering to the same market – it produced management books.

But is education profitable? It is supposed to be 'non-profit' according to the law. Most institutes run under the guise of being trusts or charitable organisations (although most of the charity begins and ends at home). In contrast, Wigan and Leigh was set up as a limited company.

The point being that the college did not seek government approval. In fact it did not apply for approval knowing its course and curriculum was radical – ahead of its time.

"We were the first ones to bring in non-academic, vocational education. Courses like fashion, design, media. Today everybody is doing it. That time no one was doing it. We succeeded because our education was tied straight to a job!"

Which goes to show it's not enough to do something new and different, it has to add value to become truly attractive. Wigan and Leigh did not just promise 'better education', it provided the concrete benefit of a job. And that was the reason middle class parents decided it was ok to spend good money on the course, even though it was not government approved.

Today many wonder whether things have gone to the other extreme where education is seen *only* as a means to a job. But that debate we'll save for another day.

The business crossed a turnover of ₹ 35-40 crore by 1999. It had its moments of turbulence. A tie-up with Empire Institute soured. There was a lot of bad press, which included Shivraman himself being called a thief on the front page in prominent newspapers. But he is philosophical about it – *hota hai*, you move on.

Despite the respectable size of the business, Shivraman says it was not hugely profitable. Yes, they charged relatively high fees but the cost of acquiring students is considerable. The profit margin was about 20 per cent (net).

The number of potential students was rising every year but so was competition. Soon there were hundreds of 'AICTE-approved' MBA institutes offering courses as well. In 2000, Shivraman realised that his business of management education was not growing at a fast enough pace. "Earlier, we were growing at nearly 50-100 per cent year on year. Later on the growth became 20 per cent".

And so was born ICRI (Institute of Clinical Research in India). The excitement had run out of MBA education, Shivraman was once again in his most productive state. He was thoroughly bored.

"My philosophy is that I am not very good at running things on a day-to-day basis. That's my weakness. I get very impatient. My goal is to set up a team, set up systems, and let the team and systems work. Give them a free hand to work. My second task is to look at new opportunities".

Clinical research was one such opportunity.

But generally an entrepreneur sets up teams and systems, yet stays on.

"That is a very big mistake. As an entrepreneur, had I stayed on in Wigan and Leigh after 1999, I would have done it a massive disservice."

Shivraman started looking for something new in 2000. In 2003, he stopped doing any work for Wigan and Leigh, except remaining on the Board. He took a separate office and spent one year 'doing nothing'. Only thinking of what next to do. He zeroed in on clinical research.

Clinical research was an area which had all the characteristics of software. All the pluses – it uses intelligence, is high on labour, low on cost and it's virgin territory. As a first step he set up a company doing clinical trials. Then, came the institute to train students who could work there.

"The company came first. We got the business and we realised, we could not execute it. There were no clinical research professionals available." If you can't find talent, you have to create it yourself.

By this stage, money for a new venture would not be an issue, I am sure.

"Money is always a problem. I am short all the time," he replies.

But wasn't education a cash cow?

"Yes, it gave me a lot of money. With that I could set up ICRI. Between 2004 and 2007, I set up four huge campuses. That ate up about ₹ 20-25 crore."

But why create campuses now and not go with the tried and tested rental model? Because this time around it was important for Shivraman to create excellence. "This time, I was keen that because I am the first entrant, I want to create an equivalent of IIM in this field."

Which is a common theme with most entrepreneurs. In the early years the *dhandha* is all that matters, but as time goes by they wish to leave behind a legacy.

It's too early to say if ICRI is that legacy but the institute is certainly doing well for itself. With 2500 students a year, ICRI rakes in ₹ 40 crore per annum. The school which was set up to service the requirements of a company is now more profitable than the company itself!

Only 70-80 students are absorbed by Shivraman's own clinical research outfit. The rest go to other companies. As always, Shivraman believes he has evangelised the idea of clinical research. "I hyped up the whole industry. The government of India should give me an award for it."

Clinical research is a $40-billion business internationally. The future prospects are bright – Shivraman expects ICRI, which is growing 100% year on year, to reach ₹ 100 crore by next year. But in the longer run, the company which runs the trials will grow substantially and become bigger than the training business.

Still, it's doubtful that will prevent him from moving on in search of the Next New Thing. The Itch is eternal, there's always another genie waiting to emerge from another lamp.

<u>ADVICE TO YOUNG ENTREPRENEURS</u>

Remember IIMs have a weakness. They teach you marketing, finance and systems but they don't teach you the importance of HR. Also they don't teach you how to raise money. There is a method to raising money. You have to be able to go and present your ideas to various kinds of institutions. You have to systematically study who are the people out there with the cash.

You have to be willing to work as a partner with people. You have to be diplomatic. And understand one thing: you are not the greatest, you are not the best. You are putting together the team, you are co-ordinating. Someone else is giving the money, someone else is actually working and it's an idea – you are all trying to make it happen.

Any good entrepreneur would have good people working for him or her or would be stuck at a low size. The control freak will remain a *dukaandaar*. You open a shop and say, I must know where every penny is going.

FOR LOVE, NOT MONEY

Shankar Maruwada (PGP '96), Marketics

He entered entrepreneurship by accident and his first venture folded up. But Shankar and his team used that failure to get it right the second time with 'Marketics', an analytics company which recently sold out to WNS for an estimated $65 million.

As I bump down Bangalore's 100 ft road on a chilly December morning to meet Shankar Maruwada I can't help thinking, "If ever there was a fairy tale in the land of entrepreneurship, it is this one."

Company is born.

Company dies.

New company is born out of the ashes.

This company prospers.

Five years later, it is bought out for $65 million.

This is not Silicon Valley, but India. Few have heard of Marketics or the work it does in the esoteric field of analytics but Shankar Maruwada and his partners have never aspired for fame.

Or even fortune, for that matter. All that he talks about, over and over and over again, is the thrill of doing 'great work'.

And it sounds like a given – we all want to do great work, don't we? But the point is to do great work for the pleasure of doing that work itself. Not in anticipation of what it will fetch you – whether in terms of appreciation or money. What the Bhagwad Gita refers to as *karmayog*.

Things happen, without your making them happen. That's the secret sauce at Marketics.

Not the takeaway I was expecting but that's the fun part about meeting entrepreneurs. They defy your expectations, make the improbable seem easy. You always leave the room thinking, "If this guy could do it, why not me and you?"

FOR LOVE, NOT MONEY

Shankar Maruwada (PGP '96), Marketics

Shankar Maruwada is the youngest of three brothers. Life was more about being a follower than a leader.

"Since I was good in my studies, they said IIT *karo*." He did. But, impressed by his dad who was a manager with Indian Aluminium, Shankar had decided to go for management in class 11 itself. IIT was just for the brand name.

Such a sensible career path. The kind every middle class parent charts for his kids. But opportunity of a different kind chose to knock on Shankar's door. The first time, he refused to open it.

In 1993, right out of engineering college, Shankar had a job offer from an unknown company in Bangalore. But he didn't join because he had already set his heart on the MBA. That company was Infosys. "I would have been one of the early employees..." he grins. "Later I used to curse myself."

But had he got those stock options, would there ever have been a Marketics? Probably not. There are no 'poor choices', sometimes life just has other plans.

At IIMA Shankar realised finance was not his cup of tea. After summers with P&G he joined the company in the marketing function and worked there for four years (1996-2000). Had a great time, good learning, great organisation. Got married in 1999, a typical yuppie life so far.

But one fine day the question popped up, where is all this leading up to?

"I had this recurring dream that I got promoted, similar kind of job. Got promoted, similar kind of job. When I am 50 years old and my son and grandson ask, 'What have you done in life? The answer was a very stark 'Sold soap, sold more soaps, sold yet more soaps.'"

Around the same time, the dotcom boom happened. A batchmate who was working with a VC came up with a business plan. He needed someone to help with the marketing side of things. And Shankar quit his job, without thinking too much.

"So one day you woke up and just decided to quit?" I ask.

"Yes... that was it," he replies.

In hindsight, for a newly married guy from a strictly middle class background, it was madness. And no, his wife wasn't working either.

But it was a time when dreams were more than enough to fill one's stomach.

The team launched a website revolving around consumer reviews. Modelled along epinions.com, apnaguide.com was a community-based site with utility value.

"Basically it was about learning from the experience of others before you go and buy. We had a good business plan. The revenue model was that companies would use the site to establish relationships, CRM and database marketing – all those things."

There were three partners – Malini, Shankar and Shailendra Malani, the prime mover behind the venture. It was January 2000, the peak of the internet boom. Indiaworld had just been bought out by Satyam for ₹ 500 crore. The world had gone a little bit crazy.

"At that time, I spoke to people and they said, be clear as to why you are doing this. If it's for money it's not a good idea. If you are doing this, because you all just want to do something, then be prepared for lots of ups and downs."

The partners quit their jobs, put in a bit of their own money and then got angel funding. Raising it was not a problem. Apnaguide.com raised ₹ 1 crore for marketing – building eyeballs, traffic and of course, the website. The money came at the height of the boom, and soon after, everything went bust. It was April 2000 and the team realised that the dotcom game was up. It was time to carefully preserve the cash that was in the bank.

And that was the first learning, "Things don't always go as per plan." It was time to think of something else to do.

Malani had a technical background, he is a Computer Science grad from BITS Pilani. So they got the idea of making a Customer Relationship module out of the Apnaguide software. The idea was to set up mini sites or some kind of technology component for companies. Apnaguide continued, in maintenance mode, but primarily it was the building block for the new CRM software. Reusing components brought down the cost significantly.

One constant, feels Shankar, is building on past experience instead of throwing it away.

The product took six months to build and it was a good product but only one company actually bought it – a leading Indian bank.

"Lots of companies showed interest but finally we realised that it's one thing to say you are interested in consumers and consumer relationships. It's another thing to actually spend money on it. Then we realised that we are talking of something which is too futuristic."

Around the same time, their paths crossed that of Intercept, a company also started by a couple of ex-P&G colleagues – Ramki and Kimi. They were in the same space and wanted their technology. Sensing synergies, Apnaguide merged and became part of Intercept. It was October 2001.

After selling two more installations of the CRM software (billing ₹ 12 lakh) Intercept too realised that selling something like this in India was very difficult. What's more, the company was running out of money. Funding was committed but then the VC backtracked at the last minute.

"So one fine day, we walked out of Intercept."

"Culture is a set of daily behaviours exhibited by an organisation. The senior guys walk the talk, others will follow. Because an organisation, especially in the beginning, is nothing but the reflection of the founders."

Clearly it wasn't a friendly parting, but break-ups and shake-ups are part of entrepreneurial life. Just about every entrepreneur has been through such an experience.

The original team had, in any case, disbanded. Malini had quit due to health issues and moved to the US. Shailendra too quit due to personal reasons and moved to the US. Which is ironic because, as Shankar puts it, "He is the quintessential entrepreneur... not me. He is the person who taught me the difference between an entrepreneur and a manager. I just happened to be in the right place at the right time and slogged it out, persevered."

That place was Marketics. The time was October 2002. Marketics was born with three partners on board – Shankar, Ramki and Vinay Mishra, an IIML graduate and colleague at Intercept. And what was its mission?

"Basically, one of the things that Intercept was trying to do at the end is sell analytics to the US. But it did not work out. We felt that it was a great opportunity but Intercept was not doing it right."

But what was it that they decided to do differently as a company to make it work?

Rule no 1: We will make sure that this time around we make more money than we spend.

Rule no 2: No VCs. We want complete operational control, to grow the way we want to.

"None of us was from the services or consulting industry. We really learnt a lot and did some great work. It was a period of more downs than ups, but those couple of years were the most fun. We started with just one or two clients from the Intercept base – that's all. And that's when it was once again time to put all the earlier learning to good use."

Having worked with P&G, the team had the experience of using analytics.

"Analytics helps you make better decisions. And we knew that kind of a service was not being provided by MR companies. There are two kinds of analytics. One is the MR analytics where FMCG companies are involved. That is survey data. Then you have transaction data from credit card companies, banks, retail and telecom."

Of course, people were sceptical. They said, 'Why can't MR companies provide analytics? Where is your counterpart model in the US? If it doesn't work in the US, it will not work here. Is it like an IT thing?'

The USP of Marketics was that it had people who had used analytics to make better decisions. And they knew that kind of service was not being provided by MR companies.

"So when we talked to clients, we talked in their language. We did not say we would build models or conduct statistical analysis. We said, 'You want to make better decisions. For that you need some insights – we will give you the insights.'"

The model would of course be built but that's not what the customer wanted thrust in his face. He wanted the end product, the pattern which emerged from the data which would help him do his job better.

And that's exactly what Marketics provided.

P&G USA was Marketics' first client. One early decision at Marketics was that it would not sell in India.

"We got some early success from the US, we realised that they really valued this service. And if you give them top-quality work, they will pay you top-quality money. That was a refreshing change for us."

"And the other thing, we wanted to create a company that will have clients who are delighted, not just satisfied. And in the

Marketics mission statement: "We will have globally delighted clients who will benefit from us being the world's best professionals in what we do. In doing so we will have fun and get rich."

process, we will make sure that we have fun also. And we will get rich. So we actually wrote down a mission that we felt was true to what we are. A lot of people I know have joined us for that..."

It was a culture thing. One of those many intangibles that Marketics got right. And not by accident, Culture was like a 'baby that was nurtured' and Shankar believes it is a strong differentiator for the company today.

"We don't care how you dress. Only one thing is not negotiable: client delight. Everything else – salary, leave, where you work from, how you work, who you are, is secondary. The brutal focus on client delight is what allowed us to grow. 80% of that was from client referrals."

Referrals was how everything was built at Marketics. Clients, employees and even investors, came through referrals.

But how do you create this magic? You get your hands dirty, get to 'know your business inside out'.

"In the beginning, because there were few people, the core team did everything... We understood what is it that makes clients happy. What is the value that they see in us? How do we deliver this proposition? What are some of the levers that we can pull to scale this up?"

But how did Marketics get these clients?

"It just happened. What we knew was that every month we are making money. See, we are just focused on making clients happy. And we had read that if you do that, they'll take care of you... we saw it happening."

Shankar recalls an email from one of Marketics early clients.

Marketics rocks. Thank you for referring Marketics to me. They went way beyond what I expected of them. And delivered things that I had not even thought of. And all this without asking for extra money.

"When people start saying things like this, what we realised is... somehow money also flows in. That client referred us to 2-3 others. I realised this business is about people. It's not about companies. If that individual manager is happy, we will be happy."

Client managers quit, went elsewhere, they gave Marketics projects from the new company. Having P&G as the first client helped – it was a large organisation with many managers who were happy to refer a good vendor to other colleagues. Given its strong brand name, other prospects easily gave them a hearing.

Marketics would not start by 'asking for the moon'. It would offer to do 'low risk' pilot projects and win client confidence. The offer was – 'See our work and then judge'.

"It took us one year to get our business model in place. We put those fancy jargons down there but basically it meant doing great work out of India – minimal cost, maximum effectiveness. So it's not outsourced work, processing work. This is a consulting kind of thing where the client throws a problem at us, we give a solution to it. But restricted to data, not general consulting based on our experience."

Marketics now works with clients; individual managers from 30-40 countries. It was hugely profitable, yet it barely had any competition.

"We kept a low profile. Because we didn't want to raise funding. We didn't need to do PR because our business had nothing to do with India."

Even today, there is some competition but not in the space Marketics occupies.

The USP was the business model the company built, which is not pure analytics, not pure consulting, not pure technology, but a combination of all of these. Crafting that model took around two years.

"It's a different kind of thrill when a client says, 'Your work has actually saved us. Your work has given us a great idea.' The closest example I can think of is what patients tell doctors."

"We learnt a lot from our clients. We work only with topnotch clients – Fortune 100 companies. And we also had advisors, investment bankers, who made sure that they asked us commonsensical questions. It was more like friends rather than a formal kind of thing. They let us be who we are, had confidence in what we were doing and showed us how and where we could do better..."

Some advisors became investors as well. Although Marketics did not need the money, their support in other areas was invaluable.

The initial capital was put up by the three partners. Shankar won't give exact figures but this is what the growth curve looks like:

"The first year, let's assume we went from zero to 400 rupees. The next year, we went to 1,600 rupees. Third year we went to 3,500. Fourth year, 7,000. Basically, we went on doubling, both revenues and profits."

It took around six months to break even in the initial phase. Of course, at the time the promoters weren't taking salaries. After that, they started making 'decent money'. Revenues came in varied forms – while some clients paid a fixed fee, others were billed per project. And a few offered retainers for work spread over a period of time.

"Our entire expansion, and we were doubling every year, the cash flow requirement, the working capital requirement, everything was funded from internal sources."

Speaking of which, intellectual capital was as important as monetary capital. And here, Marketics made an important decision – hire young people and groom them.

"When it's a new business model, and we ourselves don't know what to do, do not get in experienced guys. Because we had a bad experience earlier of getting in senior guys who would do it the way they have learnt and are not really that open. And when they are senior, you cannot argue with them on subjective things."

For the first two years, Marketics took relative freshers – one or two years out of campus. And they were literally moulded to be good at analytics. Shankar believes Marketics created a new breed of 'analytics professionals'.

This young team, mostly under age 27, lives by the 'honour system'. So it's natural to put a 'night out' for a client if required and then not come to work the next day. The community monitors itself and only occasionally do the bosses have to step in and weed out a bad egg or two. Overall, it all comes together and works.

And a great culture, great team and great work content is what drew so many high-quality people to Marketics. The company employs some 50 MBAs – mostly from IIMs. Only three of those 50 have quit over the years, which is an amazingly low attrition rate by any standard!

Cut to January 2007.

Vinay was based in the US, Ramki was travelling and looking after sales while Shankar was doing some sales effort but mainly leading delivery out of Bangalore. Building the team, setting up the organisation. By now, Marketics employed 220 people. With higher billing rates and profitability Marketics needed less people than Infosys or a traditional BPO.

And then, WNS came into the picture.

"Basically what had happened was that we were growing fast. And we were building on the experiences of the past which is that when a good thing is going, just keep in mind that bad things will come around the corner."

So Marketics had great clients, happy people, cash was pouring in, but the company decided it was time to raise money. As they say, raise money when you don't need it.

"Do you want to stay happy but small or do you want to grow? These are two different paths and you have to choose one. We made the choice to scale up."

"That's when we realised, look, what do we want to do? Are we looking at a Narayana Murthy kind of thing and going all the way?"

At the end of the day, some 220 livelihoods depended on three shoulders.

"We had got the ship here so far, with a combination of our abilities or experiences, good or bad. But we had our own limitations..."

"When you want to expand, there is a window of opportunity. If you don't utilise that, you will get left behind. And the advisors said we can raise money but the other option is that you align with somebody larger so that they can leverage the platform you have built and make Marketics much bigger, much faster."

The choice was of a strategic partner, or to raise cash and go ahead alone.

"Somewhere along the way we realised that analytics has to be sold as a part of larger bouquet of services. Clients would say, 'Oh, you do only analytics? Fine, when we need that service we'll give you our business.'"

But surely backward or forward integration was possible?

"Yes... but it would have taken a long time. We did not have the experience of doing that. That was an option of course – raise money, get in the right people, acquire companies. The other was to align with a larger player. But we were clear that we don't want to be distracted from running the business."

As fate would have it, WNS came into the picture. The company had listed the previous year and was looking to move up the value chain. What's more, Neeraj Bhargava of

WNS was once upon a time CEO of eVentures, the company where Shankar's friend and one time partner Shailendra Malani had put in a stint. The vibe was positive and WNS was convinced it was a strategic fit.

"We said it is important that the two cultures are similar, that the chemistry is right. So once we gauged that they also were comfortable, we closed the deal in March 2007. The agreement was signed and finally it was consummated around May."

And it all makes perfect sense for both parties but you can't help asking the question, "What if?" What if Marketics had charted an independent course? When the company first started up, the founders did not focus on 'limitations'. Aren't the only limits those which we set for ourselves?

But let's be honest, sometimes an immediate payout is just too attractive, weighed against a less than certain, longer term outcome. $65 million was a generous offer – 15 times the company's current profits. Marketics accepted and became part of WNS.

So have things changed?

"Well, yes and no. Now that we are part of a larger company, an NYSE listed company, financial compliance has come in. Which, after you go through initial pain, is good. You are more disciplined in a lot of things. Sales have already been integrated, HR integration is happening slowly. But again, we also realised that our culture is vastly different from WNS. They are 17,000 people, we are 250. The kind of people we have are different. It is high-end talent. So the two companies remain separate, operationally nothing much has changed."

Except that you have become rich...

"We became rich. I will not deny, it was part of the motivation."

And it was not a stock swap but all cash. Of course, many others in the company who had ESOPs also made a lot of money. And that was extremely fulfilling. Work and fun were happening all along. With 'get rich' also becoming a reality, the mission had been achieved so to speak.

Shankar says the three partners were always very clear that they and the company were two different objects. "Don't jeopardise your company's future by confusing what is good for you as a person with what is good for the company."

And that's why they were able to sell and merge with WNS without the emotional turmoil entrepreneurs go through in such situations. It was simply a decision taken in the company's best interest.

"Now the company is no longer held at the whims and fancies of the founders. There is a larger board. There is money for investment, we can recruit ahead of actual requirement. And we have scaled faster, as there is a captive base of clients to pitch to." Already, WNS has taken Marketics to over a 100 of its clients.

But the company was already growing at 100% year on year. How much incremental growth has the WNS alignment brought in?

"This year we are sticking to the plan of growing, of doubling. Next year, we want to grow even more. We had envisaged a particular window which is a few years. By then we wanted to achieve a certain scale. So aligning with WNS, as far as we see it, its part of the plan to reach there. We want to broaden the scope, not just analytics, but whatever it is that converts data to insights."

All three founders are still with the company. What brings them to office every day now? Are they as motivated?

"The thing is that is what we want to do... Globally delighted clients. We feel we are just at the tip of that iceberg. The clients we have worked with in the last one year is the envy even of an Infosys. And in some cases we have even competed with these biggies and won. So, that itself is a thrill."

"I think the thrill changes, the basic model is proven, now it is – 'How big can we get?' When money is no longer the motivation, life can be pretty good. You are more focused on work and your actions are not guided by, 'Will I make more money or not?' One thing I realised is that we complicate our lives more than we need to!"

Attitude is what you make of things that happen to you – that's what it's ultimately all about.

"We were very happy even when there were bad days because we did some fabulous work, possibly better work than this. We were very happy when we started Marketics as a traditional garage kind of start up. I remember the thrill when we bought our first AC, then first proper conference phone, first proper laptop, you go through that phase and each step is a thrill."

"But like when you are growing up, college is good but then you start work. You cannot go back to college. It was good, but it's a phase and it's over. It's that moving on which we realised is a key part of life. You have to change roles."

And Shankar does not rule out moving on from Marketics. It may happen, but right now the founding team is still on board. "Till the point we believe we can add value, we will be around."

Ultimately, every organisation aims to create a 'sense of ownership'. And the tricky part which precedes that is the ownership structure of the company itself.

At Marketics, all three partners had an equal shareholding. This can be a dicey structure, if people don't see eye to eye.

Shankar admits, "It's not as if we always had it smooth but the whenever there were differences we spoke and resolved them. But some things we had set in stone. Whatever the thing is, we will be equal in terms of ownership." Besides that, ESOPs were offered to 80 of the 200 people working at Marketics, which is generous by any standard.

"Ultimately it's about, can we look in the mirror and say that we did the right thing, we got what we deserved. What we gave to others, they deserved. Even when we knew the deal was just around the corner, we gave ESOPs to many more people. We felt it was only fair."

Fair enough and well done.

ADVICE TO YOUNG ENTREPRENEURS

It is very difficult... I wish there was just one thing. First is passion, if you are not passionate about what you are doing, then you are in the wrong place. Second is courage. The buck stops with you, does not go further. You have to make choices. You cannot say that may be, this or that. And you have to be comfortable with the choice even if it goes wrong. When you succeed, all your past and failures get wiped away.

You have to play multiple roles. You have to be egoistic, and you have to be humble. You have to be the guy doing it, yet you have to be the guy who stands back. You have to be leading, yet you have to be supportive. If the person who cleans your toilet does not come on the day of an important client visit, you have to clean it – no second thoughts.

Work experience did help in our case. The idea of focusing on a culture is from P&G. An amazing culture, with a lot of focus on values and ethics. Whatever I knew about analytics was from P&G. The domain experience was from P&G.

Passion cannot come without some knowledge around it. But there is no one size that fits all. You can always hire people with expertise.

More than VCs, an entrepreneur needs an angel. What you need at the start-up stage is some seed funding. That can come from friends, family. You just want enough money to prove your idea. VCs should ideally come in once you know what you want, the model is proven and you think the best way to scale it up is to get their investment. But you have to be prepared to accept outside control.

MILLION DOLLAR
SEAMSTRESS

**Ruby Ashraf (PGP '83),
Precious Formals**

Ruby turned her hobby of designing clothes into a
flourishing business. Her company, Precious Formals,
is one of the leading suppliers of prom dresses
in America.

It's the silver jubilee reunion of IIM Ahmedabad's class of 1983. Expanding waistlines and receding hairlines, everywhere.

Ruby Ashraf looks far too young and beautiful, to be here. A batchmate comes up to her husband Javed and remarks, only half in jest, *"Ab to bahut saal ho gaya hain…* Still I say you are very lucky to be married to her!"

They smile like they've heard this before. But as you hear the story of their life, and the company they run together, you have to wonder, "Who's to say who's really lucky?" How many men would let a bright and beautiful wife take the driver's seat and enjoy the journey together as a co-passenger?

Ruby Ashraf is CEO of Precious Formals, a $10 million company in the fashion clothing business. Javed is her partner, both in her personal and professional life.

Precious Formals sells prom dresses. For the uninitiated, the 'prom' is the high point of an American teenage girl's life. It is a kind of growing up ritual, not just a dance but a day to be remembered and treasured for years to come. The dress you buy for your prom is not just a dress, it's got to live up to a dream.

So how did an Indian woman with no formal training in fashion design enter this business and quickly make a success of it? Listening to Ruby relate how she made it happen I could only conclude, *"Dil mein chaah, to niklegi raah."*

Business plans can be made by anyone, but plans are not enough. Nor are they always necessary. Life has its own plan, you just have to flow and grow with it.

MILLION DOLLAR SEAMSTRESS

Ruby Ashraf (PGP '83),
Precious Formals

Ruby grew up in Delhi and from an early age she was exposed to business, meetings, clients.

Her father was with the Ministry of Defence before he resigned and started his own business. "I would come back from school and he would have meetings. He would take me there. I would just be sitting and listening to his discussions with clients. He was a consultant for many."

Ruby never thought that at that point she would become an entrepreneur. But, looking back, it seems like she "got trained into it without knowing it."

A common trait you notice with entrepreneurs is a heightened sense of self-awareness. And the ability to take tough decisions. So it was with Ruby. As was the done thing, she studied science and got into medical school. "The first year, when I had to do anatomy, I didn't like it. So I thought, this is not for me…"

She quit medical school and got a bachelor's and master's in science from Delhi University.

"I got admission in Birmingham, England to do a PhD in Fish Embryology. That was my special interest. Then my dad showed me an ad for IIMA in the newspaper. I was a little shy. Management means one has to be very outgoing. But I had already disappointed my parents by not continuing with medical school. So I decided to study for it."

Ruby got an admission offer and she joined. And the Institute changed her completely.

"First thing, they gave me a personality questionnaire. I think it was Professor Indira Parikh who marked out what needs to be worked on me. When you come out, you are totally groomed for the profession you have to take up after this."

There were no entrepreneurship courses on campus back then but Ruby knew she would work for about five years and then set up her own company, like her dad. Of course, she never thought it would be in the fashion business. And she never thought it would be in America.

Ruby's first job out of campus was in the HR department of BHEL.

"I interviewed for two companies – BHEL and Metalbox. I got both of them but I chose BHEL because it was in Delhi and I liked the job profile more."

Then, like so many women, Ruby got married and shifted to America. The year was 1987.

Initially, Ruby did not leave her job. "I went there and I was working on my husband to move to India. In the meanwhile, he was looking for jobs in the north, like New York."

And she was exploring the option of further studies.

Ruby got admission in Rice University in Houston to study Organisation Behaviour but her heart was set on Stanford or Harvard. She was willing to wait.

But destiny had other plans. An old and enduring love for clothes took her in a different direction.

Ruby always had the title 'Best Dressed Girl' of the batch. In fact, she used to design her own clothes. That hobby continued and she wore one such dress to an Xmas party at the university (where Javed was a professor at the time). The dress really got noticed. People said, "You have a real talent, you should be selling these dresses!"

But there wasn't much information available on the industry. There were case studies on textiles, consumer products, everything else. But nothing on apparel. So Ruby did her own case study. She travelled across America, visiting retail stores to understand fashion trends, what was selling and where her own niche might be.

"In those days there was nothing like CNN. I didn't know what the fashion trends were in the West. I really had to study it to know it."

That sounds kind of vague. Let me travel around America to see what dresses sell. Could this really be a serious gameplan for how to get into business?

"Basically my whole philosophy in life is the *shlok* from the Gita – '*Karmanyewadhika raste maa phaleshu kadachana*'. *Kuch toh karte rahna chahiye*. At the end of the day, you should feel that I have given my 120% to it. And the day should not be wasted."

So until Javed didn't get a job in the north or west (where she had set her heart on studying) or no other suitable opportunity came up, Ruby had to do something.

And it did bear fruit. Ruby understood what was selling. She started making dresses and immediately got orders from all the major stores. Ruby chose to focus on evening wear, which was very strong then. Margins were high in evening wear and design was her forte.

With the growing demand, Ruby realised she would have to set up a factory. And this meant learning about fashion itself from scratch. "I didn't even know how to stitch then. I came to India and first of all learnt pattern making."

Javed gave her company. In fact, he learnt pattern-making as well. Then they started a factory in Delhi and taught the workers pattern-making.

Why Delhi, not Texas? "Because it's all handwork, it can't be done in America. The dresses would be way too expensive to sell." This meant frequent trips between India and America, of course.

And how much money did it take to start up? A mere 5,000 dollars. As the order book grew bigger, a loan was secured from the bank.

Again, it all sounds easy. Too easy. How did she actually get orders?

"The first marketing case study at IIMA that I did with Prof A K Jain – the case of oatmeal – I got good grades in

> "As an entrepreneur you don't say that
> 'I have to reach a particular place in five
> years.' You just keep doing whatever you
> are doing. You have plans, you have goals,
> you know a strategy. But still one doesn't
> even anticipate that so much work will be
> done... you just keep doing it."

that. You have to go door-to-door, you have to do things at the grassroot level. You just can't be a small company and blow up a lot of money on something like a catalogue. I didn't do that for many years."

So she made samples, took appointments.

"The first thing in business is, you have to sell yourself. And people should trust you. They should feel that whoever you are, wherever you are from, you really mean what you say. You are sincere and you really will deliver the goods. If you have sold yourself, you will sell the product."

In the first year, the business was very small. Then it grew rapidly. Half a million dollars in the next year, then a million. Now it's ten million plus and Precious Formals is still growing.

Over the years, many things have changed. The manufacturing was shifted from India to China. And not just because of the cost advantage.

"As a designer, I realised that I have lot of limitations working in India – factories here are not so mechanised. Also, the finishing is not perfect. The equipment we need is not available."

The Chinese are also excellent pattern-makers. They could operate even from a sketch – you didn't really have to teach them.

Of course when she first explored the China option, in 1991, it was difficult. In time it became a much easier place to do business.

The nuts and bolts side of the business apart, fashion is not mere science. It is an art.

There is a Spring and a Fall season. And to succeed in fashion you have to be able to predict what will sell. In December 2007 you have already shipped 2008 Spring. And, in fact, you are designing 2009 Spring and booking orders!

So how do you do it? The answer is a certain *je ne sais quoi*, an eye for detail, a sense of what is coming next. Ruby modestly says she 'looks around' a lot. And tracks sportswear, because evening fashions follow sportswear trends.

But you and me could spend hours staring at tracksuits and trainers and still be clueless.

It takes an artist to interpret the meaning of brushstrokes and get inspired to paint his or her own canvas!

So when and how did Javed come into the picture?

Ruby had been running Precious Formals for six years when in the year 1996, she fell very sick. Javed resigned from his job at the university and joined the company. He has been with Precious Formals ever since.

If Ruby, with her expressive eyes, throaty laughter and immaculate taste in clothes, is the public face of Precious Formals. Javed is the company's strong and silent backbone.

He handles IT, as well as all the company's finances and accounts. And he's converted his own hobby, photography, into a major asset for the company.

It so happened that one year Precious Formals hired an expensive photographer and he shot a catalogue in New York City. The customers did not like it. They thought the job Javed had done the year before was better!

"Maybe because we don't treat it like work, we have a passion for it. After that, Javed has been our photographer, and he has done all the designing and touch up work as well," she beams proudly and shows me the latest catalogue.

Ruby handles all the designing and most of the marketing. Atlanta is the main hub for the evening wear market. So Precious Formals has a 10,000 sq ft showroom and does its

"We are the only company that checks every garment before shipping, in the US."

ramp shows there. Buyers come there, five times a year. Sales managers service these buyers.

"All the sales people report to me. I am their motivational force. I talk to them every morning at eight o'clock. We do targets, discuss what to do today, what we did yesterday. They give me all the figures. I hear them out, what the problems are."

A good percentage of the sales team is young girls who've graduated from fashion school. Some have left Ralph Lauren and are working for Precious Formals because they think the company gives them more inputs, more opportunities.

A 45-crore company in India would easily employ a couple of hundred people. But people cost a lot of money in America, so Precious Formals is relatively lean. Between full-time and part-time, in the peak season, there are about 65 employees.

The interesting thing is that though the dresses may be made in China, there is a strong sense that the 'buck stops here'. Precious Formals is ultimately responsible for every piece of clothing bearing its fine name.

"We are the only company that checks every garment before shipping, in the United States. In China and India, an inspection is carried out but their quality standard is different. We believe there shouldn't be even a single stain inside the lining of the garment. You are shipping such an expensive dress after all..."

Precious Formals dresses generally retail at $400-800. There is also a cheaper range, under the brand name 'Glam Gurlz' which sells for about $200. And a more premium range called 'Posh Precious' which sells above $600.

Precious and Posh Precious actually sell more. But the company developed Glam Gurlz for major stores which want to buy in bulk. They don't sell Precious because it is a conflict of interest with the boutiques.

"As a designer, I would like to design only expensive clothes. Because you can put everything you want, crystals and all. But as a strategy, you have to see where the market is going. There are customers for everything."

It's a delicate balance. You don't want to make very cheap clothes, because then you have to sell too many to make money. And you don't want to keep them so expensive that people get intimidated or do not appreciate.

What's more, you have to get stores to buy into your vision.

Some store owners said, "Oh my God! We won't be able to sell a dress worth $600!" You have to convince them, "No, no, you can!" A client will come, try out a dress, may buy, may not buy. Many a time, the salesperson has spent 7-8 hours to make a single sale.

If you sell a $600-700 dress, you have definitely made money. If you have sold a $300 dress, you have lost your money only in servicing. So Posh Precious makes great sense!

A package deal of three dresses was worked out. Store owners thought, even if all three don't sell, maybe one of their employees would buy one. So they started buying a few pieces, and as they sold, gained the confidence to order more.

Precious Formals now retails in 2,000 stores and is also selling well in Europe. There is a surge of demand from Dubai as well. "You know in the Middle East, they wear very sexy dresses. Inside the *abaaya*," she grins. International expansion is going to be a new focus for the company.

You start with a strategy, but you have to change it at so many stages along the way. Markets change, buyers change, you have to change with it.

"We started with formals for older, more mature people. We were selling at major stores. Then we shifted to boutiques, because nowadays, people in USA don't dress up for

The prom foray happened in 1996 and today Precious Formals is one of the major players in that market. At the upper end.

Christmas as much as they did before. Christmas has become more casual. So we went into prom."

"For the prom, girls spend a lot of money – it's a very big market. However badly the economy is doing, every girl will buy a dress for her prom. And that too, an expensive dress. She will work hard for it, get it from the boyfriend, from the grandparents, from wherever."

The prom foray happened in 1996 and today Precious Formals is one of the major players in that market. At the upper end.

Then, Ruby realised that this is the baby-boomer era. These days, even the mother of the bride wears strapless dresses. Earlier, they used to wear big, flouncy ones. So these prom-style dresses also appeal to older women. "Last year, for example, the wife of the Governor of Iowa bought one from us," she beams.

So a young-looking dress is actually ageless. If you modify it slightly, maybe have a chocolate-brown instead of hot pink, you can sell it to anyone. Using that customer insight, Precious Formals transitioned from the prom segment back to evening wear. Now the company is also getting into separates like jackets.

Any down phases in these 16 years?

"Things get a little difficult when we are left with more merchandise inventory. Sometimes it happens... Your money gets stuck, you have a little tighter cash flow. Then you have to manage your cash flow, get out of it and next year, you don't overstock."

Trends keep changing, and even the state of the economy. At one point, everybody wants a particular style, then suddenly people want something else!

Growth has slowed in the last 2-3 years. Partly due to external factors, partly internal.

"When I started, I did not think that it will grow so big. Since the past few years, it has got stuck at 10 million. Since 9/11 actually. The whole industry was affected by that. For many other companies, the sales went down. We have maintained our revenues... that was an achievement."

And how has it been, working with Javed? Many couples swear it would be impossible to work a single day with their spouse.

It's different for Ruby though.

"Working together is the best part actually... He takes the stress of all the accounts, the financials. It's great to work as a team because we spend so much time at work. 14-16 hours a day, seven days a week. Normally we don't travel together but we go to China together and it's very very nice."

I suspect the secret is a meeting of minds, a congruence of goals. And no ego issues. As I am interviewing Ruby, Javed sits a few feet away, patiently waiting for us to finish. He does not butt in, he does not wish to 'share the limelight'.

And I am amused (and quite in awe) of how they took the decision to actually get married. It was an arranged marriage but Ruby sent Javed the FIRO-B questionnaire (which was quite common those days to assess personality types).

"We did the personality match and we thought it's a perfect personality match... See, when you meet a person and fall in love, that's very good. But you don't know what the real person is... There are some things which are tangible – education, background. The intangible is the values, nature etc. These you hardly come to know."

So Ruby decided to 'test' their compatibility and Javed was game enough to do it.

"That was very helpful. Had I met Javed in IIMA, we would not have clicked because our likes and dislikes are very different. I like to work out, he does not. I like to go for a run, he doesn't. But it's so perfect. We have been very compatible right from the beginning... Our life is balanced. We agree quite easily."

Javed didn't want any kids and Ruby was fine with it.

"Of course there are many adjustments, little ones, like in every marriage. Javed is very adjusting. Initially, when I started the company I had to finish off so much work and Javed would come home early... We would have very little time together. Now we are together all the time."

Unlike most couples who work together, they have no problem discussing work at home.

"We are eating, reading, drinking our work all the time. This is not work for us, it is our way of life."

Ruby and Javed now want to make Precious Formals a billion-dollar company. They want to leave a legacy.

I am sure they will succeed in whatever they set out to do. Because they are so good together. And even if they don't, it will hardly matter.

Because unlike the many other entrepreneurs I interviewed for this book, it wasn't an either/or decision. Business, family, fun all has fused together. Which is not to say everyone can or should do it this way. But at least we know it can be done!

ADVICE TO YOUNG ENTREPRENEURS

You can achieve beyond your dreams, so it's OK to dream and make an action plan to turn it into reality.

There is not one formula to be successful, everyone who is successful has gone through failures in the process. It depends upon how hard we kick that failure and learn from it and take up the challenge stronger to be successful.

ORDER OF THE
PHOENIX

Deepta Rangarajan (PGP '89),
IRIS

Deepta worked with American Express and CRISIL before starting IRIS, a financial information management service.

Tough times never last, tough people do, they say. But how tough could times be, and how long would you have to last? When you go through that tough a time, every minute and every hour can seem like forever. That's the feeling I get when I walk out of the office of IRIS at the International Infotech Park in Vashi, Navi Mumbai.

There are other entrepreneurs in this book who've been through trying times. But the struggle to stay alive as a company was something I felt at IRIS most strongly. Because the body is healing, but the wound is still a bit raw.

The question that comes to mind is, why? Why couldn't IRIS raise funds after the initial cash dried up? Why did a company with great IP, great people and great vision go through this terrible patch? There is really no answer to that.

But the other question is, how? Well that is easier to understand. Entrepreneurship is a little bit like surfing. If you got knocked off by that last killer wave, you somehow cling on and stay afloat. Then, you spot the next wave in the distance and this time you ride it.

The instinct, the judgement, the courage to stand up and face the elements – that's what it's all about. The adrenaline rush at the end of it is an added bonus.

ORDER OF THE
PHOENIX

Deepta Rangarajan (PGP '89),
IRIS

Deepta Rangarajan was born in Bangalore, the youngest of four kids. Her dad was with the United Nations. Deepta travelled the world over, before finally settling down in Delhi. That's where she went to school and then college. Straight out of IIT she joined IIM Ahmedabad.

There was no business orientation in the family and while on campus Deepta never had visions of becoming an entrepreneur. But she did do something offbeat on passing out – a year off to 'explore options'.

"I thought this is too darn straitjacketed! IIT, IIM, and then a decent job with an MNC – too stereotyped! I was consciously looking to explore what would be of interest to me". In that year off, Deepta worked with an NGO, she worked for NASSCOM (which had just been set up) and also with an investment banker. "I thought I would give myself a year to figure out what I really wanted to do. I finished that one year and I was no wiser".

So Deepta went and joined American Express Bank, and later moved to CRISIL. The idea of starting something happened in 1994. The primary idea of doing something entrepreneurial came from Swaminathan, who is the CEO of IRIS, and also Deepta's husband. However, they got married after starting the company.

"Swami is an economist. He did his Masters in Economics from Yale University, worked with the World Bank, and then came back to India. He was always passionate about making a difference in the country." Swami was an Assistant Editor at *Business India*, after working with *The Economic Times*. "He is the born entrepreneur in our family." Swami spotted the opportunity that became IRIS.

It was the early days of liberalisation, Morgan Stanley had just set up shop in India in 1994 and the country seemed to be poised for growth. His idea was to set up a high-quality, independent information and research outlet to cater to the needs of institutional and retail investors.

The idea came from Swami but it was discussed and debated for a couple of months. There was a team of people from CRISIL who got interested in the idea of starting something entrepreneurial. This was the time when several job opportunities were available, with CRISIL being a happy poaching ground for foreign institutions entering India. All these companies were offering fantastic salaries.

Yet, the thought of striking out and trying to establish something on one's own was very exciting. So Deepta and some of her colleagues quit CRISIL, and Swami quit *Business India*. And that's how IRIS was born.

IRIS started with very little money – no venture capital, little savings to draw on. The team started with seed funding from some friends involved in financial markets, who liked the idea of an independent research and information house, and who trusted the team's professional competence and ethics. It really started like that.

And incredible as it may sound, the team of entrepreneurs started with no ownership in the company. Perhaps it was arrogance based on their perception that the business was so strongly defined by their IP that they could demand their stake whenever they wanted to.

The first office of IRIS was at Nariman Point, a single room in the office of the folks who had provided the seed funding. And the first few years were a huge struggle. Because it is one thing to say you will produce high-quality information, research and another to sell it. Also, as luck would have it, very shortly after IRIS was set up, the equity markets tanked, and the demand for independent research dried up.

IRIS primarily worked on a project basis in the early days, and Citibank and Morgan Stanley were some of their earliest customers. This was the time the government was disinvesting in PSUs. While interested buyers conducted their own valuation they wanted an independent valuation on whether these companies were intrinsically sound, and what price one should bid at. IRIS worked on some of the projects, made some money off these assignments and ploughed back surpluses into its information business – building large databases on Indian companies, mutual funds and markets.

Even before the business was started, all the founders of IRIS clearly realised the value of technology in an information business. At CRISIL and at the media houses where Swami had worked, there was a wealth of information. But without effective, user-friendly technology, much of the information was difficult to access and re-use. It was hard to even compare one set of companies with another on specific parameters.

So one of the earliest employees that IRIS hired was a CTO, an experienced technologist with many firsts to his credit. He was a part of the team that set up India's first wide area network, he was a part of a team that had brought the internet to India, and had worked extensively in the space of web technologies. IRIS was thus ahead of its time when it came to the technology side of setting up the databases and organising information.

Whether this was sheer luck or guided by a sense of things to come, who can say? Perhaps, both.

From 7 people who got together to form the company in 1994, IRIS grew to 40 strong by 1999. In the first year itself, three of the original founders dropped out – one died in a road accident and two left to pursue other opportunities. One was really more of a remote partner anyway, he had stepped into IRIS after his MBA at Harvard Business School, and after the

> **"One has to have a creative streak if one needs to be an entrepreneur. A strong desire to want to create something and to make that happen."**

initial few months of assisting with the business plan and early operations, decided to head back for his PhD at Harvard University.

So that left three active founders involved with the company, which was probably just as well because the company wasn't big enough for so many egos and ambitions. The third co-founder, apart from Deepta and Swami, was Balachandran (Bala), an engineer and an MBA from IIM Bangalore, and also ex-CRISIL.

"It was a small company. Extremely opportunistic also. So if someone asked if we would do allied things like market research, not necessarily our core area, we would do it to shore up our revenues. It was pretty hand to mouth". The founders took salaries, but nowhere near market levels.

Yet there was the thrill of doing innovative things, being ahead of one's time, and investing in smart technologies to handle large information sets.

For example, in 1997, IRIS helped Bloomberg set up shop in India. During the course of one of their meetings in Singapore, IRIS showed Bloomberg the India databases that it had created, and used the Mosaic browser to display the information (a browser which was popular before Internet Explorer). "We were using Mosaic to display information and link it to other relevant information sets through a click of a mouse. Bloomberg was astounded – they had never seen anything like it."

In 1999, IRIS decided to make available some part of the large information sets that it had built through a free personal finance portal, myiris.com. Suddenly, the company got noticed by retail audiences.

It was the dotcom boom and investors were looking for web-based ideas to fund. Besides, IRIS had a fine reputation. And so the company received its first major funding of over ₹ 20 crore from a clutch of private individual investors from around the world.

The founders decided to use this to massively scale up their business. The funds were invested in strengthening the operations, technology and sales teams. IRIS also invested funds in building some products, leveraging off the infobases that they had built.

Some monies were also spent in marketing the myiris.com brand, and the firm managed coups like getting the Finance Minister on the myiris.com portal immediately after presenting the union budget. It was partly the innovative use of technology, where IRIS patched the Finance Minister's voice through a cellphone on their portal. It was a smash hit, and the portal rapidly grew in popularity.

IRIS quickly grew to a little under 200 people and things were going extremely well. The company was all set to scale to the next level, establish a national presence through the portal, and build some proprietary products in the B2B information space. IRIS had also opened a new flank by starting to look at the outsourced research and information space in the United States and Europe.

All of a sudden, there was a huge crisis. The funding which was already committed by investors suddenly dried up on account of poor treasury management by the seed investors.

The difficult bit was that the founders of IRIS never really owned the company. Incredible as this may sound, they got to buy a small amount of equity just before the funding came in. But the majority stake was still with the seed investors.

So here, the company was in 'spending mode' and now there was no more money to spend! It was a huge mess. Somehow, the company managed to pay salaries and to continue operations, but every day was a struggle. Even through the worst of the crisis, there was only one time that salaries were delayed by close to a month. Else the founders managed to find resources to keep things going.

> "While we are not starving, we are not tremendously greedy, we don't constantly compare our net worth with somebody else. Having said that, it is fantastic to create wealth. Because often, it is not only an endorsement of the fact that you have done well, it gives you tremendous opportunity to do other things as well."

"It's the uncertainty that is the worst. You don't know whether you are going to have cash to meet all obligations each month, or when you are going to be liquid. This was our big lesson on the importance of cash flow."

Deepta was in fact in the US at the time the crisis erupted, trying to develop the outsourced business opportunity in research and content services. She dropped that and came back to help manage the situation. Several employees left, unable to deal with the business uncertainty. Operations had to be scaled down. Over the next two and a half years IRIS went from 180 people to 20.

"There were two options when the crisis hit us: bail out, since we anyway had such a small stake in the firm, or to look for funding to help us out of this crisis. As founder employees, we were aware of the full extent of IP in this company, and we just didn't want to give it all up".

So IRIS looked for funding and there were several offers but nothing felt quite right. "We had several term sheets, but none of them made sense to us, since the firms offering to buy us out looked at it as a distress sale. We didn't want to do a distress sale, although we had no Plan B. We also had several offers for us as a team to walk out on IRIS and join other firms to help them grow their outsourcing or web-based businesses."

However, the three partners stuck it out. Except for a moment of self-doubt when the option of 'shutting down' was seriously discussed. "However, there were two things that held us back. There was an innate realisation that there is lot of potential value in IRIS. We didn't know what the solution was going to be but we knew there had to be a solution."

The other part went deeper. Swami personally felt very morally obliged to all the other stakeholders. He said, "It's not just about the original investors of the company. It is also about the rest of the shareholders, the clients, the creditors and the employees. I can't just imagine walking off and leaving it like this. Even if we do decide to shut down this firm, it has to be from a position of strength, it cannot be from a position of weakness."

Eventually the partners restructured the business from IRIS and at a valuation better than that offered by any other investor, although it meant taking loans to clear the mounting liabilities of the company. It reflected their own faith in what they had created, and what perhaps others couldn't see then.

The assets, brand and IP were bought by a new company owned by the partners and employees, called IRIS Business. It was like a second life, a new beginning.

"We finally got lucky as well. Maybe if you wait long enough, things start working in your favour."

One of the things the founders did to get back on track was to renegotiate old contracts. A couple of fresh contracts came in from the international market as well. Bit by bit, organically, the business started growing again and cash from operations started coming in.

2004 was the roughest year and since then revenues have been ramping up rapidly. Deepta isn't comfortable sharing the figures since their company is unlisted, but revenues have jumped 17 times from 2005 to 2007. Things are now back on track.So what went right?

"Our key strength is that under one roof we combined content and a lot of cutting edge technology. And the solutions we provide are not merely standard solutions, like providing content and building websites. We offer solutions people in the market have not thought of at that point."

"Why so few women entrepreneurs? I think a lot of it has to do with the fact that women have primary responsibility for the children and family. If you have primary responsibility for caring for your family and you want to be an entrepreneur, in terms of balancing life, you could do something more cottage, maybe from home. If I had kids I would definitely re-size or re-scale the way I would be involved with the company."

For example, the portal myiris.com produces something like 160 stories every day, on a typical business day. How many stories do you think *The Economic Times* might be producing on a typical business day? 90 to 100. What's more, the output is technology driven. Myiris has built smart tools which can pre-generate the content. For example, when you report company results, it is extremely easy to write a code to automate the analysis, based on pattern recognition. i.e. comparing against past data.

Of course, analysts also provide insights based on their experience – which technology cannot deliver – but at least half the battle is won. IRIS automated the data-driven analysis six years ago whereas Thompson Financial, the global information giant, has done something on a much smaller scale only three years ago, and that is getting *Financial Times* headlines. So the IRIS story has really been about innovation, although some of the innovations did not result in as much revenues or recognition as they could have or should have!

In its new avatar, IRIS once again shifted to building products for institutional and retail customers. Another area is outsourced services – providing content and research capabilities to customers. But perhaps the most exciting thing right now is 'XBRL' XBRL or 'Extensible Business Reporting Language' is the new standard for the way in which financial information is reported. IRIS stumbled upon it about 3 years ago, when it was working on an outsourced project for a large American company.

For this project, IRIS employed an army of Chartered Accountants to take US financial data such as SEC filings and make it XBRL compliant. The idea behind XBRL is that every item in a financial report comes with in-built references and validations. This makes misreporting of data by either accident or design extremely difficult, and adds value to each element of data wherever it is used. It is extremely useful when sharing data across companies, or across geographies.

"If there is a piece of data which is XBRL compliant, the data carries the properties along with it. Otherwise if you cut paste the pieces of data from excel or export it from some application, you don't know anything about the data really – which company it belongs to, which year it pertained to, which accounting standard the data refers to and so on."

XBRL as an information standard should be the delight of regulators as well as analysts, and IRIS was convinced XBRL is the future for the information business. IRIS became a very active XBRL evangelist in India. The first thing the company did was put together a team of Chartered Accountants to create a private XBRL taxonomy for India. That is important because the Indian format of annual reports is different from the US GAAP format.

IRIS has also built a sweep of software products in the XBRL space – one solution, called iFile, is for internal and external reporting. This has been adopted by the Bombay Stock Exchange and the National Stock Exchange in India, and effective January 1st, 2008, SEBI has mandated that the top 100 Indian companies have to file using this application. This is also being deployed by IRIS for the Reserve Bank of India, where IRIS has been mandated to create an XBRL-based solution to facilitate bank reporting to the Reserve Bank of India.

IRIS has now been mandated by the Institute of Chartered Accountants of India to create the taxonomy for the country, and the firm is in the process of building that.

Meanwhile XBRL is being adopted by stock exchanges across the world. When IRIS displayed its product at a conference of regulators and stock exchanges, several exchanges showed interest. It's a virtuous cycle. Companies and regulators need software to prepare XBRL compliant returns, and users need rendering software to 'read' these XBRL documents. IRIS thus developed an entire range of products in this space and even runs an XBRL-centric BPO. In time there may be more players but right now IRIS has a headstart.

At the heart of the matter is this simple realisation: the service and consulting business is people dependent. The more you grow, the more people you need for it. Whereas once you develop products, you profit from your IP and go beyond working for specific clients and projects.

IRIS now has 240 people, plus another 60 working on a special project. The company is bigger than it has ever been and now it is self-funded. And almost completely owned by the promoters. But what of all those years of struggle? Well, as they say, when you wait long enough ordinary grapes mature into fine wine.

Additionally, for years, IRIS has focused on an India-centric content. Now that the India story is hot, there is a demand for this content from across the world. What's more, the wealth of information that IRIS built over the years is being converted to the XBRL format. "It's a huge investment and a product bet we are making once again", says Deepta. One which could give IRIS a significant advantage over other information vendors such as CRISIL and CMIE, and also make it very visible in the international information marketplace.

As they say all's well that ends well on 31st March. Enough of business – but what of the personal angle? Has all this turmoil impacted Deepta and Swami's life as a couple? How do they manage the work-life balance thing? And are separate compartments like 'work' and 'life' possible when both are so closely linked?

"I look at it like this. If you feel stressed, you want to compartmentalise something. If it is not stressful, you don't consciously compartmentalise anything. We don't work with rules like coming home and not talking about a particular issue."

So there are no rules as such but there are plenty of other things to discuss as well. And individual interests and activities. Swami is the Chairman of Bharati Vidya Bhavan, Navi Mumbai chapter, for example; he has also held positions in the Confederation of Indian Industry, and is actively interested and participates in several areas of policy making.

But if you ask two people who are married, can you work together, 90 per cent will say, "No, we cannot!" So what is it that makes it possible to have this kind of very good working relationship.

"I think there is no stock answer. I think part of it really depends on the couple's level of maturity", says Deepta. "Of course if we had kids, maybe my involvement in the business would have been less at some point in time."

Right now, the only teenager in the house is IRIS. A few more years of nurturing and it will be a fine young adult!

ADVICE TO YOUNG ENTREPRENEURS

I would say a couple of things. It is so true working for a while really makes so much of difference before you start your own enterprise. It doesn't matter where you work. When you actually work and you deal with nuances of day-to-day situations, decision-making and dealing with people, you imbibe a knowledge which is really helpful when you start being an entrepreneur basically.

I think, for us, much of what we have done has not followed a well-scripted plot. And this could be true for several entrepreneurs. You work with a broad game plan. Depending upon the availability of resources and the opportunities that present themselves at each point in time, you flexibly modify your plans and move along. You alter. But you ensure that you keep moving broadly in the direction that you want. If you say, this is my scripted plan, this is what I am going to do, if it doesn't end up happening as per that script, you will be tremendously disappointed.

On the other hand, if you are open and flexible, you will have opportunities that you never even thought of. There was nothing called XBRL when we started, and it is becoming a huge opportunity. Like a colleague of mine was saying, you need to keep the sails open and then wait for the wind to blow.

HEALTH IS
WEALTH

Cyrus Driver (PGP 2000),
Calorie Care

Cyrus quit his private equity job in Singapore to launch
Calorie Care, India's first professional, calorie-counted
meal delivery service. His own battle with weight
prompted the idea of the business!

On the job or on your own? The question just got harder for recent batches, given the vastly improved placement prospects.

And one piece of advice almost all the entrepreneurs of the earlier generation had for today's dreamers is: "Don't join a cushy job with a big brand name company. You won't learn much there, and you'll probably get addicted to the creature comforts."

Sitting in Cyrus Driver's cramped little office in Sewri, I can only think, that theory is wrong. If you have the idea of entrepreneurship coursing through your veins you will do it – anyhow.

Cyrus worked with J P Morgan in Singapore before returning to India in 2004 to set up the unique concept of 'Calorie Care'. It had been a success but like all early successes the company faces the difficult task of scaling up from here.

We don't know how he will do it, but the story is important enough even as a work in progress. Because this story could be yours.

HEALTH IS
WEALTH

**Cyrus Driver (PGP 2000),
Calorie Care**

Cyrus Driver is an Air Force child. Everyone went the doctor-engineer route, and so did Cyrus. He joined IIT Bombay. But much before that, as India was opening up in the 1990s, Cyrus found himself fascinated by business and big businessmen. "I felt these are the real 'rock stars' and knew I wanted to do something of my own early on."

With this in mind, Cyrus joined IIM Ahmedabad and that's also the reason he joined J P Morgan in their private equity division. He figured it would be a great 'learning ground', and it was.

"I worked in both India and Singapore, from where we invested in a lot of promising young Indian companies." The work included everything from hiring salespeople for investee companies, to looking into finances. It was the dotcom era when a lot of companies launched with ₹ 5-10 crore advertising budgets. And fizzled out quickly as well.

"I learnt the importance of starting small and growing big. "And I knew my company should be built the bootstrapped way."

In August 2004, Cyrus quit J P Morgan and came back to Mumbai. He had a nest egg to invest and also an idea to invest in: Calorie-counted healthy meals. "I've always had a weight problem of sorts but after I started working it became worse. I knew there was definitely a demand for such a service because I myself had a need for it." Secondly, it was a good opportunity to be an early mover in a growing space. And thus was born Calorie Care.

The first step was constituting the product. Recipes which were low in calories but tasted good as well. Sports nutritionist Lisa John worked along with two professional chefs to create a library of calorie-counted recipes. It took 10 months to put together a database of 150 such recipes across different cuisines. Everything from masala baked beans in tomato cups to grilled *hara bhara* (soya) kebabs.

"Downloading a list of low-cal recipes would take 60 minutes on the internet as there are thousands available online," says Cyrus. "The reason it took almost a year is because we actually cooked and tried out literally a thousand recipes and modified them by trial and error to come up with 150 that we thought were tasty as well as healthy".

The next hurdle was getting the sundry municipal licences required to set up a food establishment in Mumbai. "There is so much corruption! For the first time I came face to face with this whole different world."

Finding a location to set up his kitchen was also not easy. It took 5 months to zero in on a property which met the requirements and was affordable. It happened to be in less-than-glamorous Sewri and clinching the deal involved a lot of haggling and negotiations.

Next came the task of setting up a professional kitchen and this is what required a sizable investment (₹ 45 lakh, put in by Cyrus himself). Calorie Care is modelled along the lines of a flight kitchen and at its helm was chef Kamlesh Kumar, who had worked with Ambassador Skychef. And no doubt it is most impressive: gleaming stainless steel counters, uniformed workers with caps and gloves, and an air-conditioned area where salads are cut and food is packed.

Utmost care in terms of freshness and hygiene is very evident! "The meals are even delivered in our own air-conditioned vans."

You notice a lot of attention to detail. Attractive packaging, small touches like a napkin with each meal.

But the big idea is, not only are the meals calorie-counted but they are customised. This means, when you wish to order Calorie Care, you must first consult their dietician (in person, or on the phone). Next, you indicate your preferences and this could be as detailed as: "I like Indian and continental but not Chinese. I am allergic to onion and hate green peas. No salad with yoghurt dressing. Delivery at office Monday-Friday, and Saturdays at home, please."

"Technology makes it possible for us to handle this kind of customisation," says Cyrus. A specially written software conveys to the kitchen the entire list of orders daily, and how much needs to be packed for each individual as serving sizes vary from person to person.

Every meal is packed in food grade containers with individual labels, similar to inflight meals. Of course all this does not come cheap – a month of Calorie Care meals would cost between ₹ 3500-4500. But clients from the financial services sector (Deutsche Bank, Goldman Sachs and consulting companies) form the core customer base and they aren't complaining.

"We've found success with well-paid professionals pressed for time, willing to pay for health and convenience," says Cyrus.

This is certainly an achievement but also an issue. How much more can a premium service grow, and that too only on word of mouth? Currently Calorie Care delivers 600 meals a day, and caters generic 'healthy meals' to some corporate houses. The company clocked sales of approximately ₹ 2 crore in its second year and some profit – which was reinvested in the business. The issue is: where does the company go from here?

Calorie Care entered into a joint venture with Sterling Biotech, a company launching 'health malls'. The company also runs health food cafes at select gyms in Mumbai. But both these activities yield more in terms of visibility and brand awareness than any substantial revenues.

"We had ambitious plans of launching in Delhi and Bangalore, which we've dropped for now. The problem is finding and retaining senior managers. We are finding that extremely difficult." Money is not an issue, as Calorie Care raised some venture capital. However money alone is not enough...

Or maybe it is a question of being in a hurry. Graduating from a small, self-sustaining business to a large, multi-city operation with substantial scale is always difficult. A number of entrepreneurs interviewed for this book have done it, but not in 2-3 years. 8-10 years is par for the course, and it could take even longer. Cyrus, and other young entrepreneurs, may not be willing to wait that long.

"I am in talks with a couple of strategic partners. This would mean parting with a large chunk of equity but I think we will get much in return." So far the business has grown purely on word of mouth. But now it needs advertising, a sales force to market it and well, all the muscle a large organisation can provide to take it to the next level.

"If you feel you are not growing fast enough would you fight it out on your own, or would you take the practical path like me and look for a partner?" he muses. "To me 'control' is not as important as the brand becoming bigger. Something I created, living on..."

In fact, he is brutally honest when he says that at present the business is *'na ghar ka na ghat ka'*. And that also describes his own career in a sense.

Cyrus divides his time between Calorie Care and working as the India hand for 'Helix investments', a PE firm looking for companies to invest in India. "I don't take a salary from Calorie Care, whatever profit we make is put back into the business. Helix is what pays my bills," he reveals.

Again, this is something many entrepreneurs do to keep their dream alive. But one can't help wondering, is giving 50% of your time and energy to a young business enough?

There are many unanswered questions and answers as varied as the Calorie Care's customised meal plans. What works for one company may not for another. Calorie Care has lessons and learnings which will be evident – but all in due time.

ADVICE TO YOUNG ENTREPRENEURS

This is a good time to start up but keep in mind, the odds will be against you. You must carefully plan how you will be financially sustainable. Create a nest egg to draw on or, like me, make sure you have some alternate source of income. The other option is to set up after 10-15 years when you are an industry expert.

Start small and then expand, after you feel you have the product and processes right.

It's good to be a consumer of the product you are planning to launch, as you don't need to do endless market research. You know what will sell.

THE ALTERNATE
VISION

These individuals are using entrepreneurship to create social impact. Or as a platform which allows them creative expression.

THE ART OF
GIVING

Venkat Krishnan (PGP '93),
GiveIndia

He's worked with a newspaper, a television channel
and as principal of a school. Venkat then launched
GiveIndia, to promote the culture of 'giving' in India.
He is an entrepreneur but his mission is one with
a difference.

Had Venkat Krishnan got admission in a convent school in class 5, he may have been your regular investment banker type today.

But six years spent at 'Airport High School', where a large number of students came from slums and chawls, changed Venkat's life. It made him who he is.

"From class 6 or 7, I started feeling extremely strongly about inequity in society. I could see that there was a guy in my class whose father works in Dubai. So the family is well-off, they have a two-bedroom house. They would eat biscuits for breakfast which is a luxury."

"And there is another guy in the same class who lives in a slum in Kajuwadi and his father is a garage mechanic. And they would always buy *dus paise ka shakkar aur pacchis paise ka tel,* that too when a guest comes to their house."

And to Venkat that seemed fundamentally wrong.

In a country where most of us are conditioned to simply 'look the other way', makes Venkat a seriously different kind of guy. And that difference reflects in every choice in life he's made.

We are meeting in the lobby of a suburban hotel. Venkat lives somewhere close by but hesitates to call me home. "The house is too small," he mumbles. Not that he really cares what I, or anyone else, think of his life, or lifestyle.

Venkat's nickname on campus was 'Fraud' which is ironic because both in the honesty with which he speaks to me, and the actual work he does, Venkat is one of the most genuine people I have ever met.

And genuine people are always an inspiration.

THE ART OF
GIVING

Venkat Krishnan (PGP '93),
GiveIndia

Venkat Krishnan grew up in what you would call an 'ordinary middle class home', the youngest of three children.

"My dad used to work in Godrej, and I have had one of the best childhoods one could possibly have. Very caring mother, always making sure you ate all the vegetables and all that."

And yet, it was extraordinary in some ways.

"Dad is an engineer and he is one of those gizmo-type guys meaning our house is a garage at all points in time. Even now, we will have a black and white 1971 television lying somewhere in the attic because he will always aspire to repair everything."

From the time Venkat was five, he was part of these projects. Late in the evenings after coming home from work, dad would be busy tinkering with a Bush radio. Venkat would hold the soldering wire or the pliers – involved in some way.

"I think one of the best things that happened in childhood and particularly with me (I think the youngest kid in the house always gets the best treatment) was lots of exposure and learning right from early in life."

When Venkat was about 10 years old, his dad worked with a company which manufactured speakers for export to Denmark. When they had to get a die or a mould made, he would take Venkat along. Few kids get exposed to what is grinding, what is turning in a lathe, what is oil hardened natural steel and what is mild.

Later, as a teen, Venkat recalls hanging out at Sakinaka, where there are many small-scale industries. Accompanying his dad

Venkat would watch, figure out things, and give ideas on how those people could improve productivity.

"Another interesting thing – we used to play a lot of 'games' as a family when I was young. Late nights, over the weekends, all five of us used to do four digits by four digits multiplication sums and see who finished first!"

When in class 4, Venkat discovered the system for multiplying end digit by end digit numbers in one line without having to write down steps. Much later he found it was called the 'Trachtenberg System'.

The bottomline is a spirit of curiosity and of 'learning to think independently' was aroused. And that's a critical characteristic you will find in most people who are entrepreneurial in nature – they will tend to not accept what is told to them at face value but take the available information and process it on their own.

And then there was the impact of schooling.

Up to class 5 Venkat studied in what we call 'good schools'. But when his dad switched jobs and shifted to Andheri, he ended up joining 'Airport High School' which is, by all standards, a very average kind of school.

"I think that was the most life transforming experience for me. When you go to convent school, you actually don't see the whole spectrum of people. It will be middle class dominated."

At Airport High, much of the school was from the 'lower middle class', Venkat was regarded as relatively 'well off'. One day he would be playing at the house of a friend who lived in a two-bedroom house. The next day, it would be a friend who lived in a slum.

"It hits you very, very strongly when you see this first hand. Nothing shapes your future as much as the house in which you are born. That's the most significant predictor of your likelihood of success."

"There will be exceptions. There will be the odd Dhirubhai Ambani who was born poor and went on to become a star. But those are extreme examples."

No doubt something we all know, but don't feel for, because we have not personally experienced it. In fact, the trend is to protect your kids from this knowledge by sending them to an elite international school full of elite international kids like your own.

Far, far away from the 'real India'.

By class 7, Venkat was clear there was something wrong with the way things were and wanted to do something about it. At this stage Venkat studied the *Communist Manifesto* (he knew it by heart, word by word!). George Orwell's *Animal Farm* was another book which had a huge impact.

Engineering would have been a logical career choice but by class 10 Venkat was clear this wasn't the thing for him.

"I was quite fascinated by engineering, but felt very clearly that I didn't want to become an engineer. I wanted to do something that could make a difference."

So Venkat decided to take up commerce. He believed that it would help in his ultimate goal – of making a difference. Unfortunately, even though he hardly studied, Venkat managed to secure a state merit rank in the SSC board exam.

"My father is a very pushy character. He dragged me to Parle College and got me admitted to science. So *le liya* admission. I passionately hated biology so I took electronics as the option. And somehow I decided not to do commerce at that stage. In hindsight, I think that was a very wise decision. You learn far more in science."

Venkat refused to sit for engineering entrance exams and opted for a BSc in mathematics instead. Ironically, he coached several others and seven of his friends actually got through to engineering colleges. Meanwhile he essentially 'freaked out'.

"I used to play 6-7 hours of cricket every day. And I had also started smoking. So a typical day would be sitting on a *katta*, outside the college, looking at girls, eve teasing them, smoking, and lots of cricket and whiling away one's time." An admission which will shock and awe most kids today, who dream of someday making it to an IIM!

However despite failing in all subjects in the prelims and studying for about a week, Venkat managed a 92% in the HSC. Once again, dad tried to interest him in joining a local engineering college but by this time he had grown in conviction and learnt to say 'No'.

> **"We also set up a Rotaract club in the college, which was very very exciting. I would say my first entrepreneurial experience in a sense."**

"I was passionate about mathematics as a subject, still am. You can get me excited about maths like this in thirty seconds."

Venkat secured a merit scholarship for studying maths. Of course, he hardly ever went to college; instead excelled in extra-currics.

"At the the end of every term, I would go with a long sheet with day-by-day details of where I had represented the college – in chess, debating, dramatics, JAM and so on. We also set up a Rotaract club in the college, which was very very exciting. I would say my first entrepreneurial experience in a sense."

Parle College was a fairly traditional, Marathi kind of a place where there was no culture of participating in intercollegiate competitions apart from classical music. The Rotaract club made a huge impact in terms of transforming the environment in the college, making it more cosmopolitan and encouraging young talent.

"I was the founder and president. It took a lot of effort to convince our college authorities to allow something like this. According to them, it was very western. They believed that girls wearing skirts is not a good idea and with Rotaract all these skirt-wearing girls would come to the college."

In hindsight, Venkat realises he was good at understanding people from opposite ends of the spectrum – the 'pseud' category and the *'dehaati'* category. He had the knack of seeing the perspective of others, and somehow balancing it all.

The activities of the Rotaract Club included going to TOMCO (Tata Oil Company), meeting the GM and convincing him to come and give a talk on marketing as a career to students.

"We actually used to meet people, get them excited, get them to college and organise a career guidance fair entirely on our own. Coming from the classic middle class upbringing, it was a liberating experience, being able to do my own thing, meet new people, take risks, buy things, succeed, fail, whatever."

The result was that Parle college blossomed. In fact, they won the 'Best College' trophy at Mood Indigo in a particular year.

Which again goes to show that it's not important to merely get into the 'Best College'. But to make the best of your college life, wherever you experience it.

So after all this, how did IIM happen?

"That's an interesting story. Three weeks before my second year finals exams in college, our head of department in statistics called me and another guy said 'I don't care what you have done in intercollegiate bullshit. You have not attended any statistics classes, I am going to fail you.'"

Finally he relented and gave them a separate test as a 'pre-qualifier' to even attempt the exam. Venkat got 20 out of 20 on that test and the crisis was averted. But as a consequence, he got deeply interested in statistics.

"Firstly, because it is so much about numbers and I am passionate about maths. And secondly, you realise how much impact it has on peoples' lives. Look at the green revolution that has happened, or the top scientific discoveries..."

"What does a scientist do? He designs the experiment. But that is actually only 25% of the job. 75% is analysing the data you got from the experiment, creating hypotheses and testing them out. Which is all statistics actually."

Venkat gave up his maths scholarship and decided to major in statistics. Side by side he studied French and Cost Accounting. "People say a balance sheet is difficult but I have never been able to create a balance sheet that doesn't tally," he says matter of factly

"So basically things came quite easily to you," I observe.

"Yes, things came quite easily to me."

"Then that becomes difficult because you can do anything," I add.

"To say that it's difficult is not fair. I would say it makes life easy. You can pick and choose what you want to do."

> **"We actually used to go and meet people, get them excited, get them to college and organise a career guidance fair entirely on our own."**

And at some point Venkat chose to take up management, although not for the usual reasons.

"One of the fears I started having while doing BSc is, am I being extravagant? Because I am not from a rich family, right. I had to build my life."

The idea of becoming a sales rep running around selling pharmaceuticals did not appeal. So more as a 'de-risking' thing, Venkat took the CAT exam.

"I managed to get section A of IMS coaching material from one of my seniors, free of cost. I studied from that. My CAT entrance was terrible. At IES school in Dadar, I was put in a KG class where the benches were so small that I had to sit with my legs outside for the whole two hours."

"Calls came from all four IIMs. At the IIM Ahmedabad interview, Prof G S Gupta was on my interview panel. In those days, on Doordarshan, in weather forecasts, they used to give decimal temperatures of all cities."

"Gupta asked, 'You are a stats grad. Tell me, what is the probability that all eight decimals will be different. A guesstimate.'"

"I said, 'Less than five per cent.'"

"He said, 'I am delighted. You are through because this is the first time anybody has given the correct answer to this question.'"

Venkat had also taken the Indian Statistical Institute (ISI) entrance test. On 3 July 1991, when he was on the IIM campus, the MStats admission letter came.

"I think that was the toughest decision I went through in my life. From six in the evening till three in the morning I was agonising over what to do. My passion was to do statistics, I wanted to go to Calcutta. But somehow the idea that the MBA degree gives you much more access to more opportunities, financially you will be much more well off, that in turn is empowering."

Finally, he opted to stay at IIMA.

"First 1.5 months, I was very scared because everybody is a Stephen's topper and IIT this and IIT that. I did extremely well. My first mid-term's GPA was 3.7 or something like that. Then I stopped studying."

Why?

"I am not interested in doing well academically."

So what was he doing?

"I was sleeping. You can ask anybody in my dorm."

And thus, Venkat was nicknamed 'Fraud'. People used to believe that after everyone slept, he must have been switching on his table lamp and studying. Because he did so well, getting As in tough quant courses without 'any apparent effort'.

As usual, Venkat did find ways to use his time constructively.

Learning to play the keyboard; reading in the library, whenever he had free time. Much of it on the subject of higher education. The system of memorising dates and formulas, he strongly believed, was killing human potential. If you let young people fall in love with a subject, imagine what they can do to a build a better world!

Clearly, Venkat was not headed for a mainstream corporate career. The idea was how to leverage this degree to make a difference. The IAS was one possibility. A summer job with Khadi Village Industries followed. The project was to develop a model to market khadi without rebate.

Soon enough he realised a similar project had been done by IIMA's Prof Vora and it was gathering dust in their library. What's more, working with the CEO of KVIC, an IAS officer, made Venkat realise how weak the bureaucracy was in terms of decision-making. He realised that the IAS was not his cup of tea.

Then, LEM happened.

Venkat had opted for the entrepreneurship package – courses like New Venture Management, PPID (Project Planning Implementation and Development) and LEM (Laboratory in

> **"... somehow the idea that the MBA degree gives you much more access to more opportunities, financially you will be much more well off, that in turn is empowering."**

Entrepreneurial Motivation). Plus, he did two IPs (Independent Projects) on entrepreneurship.

The first IP was on the feasibility of private enterprise in education, especially vocational education. The second was on the feasibility of the private sector in rural finance (the term microfinance was then unheard of).

By this time he was quite confident about wanting to become an entrepreneur, at some stage in life. But it was also clear that even if he became an entrepreneur, it would not be something like IT, but about 'making a difference.'

"I remember my first reflective note for the LEM class – I see myself as an instrument or tool that is available to society. And my choices should be guided by maximising the returns that I will give to the society. So I will not do something just because I like it, but because that is the best use of my time for the society's benefit."

"If I think that I will serve society best by becoming a teacher, then I will teach. If I think I will help society best by becoming a businessman, then I will become a businessman. I will do whatever it takes." The guiding principle was, and remains, to restore the maximum amount of fairness to society.

Come placement and you know Venkat is not going to go for the usual companies.

Actually, he almost joined an *aatawallah* near Vapi who had participated in placement that year. He was offering a fancy salary, but the chap said the job is to help run the *aata chakki* and help him to save income tax. That put Venkat off completely.

"I would have joined him, if he had been an honest guy. Because he was asking you to run the business as a CEO," says Venkat wistfully.

And that's something which makes a lot of sense for any MBA

with ambitions of becoming an entrepreneur. Joining a company which may not be the biggest or most glamorous name in the business, but a place where you get to be hands-on and get a 360 degree experience of actually running a business.

Eventually he settled for TOI – a day six company – as media too is an opportunity to 'make a difference'. And like every experience, he sought out and savoured for its duration, this stint too was about learning, about growth, about invention.

Being EA to Mr Arun Arora, a director on the board, Venkat interacted closely with Sameer Jain, Vineet Jain and Ashok Jain. He worked on IR problems faced by the company, drafting the letters sent to the union during a strike.

Then there was a salary restructuring project where Venkat argued that journalists should be paid better. He also helped write a far reaching document called 'Looking Beyond the Horizon' which envisioned the technology strategy for the company. Much of which actually got implemented.

Then Venkat's boss joined Sony Entertainment Television (SET) as CEO. The condition set by the Jains was that Mr Arora could not take away more than one employee. The person he chose was Venkat.

"I was not keen to leave but he had already asked for me. Plus SET paid me 40k a month which was big money in 1995. My brother and I had both taken student loans, plus dad had quit his job, tried a business and failed at it."

The SET job held the opportunity to clear off the family debts, allowing Venkat the freedom to then do whatever he wished. Four months' salary was all it took to pay off everything. And as always, Venkat is grateful for the exposure he got at SET.

"Even though it was a very short six-month stint, I got to work with the promoters and build the business plan of the company. I made the most critical sales pitch to Fulcrum, and to M Venkataraman, the head for media at HLL."

But it was time to move on to something else. In a field much dearer to him. The field of education.

In 1995, Sunil Handa sent out a note to a number of IIMA alumni and former LEM students about a proposed school project. However, the idea was a residential school for the middle class

"I remember my first reflective note for the LEM class – I see myself as an instrument or tool that is available to society."

and that did not excite Venkat. Until close friend and batchmate Sridhar (DD) stepped in.

DD was working with IBM at that time and he was excited. He said, "Let's go and meet Sunil Handa. Let's offer to volunteer the weekends."

Venkat was very passionate about teaching and said, *"Chalo, jaate hai."*

But once they got there, something happened.

"I told Sunilbhai that residential schools are cut off from real life. Even IIT and such places, you are so cut off from reality that you tend to live in islands. You don't know what it means to be a poor guy in India. You don't know what it means to live in slums. You don't know what it means to struggle to exist."

Why not instead set up a day school? What's more, there would be a certain quota of students from the poorest of poor families. Sunil agreed and by the end of the meeting both Venkat and DD decided to quit their jobs. This was in August 1995.

"Both of us were in the middle of product launches, so when they said please stay back till the launch, it seemed like a fair kind of thing to do. I finished work at SET on 14 January 1996 at 7:30 pm. At 9 o'clock I took the flight to Ahmedabad."

And thus started the Eklavya chapter.

"We spent about a year and a half researching education, figuring out what is a good school. So we travelled all over India. We spent three weeks in Europe also, doing some things together then branching off. Having conversations till three in the night on everything from what is the best method of education, to what should be the discipline policy of a school. Right down to how we should design our chairs."

The point being that whenever you look beyond business, into the things that make a difference to the quality of our lives, we somehow think there's no need to apply scientific thought.

"In India you find that the guy who is designing a mall is designing a school the next day. And that architect will have zero understanding of what you mean by an educational environment. So kindergarten children are climbing six-inch high steps, urinals are designed at a height where the child actually has to stand at the edge of his toes."

Which is why the 'immersion' experience was so important.

"Between us, we must have read at least a thousand books, I am not exaggerating. We would read an average of three books a week, on pedagogy, on the Montessori method, and so on."

Responsibilities had been divided – Venkat was setting up the day school, Sudhir (an IIMA PGP '94) was setting up the residential school, and Sridhar was setting up the teachers' training institute.

In March 1997, the day school was ready to launch. And it was an absolutely humbling experience.

"All four of us were IIM grads, right! So we had this huge thing that the day we announce admissions, there is going to be a mile-long line of people who want to get admission to our fantastic school. So 27 March 1997, we put ads in the paper and Sunil Handa came with a camera to video-record the queue."

A total of five people came to inquire. The team was shattered. At 1 am they convened and wondered aloud, "*Boss abhi karna kya hai,* it seems as if the world doesn't want us to set up the school." Then they decided, come hell or high water, if we get even 10 kids, we are going to start our school.

For two months after that, they did door to door sales. Sridhar, Sudhir, Venkat and their teachers.

"We would knock on people's door, with a brochure in our hands and say, 'Good afternoon madam, we are here to talk to you about a new school that we are setting up in your city. Would you like to know about it'?"

"The good thing is, more than 70% of the people let us into their homes. They would sit, they would hear us, give us *chai* and biscuits. The fact that we were from IIM made a big difference. After two months of door to door calling, we closed the admission with 34 kids for class one, two and three."

> **"… whenever you look into the things that make a difference to the quality of our lives, we somehow think there's no need to apply scientific thought."**

The goal had been to get 24 + 24 + 20 so getting 34 students, that too with great difficulty, did not feel like an achievement.

"If you ask me, this was my closest brush with 'failure' in life. But we saw through it – having each other for support was of huge value."

Of course, this was just the beginning. The school started and a fascinating journey began.

It was all about teamwork. There was a great sense of togetherness, a team of teachers who were extraordinarily passionate. Some of them would work till two in the morning, then leave their homes at 6.30 am to reach the school at 7.15 am. All bound by a sense of purpose, a commitment to something larger than themselves.

Parents were delighted with the experience. The following year when admissions opened, all 240 seats filled up. Some had to be turned away. Eklavya was the 'coolest school of Ahmedabad' within one year of existence.

How did it all happen?

"I think if there is passion in the environment, people pick it up. I have seen it in every place I have worked in. Nothing energises people like seeing other positive people, and integrity of course. Integrity is a very big booster of morale. People see that the others involved with them are doing something with the desire of doing something good and not their own gain. That drives people extraordinarily."

Four years after getting into the Eklavya project, two and a half years as principal of Eklavya school, Venkat decided it was time to move on.

Why?

"I am a my-way-or-the-highway kind of guy. And I guess I decided it was just time to move on."

Like every time he started a new chapter in life, Venkat had no clear plan of what next. But some thoughts were in his head.

During the one and a half years of travelling for the Eklavya project, Venkat recalled meeting a lot of organisations including NGOs that were doing really good work. Very committed, very passionate people, yet somehow nobody had even heard of them. That bothered him.

Then in 1998, Venkat spent two months in the US, travelling all over. It happened like this – Sudhir, Sridhar and Venkat had all been saving to buy a house. But it dawned on Venkat one fine morning that he didn't really want to own a house. A rented house would suit him fine, especially because he did not plan to marry.

Soon after, Venkat noticed an ad for a round trip to New York by Royal Jordanian Airlines, for ₹ 26,000.

"I was always fascinated by the US as a country, especially after the Soviet Union collapsed. I wanted to find out, what is it that makes US as a country tick. I also figured that I was not doing any of the conventional things that people do for their parents, right! So I decided to encash the lakh and a half rupees I had saved, and bought three round trip tickets to the US where my brother was then based."

With the remaining money Venkat bought a VUSA pass to travel to 12 cities across the US – Cincinnati, New York, Washington, New Jersey, Burlington, Minneapolis, Philadelphia, Boston, L.A., San Francisco. Crazy amounts of travel at dirt cheap prices.

In every city he knew somebody, so he wrote them a mail saying, "Let me stay at your place for two days." And every place he went to, Venkat would go to a school.

"I was running a school and trying to understand the American education system. One of the things that hit me really hard about the US was that people in that country have a sense of ownership for their country. People care."

"That really hit me hard and I felt, that's what we need back home in India. You take a typical guy who goes to IIM, who comes out, works in an investment bank or wherever. We are obsessed about our own careers, and we couldn't care less about our country. I think that has to change, that's not on."

"I think if there is passion in the environment, people pick it up. I have seen it in every place I have worked in."

"After all, those of us who have gone through IIMs and IITs have been subsidised by the poor – the guy living on the road, when he buys his two bit of a matchbox and pays sales tax. The second part is that we were lucky to have been born where we were. What if I were born as a garage mechanic's son?"

On returning to India, Venkat did a lot of research. At one level he found the Rockefellers, Carnegies and now Bill Gates who've given away their wealth. But what about the contribution of ordinary citizens towards the betterment of society?

"In America, every school that I went to, every working day, there would be mothers from middle class families, sitting in the classroom and helping the teacher with a group of Hispanic students who are weak or children with learning disabilities.There was this sense of civic responsibility, that as a citizen it is our duty to help."

"In a town called Burlington in Vermont, they were going to close down one of the three high schools. And they had a town hall meeting. That's the first unthinkable thing, right! If BMC wants to close down one of its schools, I don't think they will actually organise a consultation. But here they actually had a discussion, and it was well attended."

"Most importantly, the affluent people in town said 'Close down the school nearest to ours, because we all have cars and we can afford to send our kids there.' Whereas in India, Malabar Hill people will say, 'Suck the water from Vaitarna and give us water 24 hours a day. And too bad if Mira Road, which is a few kilometres away doesn't get water more than half an hour a day'!"

In the 'Market is Everything Era', the middle class in India has lost that sense of purpose. And Venkat is passionate even in his dissection of the problem.

"It is the middle class who were the authors of the freedom struggle, not the rich, not the poor. Gandhi was spot on."

"I cry every time when I think of 15 August when we were all celebrating freedom and he was in the middle of a village near Calcutta saying, 'Now is not the time to celebrate freedom. Now is the time to fight the next enemy that we have, which is religious intolerance'. What courage it takes for a guy to think like that!"

Freedom from the British is the first milestone in my life, my next milestone is freedom from poverty, my next milestone is freedom from intolerance, that is what we need!

"We need the best minds in the country to think, 'What is the human ideal that we aspire towards?' Rather than what is the next 30-crore flat that I can buy for myself, or whatever else that I can do for myself."

He hastens to add, "Please have a 30-crore flat, but don't be blind to the world outside your window."

The time was ripe. A growing number of Indians were beginning to do well for themselves. They were going to have everything that they could possibly want very early in life. Could we not then start building a culture that helps give back?

And thus was born 'GiveIndia', an organisation dedicated to promoting and enabling a culture of 'giving'.

When Venkat quit Eklavya, a couple of things fell in place. He had just bought a home PC and was fascinated by the power of the internet.

The net was also a useful source of information. Venkat found out that in the US 'giving' – in all forms – formed 1.8 per cent of GDP or $180 billion dollars in '99-00. The corresponding number in India was less than 0.1 per cent or 0.2 per cent.

And here's a startling fact – the poorest people give the most, as a percentage of income. This is true not only in the US, but all over the world.

Venkat realised that on the one hand there were organisations and people who are passionate and doing amazing work which nobody has heard of. On the other hand, there is an opportunity to give back.

"I used to write to batchmates, friends, people I know who are doing well asking them, 'Why you don't give more?' The first question was, 'Who can I give to? I don't know if my money will

> **"In America, every school that I went to... there was this sense of civic responsibility, that as a citizen it is our duty to help."**

be used properly.' That typical cynicism that we have in our system is perhaps justified."

So the idea was born that one can create an organisation that showcases NGOs doing good work and enable those who wish to 'give' a platform to connect with them. And thus, help create a culture of giving back.

One good thing that Venkat learnt in Eklavya, and credit to Sunil Handa for that, is whenever you have a good idea, write a note, circulate it, show it to people, get their thoughts and reactions. So he wrote a two-page concept note, mailed it to some people and got a lot of interesting feedback. And then Venkat started meeting people to turn the idea into action.

He went back to *The Times of India*, they were not interested. He met Shekhar Gupta at *The Indian Express*. Shekhar loved the idea and said, "Come and help me run the paper and use *Indian Express* as a vehicle to build the idea of GiveIndia." Venkat declined.

Gagan Sethi, who runs an NGO in Ahmedabad called 'Jan Vikas', was very encouraging and even offered to seedfund the idea with ₹ 10-12 lakh.

"In hindsight, one of the best things that happened with the IIM degree was, it gives you access. It opens doors for you like nothing else does. I don't think a person who doesn't have an IIM degree would have been able to get access to Shekhar Gupta, be able to convince him, to support an idea like this. And I think the kind of networks you get being in the IIM system are invaluable."

Through this network, Venkat met Nachiket Mor of ICICI. He said, "You know, we at ICICI have been thinking of doing something exactly like this. So why don't you set up the organisation! We will fund you, give you all the support you need, help build it. We will give you the license to use our brand if you want it."

"And I would say I have been really lucky. The amount of support I have got in my life is mind-boggling. ICICI and Nachiket in particular, hats off to the support they have given. Unquestioning support. Any time I need his help, he is available. Anytime we are going through a difficult patch, they are with us."

And they have never sat on our heads and said, "You have to do it this way and why aren't you doing this."

With this support, GiveIndia formally started in April 2000, five months after the idea was born. GiveIndia is structured as a philanthropy exchange. Just as you have a stock exchange which connects companies with investors, GiveIndia connects worthy NGOs with donors.

"I would say GiveIndia is actually one of the founding organisations of the idea of philanthropy marketplaces globally. After us, a lot of other organisations were born. Like Global Giving in the US, there is now one in South Africa, in the Philippines, in Columbia, Argentina etc. Most of these organisations were set up between 2000-03."

The first version of GiveIndia was a simple website which listed five organisations doing good work. Using the ICICI network and online banner advertising GiveIndia started reaching out to potential donors.

The first eight months were a disaster. GiveIndia managed to raise ₹ 1.31 lakh in 34 transactions. On 26 January 2001, the Gujarat earthquake happened. The site crashed, after receiving three million hits in a single day. GiveIndia raised ₹ 97 lakh in one week.

"We set up an earthquake relief fund and at that time, we were the only online vehicle available to donate in India." The sad truth is that when something happens, people give far more than is required. What they don't realise is that a country like India is a daily living disaster. Diarrhoea is a much bigger disaster than earthquake, tsunami, cyclone, the Orissa cyclone, all of them put together."

So 26 January 2001 was really an aberration, not a 'turning point'. In the next financial year, a year without an earthquake,

"Diarrhoea is a much bigger disaster than earthquake, tsunami, cyclone, the Orissa cyclone, all of them put together."

GiveIndia raised only ₹ 25 lakh. However, the amount of money raised was not the only measure of the success of the project.

Venkat explains: "We evaluate GiveIndia on the basis of three parameters. One is the amount of money we are able to channel. Second is the number of donors we are able to engage. Every individual donor chooses what he wants to do through GiveIndia, and therefore we can't measure the impact at the end destination."

GiveIndia believes that a large number of individual donors making choices will collectively make a much better basket or portfolio than one smart foundation giving grants. So its own success lies in getting more and more people engaged. Getting more and more people to care.

"You must keep in mind that the amount of money we will raise will always be insignificant. Even if GiveIndia becomes rabidly successful and raises ₹ 1,000 crore a year, the Government of India gives ₹ 18,000 crore every year to NGOs alone."

So it's more about instituting a culture of giving.

"Yes, but more important than that is the idea of building ownership. Why is that the tax rupee does not get used effectively? Because most of us look at taxes as a license to exist. We are paying taxes and telling the government, 'I don't care whether you are doing anything with this money or not, leave me alone.'"

The middle class response to every national problem is, privatize! Government schools suck, so we put our kids in private schools. Water starts getting bad, so we consume mineral water. In the year 2006, India's expenditure on water, privately paid, exceeded the combined water budgets of all municipal corporations!

At this point I wonder if I am speaking to Sitaram Yechury but Venkat is simply stating the problem. And he's not got a closed view about the possible solutions. So privatise all you want but do not disconnect. Do not abscond from your duty as a citizen.

"That is why GiveIndia insists that everybody has to choose where their money will go. Because even making the choice that I think education is more important than health, or livelihood is more important than education, means an individual has thought about and acknowledged the problem!"

Every individual donor gets a report describing how their money was used. Which makes people realise that even a little contribution can make so much difference. For example, it takes just ₹ 180 to give a smokeless *chulha*!

"When I was a kid, I have seen my mom sometimes use firewood, and I remember how much she used to cough. So imagine somebody else's mother, three times a day in the village, is inhaling firewood, coughing, coughing, coughing! And we have spent more than hundred and fifty rupees on this coffee right now! That's all it takes to change!"

Backing all this passion and conviction is systems and management science. GiveIndia now certifies 120 voluntary organisations. It provides the due diligence and the platform. And Venkat believes that the market will correct everything else.

"If an NGO comes and gets listed on GiveIndia today, they typically start getting some amount of money every month. Somebody will get 1,000 rupees a month, somebody will get five lakh rupees a month. What they start seeing is the power of engaging individuals as against depending on one large donor (as charities have traditionally operated). They see the value in being transparent in their accounting."

While earning a 'profit' is not crucial for GiveIndia, the goal was to ultimately become self-sufficient. Today 94% of GiveIndia's revenues come through the transaction and service charges levied to donors. Only five per cent of the expenditure is borne from the seed grant that ICICI had initially provided.

"My idea is that in the next 3-4 years, it should be a 100% viable organisation standing on its own feet. If my cost of fund raising is about 20 per cent, ICICI wouldn't bother too much. But an individual donor, giving 1,000 rupees will jump up and down and

> **"In 2007-08, GiveIndia expects to channel roughly ₹ 18.5 crore from 50,000 individual donors. Of these, 25,000 are payroll giving donors."**

fuss about it. And that's exactly what I like. Because his pressure will drive us to be efficient. It will not give us the space to take things easy and set unambitious goals."

That is why much of the ₹ 4 crore provided by ICICI after the initial funding (₹ 72 lakh) is lying unused. The challenge is to not need to use it!

In 2007-08, GiveIndia expects to channel roughly ₹ 18.5 crore from 50,000 individual donors. Of these, 25,000 are 'payroll giving' donors. This is a programme GiveIndia has been promoting to corporates where employees can choose to have a small fixed amount deducted from their salary and channelled to a cause of their choice.

'Payroll Give' was born out of the insight that people want to give, but it is not high on their priority. So, we will have to reach them, and not vice versa. But how? The most common method of fund raising used by NGOs is face-to-face. This is horribly expensive. For every 100 rupees, the cost of raising the money is 40-70%.

Venkat's analytical mind broke down the problem.

"The cost of raising funds can be broken down into the cost of establishing credibility, cost of doing the transaction, and then the cost of servicing the relationship with the donor. The idea of Payroll Giving is – I go into a company and the CEO sends out a mail to all the employees saying that we have signed up for this programme. Cost of credibility is zero."

"The second thing with Payroll Giving is that you acquire a customer once, but he stays with you for a lifetime. Once he has signed in, by default he is on the programme. So the only thing left is the cost of servicing the donor. You have straightaway brought your cost down substantially. That's one of the reasons why it works."

Currently more than 20 companies including HSBC, HDFC,

ICICI bank, YES bank, Deutsche bank and many others have signed on. But Venkat admits, it was not an instant, runaway success. Few new ideas are!

The initial pitches were made to friends and wellwishers. In the initial one-one and a half year Payroll Giving saw market response but struggled to crack the sales model. Eventually they built a classic retail sales organisation driven by targets. But it remains an intense effort. One mail from the CEO and HR department is not enough to move 10,000 people. You need to go and meet people from desk to desk – there is no two ways about it!

The power of a person-to-person sales pitch is never to be underestimated. It's one of the arrows in the arsenal of every entrepreneur, unmatched by automation and corporatisation.

The most visible form of fund raising however, remains the Marathon. GiveIndia is the official charity partner for the events in Mumbai and Delhi with around 15,000 individuals raising funds through this channel.

"We saw how marathons in the other parts of the world raise a lot of money. Standard Chartered bank was sponsoring the Mumbai Marathon and Procam was organising the event. We went to them and said, 'Why don't you let us use the event as a platform? The benefit is that your event gets a nice feel, a social conscience. You will find it easier to push things through with government and the media, press, everybody will be more interested.' So they got excited."

In 2007, the Mumbai Marathon raised ₹ 7 crore and the Delhi Marathon ₹ 1.5 crore.

65% of this was through individuals, as that is GiveIndia's focus.

"We don't want to focus on companies. See, companies don't change the nature of a country. It's individuals who change the nature of the country. So if you want to change the caring nature of the country, you have to work with individuals."

And thus came the idea of raising pledges. Instead of an individual simply donating to charity, he or she would run for a cause. And raise money for this cause from other people.

The best thing, exults Venkat, is that there is zero event organising cost, so the total fund raising cost for GiveIndia is a mere 3.5-4%. Which is an industry benchmark!

Lastly, around 5,000 people give purely through the online route, contributing 15-20% of GiveIndia's overall inflows. The big challenge now is scaling up, and this requires investment.

"We are investing almost a crore in IT. Our payroll programme has worked only because of technology. People sign on and sign off online. We process that and send the company a file which they upload into their payroll processing software, whichever software they are using."

Payroll Giving is not the first attempt of its kind but it has worked because it understands the end user's needs. Then there remains the challenge of attracting good people.

"By NGO standards we pay reasonably well. But of course nothing close to the corporate sector. Also we require people who are going to do very corporate type of jobs. They are not working with children and receiving emotional fulfillment on a daily basis. Yet we do attract people with a huge sense of commitment."

There are many high-calibre professionals willing to work part-time. Finding such people willing to work full-time is the challenge.

"In many ways, what GiveIndia is today is thanks to people like Mathan Varkey (who was Triton's Media Head) and Pushpa Singh (Sr Mgr at Anagram) who gave up successful and lucrative careers to work for a cause," says Venkat. There are at least 15 such people in GiveIndia who've said 'no' to megabucks for a chance to make a difference.

So what is the future looking like? Very bright!

"I think the next generation has a much greater orientation of giving. We have all seen difficult times in childhood. So there is this fear that something could happen, there could be a recession, etc, etc. But the youngsters today are so confident, so secure. They feel confident that we will be able to take care of ourselves, so let's share a bit."

In fact, at BPOs like Genpact and WNS, young kids, 22-23 year olds earning ₹ 6,000 have signed up to donate ₹ 100 a month. And conversion rates in these BPOs are 70-75%!

So the culture of 'giving' does seem to be taking root.

Venkat recalls GiveIndia's first ever annual report, which contained a paragraph which he wished to see in the 2020 annual report. It's a letter which read as follows:

Dear Stakeholders,

We are delighted to inform you GiveIndia has closed down.

Donors are now active, they are finding NGOs, they are engaging with them, they are giving money directly and they don't need GIVE INDIA.

"We love what we do, but ideally we are an undesirable element. The existence of a GiveIndia is a reflection that people in this country are not able to do what they should do on their own. There is a need for people like us. I wish there wasn't. So we could also go and make money in the corporate sector."

Not that such a thing will ever happen! Already Venkat is deeply involved in a company called E-I or Education-Initiatives run by DD and Sudhir. In fact, he draws no salary from GiveIndia at all.

"I spend 25-30% of my time on EI. EI pays me, I got a big salary hike this April – from 12,000 bucks, I now make 20,000 bucks. I stay with my parents, so that's more than enough."

"The best joy comes when we are able to do something and prove an idea. Right now we are working on a product called ADEPTS. It is an online self-learning tool, that kids can use to teach themselves a subject."

"We are doing it with great depth of understanding. Really sophisticated statistical tools. Only four or five people in the world are using those kind of tools. We have a depth and granularity of how a child learns. That's fascinating, commercial success is actually not important."

And yet, you know it will come. And that Venkat will eventually move on.

"Next August I will be out of GiveIndia," he promises. "I genuinely believe that I am now counterproductive to the organisation."

As usual, there are no definite plans but you can be sure something new will fascinate him. But, of course, it will be all about making a difference.

ADVICE TO YOUNG ENTREPRENEURS

My advice for IIMA alumni – the IIMA qualification is the best possible 'income insurance' you can get in India today. So if at all there is anyone who can take risks with a low downside, it has to be you!

My advice to 'would be' entrepreneurs – nothing is perhaps a greater truism than the '3-year rule' – if you are able to hang in and survive for 3 years, you'll be up and running and by the fourth year, you will be better off as an entrepreneur than you'd have been in a job. I've seen this happen in my own three efforts that I've been involved with as start ups, and with several friends I've seen build businesses as well.

For '4 yrs+ old entrepreneurs' – I want advice FROM you on how to take yourself out of an institution and leave it better off without you than it is with you.

And my advice for the world at large – Just try and experience the joy of 'giving' first hand. Give your time, money, skills to people who need it, and help improve their lives, and trust me, you will get far more joy out of it than anything else.

SMALL IS
BEAUTIFUL

Anand Halve (PGP '77),
chlorophyll

After two decades in advertising Anand set up a
brand consultancy called chlorophyll. He believes
'small is beautiful' because in the quest for size and
scale you lose out on the joy of creation. This is an
alternate model of entrepreneurship.

When you use the words 'successful' and 'entrepreneur' in the same sentence the image that comes to mind is someone who's built up an empire of some sort. A listed company, with a few thousand employees and several millions in revenues, or even in billions.

These are success stories, for sure, and several of the entrepreneurs featured in this book fall in just this category. Scaling up your company from a 12-man operation to 1200 is certainly an achievement. But every entrepreneur who's done it admits he's lost something in the process.

Everyone starts small, and struggles. But there is the joy of being hands-on and personally involved with every aspect of your business. With size comes detachment. Delegation. And an insatiable appetite to 'grow'. Because the stock markets demand it.

'Think big' and somehow get there remains the ambition of most entrepreneurs. But there are a few who consciously decide to take another route.

These entrepreneurs want control over the quality of their lives, and the quality of the business. They would rather be a boutique than a faceless corporation. Such a business is driven by the knowledge and expertise of its founders, and hence remains inherently unscalable. But the creative satisfaction and meaning the entrepreneur derives from his or her work makes it worth the while.

Anand Halve is one such entrepreneur. He jointly runs chlorophyll, an 'end to end brand consultancy'. With over two decades of advertising experience, he could have set up a traditional agency, driven by billings and commissions. He chose otherwise.

Anand's story illustrates that there is no one definition of 'entrepreneurship'. Ultimately it is doing what you want to do, the way you want to do it. If that means size, dilution of equity, outside capital and attendant pressures, so be it.

But there is another way which you could explore. The small and beautiful.

SMALL IS
BEAUTIFUL

Anand Halve (PGP '77),
chlorophyll

Know thyself and the rest follows, they say. As a first year student in medical college Anand Halve knew he could not spend every day of his working life surrounded by people who were 'basically looking miserable'.

So he dropped out of medicine and completed a graduation in science. The choices ahead him were the IAS ("my dad was an IAS officer"), probationary officer exam for banks, or the barely-heard-of-new-degree: the MBA.

There was no burning desire to do management but Anand gave the CAT and made it to IIMA.

"Not having a quantitative or finance background, marketing became a choice by elimination. But it became exciting by itself because of two people who influenced me greatly: Professor Labdhi Bhandari (who had earlier worked with Levers) and Subroto Sengupta from advertising".

At placement, on the first day, Lintas made an offer while Levers selected him for the final round to be in Mumbai ten days later. Anand took the Lintas option. It was a hugely exciting place at that time, led by Alyque Padamsee.

Anand joined the research division of Lintas and quickly fell in love with advertising. He spent three years understanding consumers and seeing that understanding get translated into great advertising. He then switched to client servicing and account management in the front line.

The idea of 'account planning' as a function was beginning to take root with JWT internationally. Anand tried to implement it at Lintas India but it did not quite happen. So after 8 years with the company he left.

After short stints at agencies like Clarion and Rediffusion, Anand joined Enterprise. The year was 1988.

Enterprise was an agency run by the charismatic Mohammed Khan. Earlier Khan, along with Ajit Balakrishnan and Arun Nanda had set up Rediffusion. In 1983, he started Enterprise,an agency with a distinct identity and flavour of advertising.

"I saw the quality of work the relatively smaller and higher risk-taking agencies were doing. The JWTs and the Lintas types were guided by the formulae that their major clients had laid down – the Unilever way of doing advertising, for example."

"The other interesting thing that Mohammed had said and which stuck in my mind was that if you have pots of money, you don't need good advertising. You can just hurl enough advertising rupees at the customer, until almost in sheer panic, the consumer gives up and says okay, I surrender".

'Washing powder Nirma' is one such example, he says.

To Anand, the heart and soul of being in the advertising business was what you do that finally connects you with the customer! All the rest is background music. That's what attracted him to join Enterprise – Mohammed Khan essentially believed the same thing.

But what role would a management graduate play in an agency where the creative process was placed on a pedestal?

Well-wishers told Anand joining Enterprise was not a good idea. You represent the left brain and Mohammed Khan represents the right brain. The twain shall have fireworks, but it's unlikely to be a partnership, they said.

But Anand was something of a maverick.

"I had never found management education interfering with my need to be wacky. Besides I had always found that if your end goal is the same, there isn't any conflict. Even with the nuttiest creative people in Lintas, I got along very well. So I said, there is no reason why it shouldn't happen here."

The partnership actually flourished. The formula went like this: If there was a disagreement regarding the 'What' of the communication, Mohammed would go by what Anand had to say. If the disagreement was regarding the 'How' part, Anand would go by what Mohammed had to say.

"For instance, should the proposition be built around durability, or style? That would come out of understanding the customer and I would have the last call on that decision. Whether we should take a more serious approach, or emotional approach – that was Mohammed's decision. Because that is a finally an intuitive call on what is it that people will respond to."

An example of the work produced by this left brain-right brain partnership was the promotion of egg consumption for the National Egg Co-ordination Committee that Enterprise did for ten years. In fact the line "*Sunday ho ya Monday roz khao anday*" written by Anand became part of popular folklore.

There was also an education component on the nutritive value of eggs, and a recipe campaign suggesting how you could make eggs in different ways. It was a 360 degree approach to communication which Anand would later implement in his own company chlorophyll.

In 1994 Anand became a director at Enterprise advertising and even got an ownership stake. By this time all leading agencies had sold part of their stake to a multinational agency. Mohammed Khan was one of the last legends in Indian advertising who had still not made his millions.

"So there was this sense, though he didn't say it in so many words, that I am missing the bus! We told him, selling out is not such a good idea."

Enterprise embodied the whole spirit of doing your own thing, and not having to work on quarter by quarter performance review of billings. The multinational, billings-driven agency is a different work style altogether. You can't start doing it when you are 53 years old.

"The buffer that we talk about is having enough money in the bank to pay fixed expenses for two months. You need to have it at any given point."

But Mohammed took his chances and began discussions with London-based Lowe. Meanwhile, another small agency called Nexus, started by IIMA graduate Rajiv Agarwal was also speaking with Lowe.

When a merger happened in 1996, Enterprise Nexus Communications came into being. It had three major shareholders – the founders of Enterprise, founders of Nexus and Lowe.

The merger was a disaster from the word go. Mohammed and Rajiv had a personality clash, and their work styles were vastly different. One was more laissez faire, while the other had a high need for control. When people from both sides began working together, there was pandemonium.

Mohammed could not accept the much younger Rajiv as an equal. He was also used to running the agency in a fashion where there was no need to be answerable to anybody. The foreign partner quickly started breathing down their necks for quarterly results.

There were other, practical issues. Nexus was a smaller agency with a higher salary cost for a smaller number of people. The salaries of people who had worked for Enterprise had to be raised to match this. So, on day one, costs went up by 30 per cent.

On top of that there was no new business coming in. Lowe had a 24% stake but no international clients who could quickly be realigned and fall into the new agency's kitty. In fact, Enterprise Nexus lost one of its biggest accounts, Raymonds, within the first 6 months.

Another disturbing thing happened – a large number of people got sacked because you didn't need two people to do the same job in the merged entity. "The owners have screwed up and the burden of that has been put on somebody else," Anand thought to himself.

The high price of 'growth at any cost' became very clear to Anand. It was a lesson that would stay with him.

Anand stayed with Enterprise Nexus for a year and a half. The agency actually shrank in this period.

What next? Entrepreneurship had never been on Anand's mind. He was an advertising professional with two decades' experience so he explored options in advertising. Lintas was in the process of buying Pratibha – a family-owned agency of the Kirloskar group and they made Anand an offer.

"Lintas wanted Pratibha to get used to international norms and I was given the job because I was familiar with the Lintas system and am a Maharashtrian. Remember, Kirloskar is essentially a Pune agency. So it was thought they would be comfortable with me."

Most second or third agencies are clones of the mother brand and designed to handle 'competing business'. Anand thought the sensible thing to do was to position Pratibha differently. He took up the offer to run Pratibha.

"The working title of my presentation to Geetanjali Kirloskar and Prem Mehta was: 'The Agency for the Rest of Us'. By that I meant the agency for those who are not in South Bombay. And my idea was to build a second network in Pune, in Nagpur, in Jaipur, in Kanpur, which is essentially staffed by regional language creative directors. Not the smooth-talking South Bombay culture represented by Lintas."

The idea was shot down.

"That's when I said, 'The time has come to get out of this circuit. Somebody else is going to run the agenda as long as you are not driving it.' This was the first time the thought came to mind: 'Let me become an entrepreneur.'"

"At Enterprise, for those 11 years, I actually had the best of both worlds. We were not owned by an international network, so we had complete freedom. By temperament Mohammed

> **As Jay Chiat of Chiat Day (the agency which produced memorable commercials for the likes of Apple and Nike) once said: "How big can we get before we get bad!" Chiat Day had only four very large clients.**

did not want to get into decisions like whether to open new branches or not, whether to have a new PR division or not, whether to start production of television commercials or not. All these were my decisions. So, I had the advantage and freedom to do all that. It was great fun".

But that freedom was no more and it was unlikely that Anand would get such a role in any agency now because it was a whole new era. All the big agencies were owned by the international networks. They were subject to the same kind of pressures.

After a year shuttling between Mumbai and Pune (where Pratibha was based), Anand decided it was time to branch out on his own.

"So you became an entrepreneur out of circumstance?" I ask.

"You will have to say that".

"It's not as if you had a great desire to be one?"

"No."

A decade later, of course, there are absolutely no regrets.

The decision to take the plunge was all very well but what would the enterprise do? Anand had ruled out the agency option. Even as he was toying with ideas he got a call from old friend Kiran Khalap, the CEO and CCO of advertising agency Clarion.

It was 11 pm and Kiran asked: "Are you enjoying your work?"

"Absolutely not," replied Anand.

Kiran was experiencing the same sense of 'this is no fun', as

Clarion had been bought over by an international company (Bates). So Anand and Kiran sat down and formulated a plan. They would start a communications consultancy with a difference.

The first thing they decided was that they would work not on commissions, but for a fee.

Because that would free them to focus on unadulterated communication.

"For example, if a client comes out with a great throat lozenge, maybe the best thing to do would be to just distribute it to any guy you see at the *paanwallah* buying a 20s packet of cigarettes because he is going to have a throat problem. But you can never suggest that if you are working on a commission basis because there is no billing in it. So you say, let's do a television film."

The second key difference would be the direct involvement of the top management with every client and campaign.

"In the agency business, the most experienced and knowledgeable resources actually spend most of their time on admin work. Such as in recruitment and replacement of people. Managing ego conflicts and hassles. Worrying about collections. So you actually spend much less time in rolling up your sleeves and doing your work. That is left to the next rung."

No wonder people actually lose the initial joy they felt working in advertising. And this phenomenon applies to every industry but the sense of loss is all the more acute if it happens to a creative professional.

There were five people in the founding team: Anand, Kiran, an art director (Nalesh), copywriter (Gangadharan) and an account planner (Manjunath Hegde). It was thus not accident but design that ensured chlorophyll would not be a very large company.

"My view about the communications business is that finally it depends on human skills, and those cannot be replicated and cloned. So the growth of this company can only be up to human scale."

"The name chlorophyll embodies our core values: creativity and efficiency. The molecule is exceedingly efficient because it uses every photon and it is creative because it combines two unrelated things – carbon dioxide and water – to create something new."

As Jay Chiat of Chiat Day (the agency which produced memorable commercials for the likes of Apple and Nike) once said: "How big can we get before we get bad!" Chiat Day had only four very large clients.

Well and good, but how did chlorophyll actually get started?

The easiest way to get business is to steal some clients from your former agency.

Anand and Kiran had decided they would not talk to these clients for at least 6 months.

"We did one thing that was quite unusual for setting up a new place. We launched on 15 August, Independence Day. So the party was on 14th night, 1999. Madan Bahal, a friend who owned Adfactors, said I am going to give you great PR coverage. And chlorophyll got great PR coverage."

Anand and Kiran called all their past associates, co-workers, clients etc. The first inquiry came from Marico. The company was developing a new Parachute variant and soon after gave some work on Sweekar cooking oil as well.

The Parachute launch included coming up with the brand name, packaging, positioning, everything. Just the kind of work chlorophyll had set out to do. Whereas Sweekar was the usual advertising campaign only. But Rome was not built in a day; they took both assignments.

However there were problems. Although chlorophyll had a flat structure, Marico was a hierarchy. Anand and Kiran found themselves interacting with product executives. And there was an expectation that they would be available anytime, anywhere for meetings – that's how client and agency traditionally functioned.

The biggest problem was the assumption that because you are a small agency, your cost structure is low, and therefore your fees should be low.

The sheer operational pressure made by an advertising account was huge. There was another issue. "We didn't want to go the advertising path because we had seen, in a business downturn, you are taking on the responsibility for your employees' lives. And we are not human beings who can go home and sleep after sacking five people and say, 'Screw you, buddy, fend for yourself'!"

"It took all of 3 years, from 1999 to 2002, to figure out what areas made both creative and economic sense for the company. chlorophyll found its niche by focusing on brand and corporate identity – a completely new and virgin territory.

Luckily for all concerned, 1999-2000 was a period when many people were setting up internet-based companies. And there were enough VCs throwing money at them. So the need for corporate identity was going through an absolute boom – chlorophyll did 20 brand identities in 18 months.

chlorophyll also worked on projects stretching over a longer period of time. The Taj budget hotels project for example was spread over two and a half years. It was also decided that at any point, the company should have a retainer business that would take care of 30 per cent of costs. So there should be at least some cushion.

The idea was to be small but viable. The founding team decided that at the end of 18 months, there must be at least one rupee of profit. And this was after all the partners took a salary equal to their last paycheque prior to joining chlorophyll. Any surplus would be shared by the partners. Yet they would not pressure themselves to take on any and every business.

Clarity of thought on what the company should do meant saying 'no' to certain kinds of business. But over time clients respected this approach, and the kind of business chlorophyll desired came in through client recommendations and word of mouth.

With time chlorophyll did expand to 18-odd people. But they did not hire the standard agency types. The idea was to get on board people from interactive media, packaging design or with an understanding of the mobile and web world.

Much of this talent was drawn from colleges where Anand and Kiran gave lectures, as well as former colleagues who had pleasant memories of working with them. Of course the attraction of the quality of work they would do was also huge.

Attrition is not much of an issue.

The chlorophyll office is such a pleasant place I am not surprised. It's trendy without being wannabe, a place where thoughts and ideas float in the air and people seem to be genuinely happy.

Great, but coming back to the money aspect...

"Madan Bahal once said something very interesting: 'You don't make big money by doing more work. You make big money by selling companies'. And that is not our objective."

In 2007, chlorophyll generated ₹ 5 crore in fees. Most agencies still report a turnover in the form of gross billings, on which they earn anything from 2 to 15%. A '₹ 100-crore' agency may actually only be making a profit of ₹ 3-5 crore. So chlorophyll is a profitable agency, but prefers to use different yardsticks to measure that profitability. "Instead of per capita billing, we use 'per rupee manpower'. How productive is each rupee of manpower?, we ask."

Ultimately this is a case of small by choice not by default or the result of a 'failed attempt to scale'. Every decision is driven by the satisfaction levels as well as lifestyle desired by the entrepreneurs. It's a space they have created where they can just be, not forced to be.

"I think we smile a lot more. I don't think we have had so much fun on a day to day, month to month basis as we had at chlorophyll. Because there is no source of stress. We don't have any external masters whose wishes have to be fulfilled, if we don't want to take on any projects we simply don't."

"We use three yardsticks and we know it is very unlikely that any project will fulfill all three. But let's hope for at least two in every project. If it's only one, then it better be superlative on that one dimension. And the dimensions are: *It must give us money, or it must give us fame, or it must give us great joy.*"

So there are projects chlorophyll has done for the fun aspect. Because they like the idea, or the people. "For example we are working for the Maharana of Udaipur, looking after his 'brand'. Is it great amounts of money? No. But it's great fun... How many chaps can say my client is the 76th in the line of kings of Mewar, unbroken from 734 AD? And I was having a cup of tea with him last week."

And in the midst of all this, Anand also managed to write a book, *Planning for Power Advertising.* "It's a textbook in communication courses. I know for sure, there is no way in which I would have been able to write that book if I was working and reporting to Hongkong or APAC or whatever it is."

Reporting to your own conscience is the highest and most rewarding form of servitude. And you can even make a good living out of it!

<u>ADVICE TO YOUNG ENTREPRENEURS</u>

Goals

* Follow your heart. (The brain can do many things, but only the heart can answer the meaningful questions of life!)

* Think of the intangibles you value first – and let them determine the tangibles. (Steve Jobs and Michael Dell are driven by different intangibles...figure out who you'd rather be.)

* Don't defer your joy at a beach today, for some imagined future weekend in Acapulco – by the time that happens your diabetes may not let you enjoy the pina coladas.

Money

* Money is not an end in itself. (Anu Aga, ex-Chairperson, Thermax, once said: "Profits are important but not the only thing... without breathing, you and I can't live, but if you ask me what is the purpose of my life and if I say breathing, it is such a narrow way to define it.")

* Create love and affection in your workplace. (People give up their lives for what they love but no one will do it for an EBIDTA.)

People and values

* Surround yourself with like-minded people. (You can't plan together, if the guys at the table are Gautam Buddha and Genghis Khan.)

* Define your Do's and Don't's, before you start. Post-facto, any act can be justified.

* No deal is worth losing your self-respect.

The last word

* Finally, if you don't laugh enough, your business model is probably wrong!

A SENSE OF OWNERSHIP

S B Dangayach (PGP '72), Sintex

He is not the owner of the company but in every other sense works like an entrepreneur. The man behind the iconic Sintex water tanks believes in constant evolution and creation of new products. And after 34 years with one company he is still passionate about it!

It is a bit of a shock when you are interviewing someone for a book on entrepreneurship and the very first sentence he utters is: "I'm sure you know… I don't own this company, but in every other sense I am an entrepreneur."

Honestly, I did not know, and that's why you were shorlisted, sir. But I am intrigued and we get on with the interview. And I am glad, because Mr S B Dangayach of Sintex is a truly fascinating subject.

Management books often talk about being 'entrepreneurial' within a large company. Some refer to this as being 'intrapreneurial'. Both terms sound like terms from a Dilbert comic strip, to keep cubicle workers happy.

The idea of an 'entrepreneur' who is not an owner but completely synonymous with the success of the company seems equally farfetched. Sure, anyone from a trainee to the CEO can feel a sense of 'ownership'. But for how long? 3 years, 5 years, 8 years?

S B Dangayach has been with Sintex for 34 years. As he tells me the story of how he built this company he has all the fire, the feeling and all the fondness of a founder.

Like a parent who deeply loves an adopted child and believes this is his own flesh and blood.

In the cutt-hroat world of business, a rare and beautiful thing.

A SENSE OF OWNERSHIP

S B Dangayach (PGP '72), Sintex

S B Dangayach grew up in Rajasthan. After completing his graduation from Bombay he joined IIM Ahmedabad, and then Asian Paints. The year was 1972.

"Asian Paints was a very famous company back then… It was structured and very well managed. The company had fantastic systems, it had fantastic controls – they were ahead of even Hindustan Lever in some of those areas."

Asian Paints was a very prestigious job to join at that time. And Dangayach is surprised that they actually took him. The job profile mentioned that only engineers with an MBA will be considered. Dangayach was a science graduate. Nevertheless, he applied.

He was asked: "You are not an engineer. How do you justify being here?" And he had a simple answer: "Many of the engineers who are from IIT take lessons from me in subjects like OR, and quantitative methods." It was an audacious but true statement and should have got him the job.

But there were further doubts, regarding his age. Dangayach was not even eighteen when he joined IIM. He was in fact under 20 when he sat for placement.

The interviewer, one Mr Chari, asked: "You are such a young boy, how can you justify being here?"

Dangayach replied, "Youth is on my side and the fact that I have competed with so many older people and succeeded should tell you that I must have something in me."

A third question was asked: "You are a Marwari. Marwaris never work for too long with anybody. They go off to set up their own business."

Dangayach's answer to that was: "I don't value money as much as Marwaris do. If you give me an independent workplace, I will be all right."

He secured the job. A trait you see in so many entrepreneurs: when they really want something, they fight against the odds and get it!

Dangayach worked at Asian Paints for two years but he was not very happy. The company had been in business for 30 years and was a leader in the paint industry by that point of time. There was little freedom or latitude to think independently, or innovatively. The young MBA – like most young MBAs – felt constrained.

Dangayach realised that working at such a place was not conducive to his temperament.

Through an ad on the notice board of IIM Ahmedabad he first learnt of an opening at a company called the Bharat Vijay Mills Pvt Ltd. It was a textile company starting a small division in plastics.

"I applied and I obviously got a chance because there was no other person who was willing to join Bharat Vijay Mills," he says with a twinkle in his eye.

Bharat Vijay Mills was located around 30 kilometres away from Ahmedabad in a mofussil town called Kalol. It was a small place but that's precisely why it attracted Dangayach. He had seen life in the 'big' lane and knew his future lay elsewhere.

Bharat Vijay Mills was focused on textiles. With an eye on the future, the company thought of venturing into chemicals and plastics. The idea was to put up small ventures which somebody could manage as an SBU. For the plastics division that person was to be Dangayach.

"The Patel family promised me latitude, freedom of action. Once I proved myself, there would be no interference from the owners."

The business was started with a seed capital of ₹ 30 lakh. And within a few months, Dangayach had built an excellent equation with the Patels.

"I was comfortable, they were comfortable. And since then I have been continuing and it has been almost thirty-three years that I have been here. And obviously I have been managing the business like any entrepreneur will manage, barring the fact that the entrepreneur sometimes puts in his own money."

Dangayach put in no money and owns an insignificant amount of shares. His kick was to manage the business independently and autonomously. And he got that.

Joining as marketing officer in September 1974, Dangayach was promised 'complete charge' – if he proved himself. And that's what happened. By December, he was made General Manager. Of course there was no great structure in the company. So it was more an endorsement of the fact that a 22-year-old can manage all the functions – manufacturing, marketing, finance, accounts.

The entire gamut of business decisions from which products to make, the strategy to follow, securing the finance from institutions like GSFC, putting the production team together – everything was in Dangayach's hands.

And there was no interference?

"Once I convinced them that I can manage, they played only a notional role."

The irony is that the small plastics division Dangayach took charge of became so big that Bharat Vijay Mills became synonymous with it. The name of the company was one day to change to 'Sintex'.

The name 'Sintex' comes from 'sintering', which is a process. It was also apt because it combined the two products of Bharat Vijay Mills – sintering and textiles.

What's more, it seemed easy to pronounce, easy to recall.

Today the brand 'Sintex' is synonymous with plastic water tanks. Almost like Xerox with xeroxing. But Sinter Plast containers actually came into existence to make industrial

> **"People know my integrity, people who are into headhunting do not approach me ever. Possibly they have some report about me, some reference about me, so they are aware of what reaction they may get."**

articles for the textile industry. Things like 'card cans' which are meant to handle cotton slivers.

But as luck would have it, the company did not succeed in marketing card cans. So it had to think of some other use for the plant. Sintex diversified into industrial containers – for storage, transportation, processing and material handling.

It became a decent-sized business. In 1975, Sintex did a turnover of ₹ 3 lakh. The next year the company did twenty lakh, then sixty lakh. In 1977 they had achieved break even.

"So we thought why not use this process for making something which has a bigger application?" And thus both a water tank and an enduring philosophy was born.

The moment one product stabilises, think of something new!

But how does one come up with ideas?

"We had a rotational moulding plant, which is very good for making hollow articles, especially large ones. The shape reminded me of a water tank. So I thought, why not try that product."

Of course, a lot of thinking went into the design and market analysis. They talked to government officials, water bodies experts, building research institutes, building organisations – all kinds of people. Everyone expressed the need to look beyond cement and steel water tanks. However, when the company conducted a market survey it found that there was no market for plastic tanks. At least not at the price proposed by Sintex.

But Dangayach believed in the product. Sintex defied conventional thinking and went ahead. Willing to lose money in the initial period, if necessary.

There were no other competitors, which was both good and bad. Sintex created a new product category altogether and spent the next 4-5 years doing aggressive marketing. Side-stepping the obvious target group and focusing on actual end users.

"Architects are the people who design buildings. So we talked to a few of them to get a reaction. We soon realised that architects are very individualistic and artistic kind of people. They did not like the idea of an oddly shaped black tank on top of their buildings!"

So Dangayach decided to address a different kind of user: the government. There was a mandate from the government of India to look at substitutes for cement and steel, so *sarkaari* departments were willing to look at Sintex. Structural engineers and project engineers were also more open to change, because of the bad experiences that they'd had with the other tanks.

Meanwhile through advertising and publicity Sintex kept building up public awareness about the plastic tank being leakage free and corrosion free. There were issues of hygiene, contamination and also the effect of cement tanks on the building structure.

It's hard to believe for those of us who grew up in a later era and saw Sintex tanks on the top of every building. We never stopped to think whether they were ugly! We simply accepted that water has to be stored and this is the way to do it.

It pays to push an idea ahead of its time if you genuinely believe it addresses a pain-point with your customer. Getting the initial momentum may be an effort but then it simply takes off!

It was a difficult five-year period. Even as Sintex water tanks were in the 'educate the customer' phase, the industrial products business continued. But that's the interesting thing about Dangayach. There's a bee in his bonnet that keeps buzzing.

"If you ask me, I have been a serial entrepreneur. We have come up with new things every 2-3 years and there are quite a few things that we are doing that we couldn't have imagined

> **"I have a very simple mantra which is to combine four I's. The first I is Initiative. Second I is Intelligence, correct choices. Third is Industry, which is obviously hard work. Fourth I is Integrity. I work with total integrity. If I take up something, either I will give my whole of it, or I will not take it up."**

10 or 15 years ago. So it is the question of coming up with something different, something that is challenging, that is creatively satisfying."

Dangayach believes an entrepreneur must constantly play the role of 'trinity'. On the one hand you have to realise which products are not working or declining and eventually get rid of those lines. Simultaneously you need something which can sustain the current revenues and something which can be big in the future.

So from industrial products to plastic water tanks – what next? Sintex decided to get into another building-related product. Something which could be a substitute for timber and wood. In 1984-85, the company created a whole new category of products based around plastic extrusions and then forayed into plastic doors, partitions and windows.

"We succeeded in doors, we succeeded in the profiles that can go for panelling and partition. But we did not succeed in PVC windows. It has been almost 20 years and we are still struggling with plastic windows."

PVC windows are the number one windows worldwide – in the US, UK, Germany, China. Dangayach hasn't lost hope yet. The market just wasn't ready.

"First we positioned it as a higher-end product, then we positioned it as an energy-saving window, then we positioned it as something which can substitute aluminium. We said it is going to be colourful, it is going to be better, etc etc. So far we have not succeeded. It has been a dormant line, just doing marginal business."

Twenty years of struggle with this product, and yet he isn't quite ready to give up. And maybe he will be proven right. With energy conservation becoming a central issue in building design, the plastic window is poised to take off once again.

The ability to take risks, the courage to admit your mistakes and the gumption to 'think big' are the hallmark of any entrepreneur. And Dangayach has all those qualities.

He's not stuck to the idea of plastic, for example. The next big thing, he thinks, is prefabricated buildings. These could be PVC, concrete, metal or cement sandwich panels.

"We are realising that we need not be stuck to one set of materials. We are now material agnostic and technology agnostic. The key thing is to work in areas which are appropriate for the overall environment and which will have a very good future."

Already, Sintex is a leader in small to medium-sized prefabricated structures in the country. Prefabricated schools, prefabricated houses, prefabricated medical centres – that is what Dangayach believes is the future.

And as the original business of water tanks becomes hypercompetitive and commoditised, one man can sleep without any worries…

Clearly Dangayach is the prime thinker and mover at Sintex. What kind of technology should be selected, what product lines, what marketing strategies, what finance should be brought in – he is integral to everything. So what is the role played by the owners?

"We don't have a structured understanding but there is a tacit understanding that I am a person with an entrepreneurial bent of mind. The promoters – Mr Dinesh Patel and Mr Arun Patel – share a very good chemistry with me. That chemistry gives them the confidence that here is a guy who is not going to give a wrong suggestion."

"And obviously I have got the necessary reasoning for it. It may not be a very long report. We sit for half an hour, an hour, relevant questions are shared and we take a decision. Often it is a very informal decision taken over a cup of tea or lunch.

Within fifteen minutes, we decide that this is what we want to do, fund calculations are made and naturally, periodic meetings are held as well."

That's the kind of rapport few partners in business share these days – not even brothers!

Another milestone for the company was a private equity investment by Indocean in 1998-99. The fund, headed by Pradip Shah, zeroed in on Sintex as they believed it would grow in value. And that further value would be unlocked over a period of time. At that time, the turnover of Sintex was around ₹ 170 crore.

Indocean wanted Dangayach to be with the company as a 'promoter'. "The agreement mentioned 'us', meaning the owning family (the Patels) and I."

"So at that point you became more of an official owner," I ask.

"No, I am not an owner," he reiterates

"But you have an ownership stake."

"No, it is very nominal. But, I behave like an owner. The point is that even without the ownership, you try to bring in the best to your job. That is what I have been doing… Money is not very important to me in my personal life, barring a certain level. Money has never driven me, or what I will be doing next."

It's the 'open format' of work which excites Dangayach. And the format has worked for all concerned.

Some years ago the company changed its name from Bharat Vijay Mills to 'Sintex', taking advantage of the brand name recall enjoyed by its most famous product. This year the Sintex plastics division will cross ₹ 1,000* crore in turnover. 70% of the company's revenues come from this division. The remaining comes from the textiles division, which is managed by the Patel family.

"We have divided our responsibilities. That is why all of us have space and all of us have independence and autonomy.

* Sintex Industries' net profit was ₹216.33 crore on a total income of ₹1,700.26 crore in the year ended March 2008.

I have autonomy in my domain. We must have made many wrong moves. And we have made some correct moves. Overall we are doing all right."

A typically understated statement!

Apart from the fantastic symbiotic relationship Dangayach has sustained with his promoters (or 'venture capitalists' so to speak) it's fascinating to observe how his mind works. Every product idea he thinks of is linked to macro trends.

With prefab, the vision is linked to the idea of affordable housing. And to make prefab more viable Sintex has pioneered a method of rapid construction. Utilising a plastic former, they created the idea of 'monolithic concrete construction'. All the walls, the roof, the partition, the loft – everything is cast in one shot. It is literally casting the house on the construction site, in one single shot, out of concrete.

An entire floor can be completed in 4-5 days. The method has been implemented in Ahmedabad, and other areas of Gujarat. There is a mandate from the government to construct 10,000 such houses in Delhi. Given the focus on slum redevelopment in all major metros, this could be a huge opportunity. It is, Dangayach believes, the most cost-effective method of creating mass housing.

As with the water tanks, it is the government which is adopting the innovation before the private sector. An insight which could benefit other entrepreneurs.

Dangayach adds: "See, the government today is the biggest buyer. Within the government, I would say some of the engineers, some of the key decision-makers, are as efficient and open to accepting new ideas as in the private sector. From my experience I can say that on many occasions it is easier to convince them."

As for ideas, Dangayach admits he's had a lot of pet projects which have not worked.

"Solar water heating is very dear to my heart. I have been thinking that we should be giving cost-effective, affordable, solar water heating solutions in the country. Copper was very expensive so we thought why not make it out of plastic. I designed such a product with the help of my team. We made the panel out of black plastic as it absorbs better."

The water tank for the heating system was made out of plastic as well. It resulted in a sizeable business 3-4 years ago.

The company sold 10-12,000 units a year. But servicing and issues like installation and leakage became problems. So the product was withdrawn. But it is now being relaunched.

"My idea was that if Israel can have a solar water system in every house, Turkey can have, Greece can have, Cyprus can have, why not at least in some parts of India which have abundant sunshine and a similar temperature profile?"

You would think, to achieve all this, Sintex must have a crack R&D set up. The reality is, a small team makes it happen.

"Many a times, I am functioning as an ideation man and as a designing person. I am a 'fraud engineer' (grins), so I also help with how an idea has to be taken through the process of engineering, and converted into a product. I also look at the after sales service aspect."

"If a solar water heater does not work for two days, the housewife is generally going to make a noise about it. So there are going to be quality issues, there are going to be service issues. We need to go through all that, but I don't have a big team."

The company's mission statement is 'meaningful innovations.' Any domain it works in must have a large and relevant problem affecting the masses. One such idea is a 'rainwater harvesting system' providing a total solution to water problems.

Of course it's also a huge business opportunity. "This may turn out to be a big growth driver for our core product of water tanks. Today people buy a tank of 1,000 litres for 3,000 rupees. If I give a rain water harvesting system, then you need a tank of 7,000 litres, and the entire system may cost ₹ 60,000. If that succeeds, we will have a fantastic business model!"

Dangayach's eyes shine as he explains how it's all going to work:

"We can create a very durable, underground water storage

structure at a very reasonable cost, for a multi-storeyed building. Under a parking lot! Not from concrete, we will create from something else. We have already devised a special technology, we have already validated it."

"I feel very passionately about each of these things. That is the reason why we keep on innovating."

And passion as they say is infectious. On a flight, a couple of days before our interview, Dangayach met the legendary architect B V Doshi and got him interested in green building materials.

I find it amazing that a grey-haired, fifty-plus man is still so excited about his company and its many businesses after a stint of 35 years. And I hate to repeat it, but it's not even his own company, technically speaking. 'Actually neither is it the Patels'. Over 50% of Sintex is now 'owned' by FIIs, funds and other investors.

Dangayach makes one final attempt to clear the conundrum: "We associate ownership with the money. Correct or not! You feel that you have probably 30-40-50 per cent stake. And you continue with the thought that this is what is making you powerful."

"But if I am able to take an idea, maybe take a project, which I can nurture, which I can grow, which I can take forward, I think it's as good as what an owner would be doing. The profit motive is probably making him work an hour or two hours more. I can assure you, that on all these ideas, my work is no less than anybody who is driven by or who is crazy about money."

Amen to that.

ADVICE TO YOUNG ENTREPRENEURS

I think, first of all, you should do what you like the best of all. Number one. Then there should be convergence and there should be compatibility with what you think your conscience tells you, and what you want to do.

I do what my conscience tells me to do. That is what I mean by integrity, total integrity. That is what I advise young people as well.

BASIC
INSTINCT

Vijay Mahajan (PGP '81),
Basix

An IIT-IIM graduate, Vijay has devoted his life to addressing issues of inequality and social justice but through management techniques. He pioneered the concept of microfinance in India through an organisation called Basix which gives loans to the rural poor.

Entrepreneurship is generally associated with money. Lots of it.

But just about every entrepreneur I interviewed went to great pains to explain that the thought of making more money is not what charged them up each morning. Money is important for what it allows you to do as a company. But it's not what makes you fall asleep soundly each night.

All these entrepreneurs, whether in the business of sugar, retailing groceries or job listings actually derive meaning from the impact their business makes on people's lives – the jobs they create, the value they deliver, the good work they do in the communities they serve directly or indirectly.

What if the equation was turned on its head? What if making a social impact was the primary indication of one's 'success' and money became incidental, although important in order to keep the good work going?

Vijay Mahajan is a living answer to those questions. Dressed in the trademark Fabindia handloom *kurta* he looks every bit the social worker. But the work he does is what any MBA could be doing: addressing a need gap in the market. It's just that his market is one which was never thought to be worth addressing.

Ten years before C K Prahalad came along and sexed up the whole notion of serving the 'bottom of the pyramid', Vijay had established an organisation doing just that. Basix is not the biggest institution of its kind but it created the culture of microfinance in the country.

And like any other new idea, it took one man's strength of conviction and perseverance of spirit to get it accepted. This is the story of what it means to stick to what you believe in, not for months or years but as long as it takes.

BASIC
INSTINCT

Vijay Mahajan (PGP '81),
Basix

Vijay Mahajan was not born or brought up differently from the rest of us.

"I don't think I have had any strong role models either on entrepreneurship or social entrepreneurship within my immediate or even my extended family. My father was a civilian in the army, my mother was at home. I had three elder brothers, all in the defence services. In fact if anything, we are a *fauji* family, that's where I should have gone."

Instead, by the time he graduated from IIM Ahmedabad Vijay was sure about what he wanted to do: address the issues of inequality and social justice.

There was no eureka moment, the process of sensitisation took many years and many forms.

"I finished school and my last five years were in St Xavier's in Jaipur – a Jesuit school. My first encounter with poverty, rural people, the concept of social service, happened at this school."

There was a period called 'Character'. During the character period, students would go to the general hospital once in a week. Their job was to go around wards and ask patients if they needed something – any letters to be written home or medicine to be bought.

But this is hindsight. Back then, life continued on the generally prescribed course. Vijay joined IIT Delhi after completing his schooling. 1970-75 was a time of great turmoil in India, as well as globally. India went to war over Bangladesh and in 1973 there was the Navanirman movement in Gujarat followed by Jaya Prakash Narayan's 'Total Revolution'.

Vijay was just a regular student, not an activist of any sort. But there was a certain let-us-do-good feeling in the air and the influence of Schumacher who wrote *Small is Beautiful*.

"There was this view among some of us, idealistic fellows, that technology can solve a lot of problems. So it was with this belief that one started going to villages and looking for technology solutions." It was something a group of IITians did off and on, during their summer holidays.

But after graduating, Vijay continued on the straight and normal path. He worked with the marketing department of Philips in eastern India. The job involved a lot of travel through the hinterland.

"In those days, Bihar, Orissa, Bengal, the North East were quite poor. Like Satyajit Ray's movies. I was already sensitised to so many issues, so there was this continuous inner dialogue going on."

What to do? Where to start doing it? Around three years into the job Vijay decided he would work in development on a full-time basis. But he could not actually make the switch. Blame it on 'middle class insecurity', he says.

At the same time Vijay had heard of Prof Ravi Mathai who had stepped aside as the director of IIMA and had started the Jawaja project. "So I said let me go to IIMA. It will be a) career insurance, and b) in the best case, I might work with Ravi and his colleague Prof Ranjit Gupta and understand rural development better."

"So you can say by the time I went to IIMA, I had made up my mind 80 per cent that this is what I will do. I was more than quite sure."

While at IIMA, Vijay basically 'freaked out' and took full advantage of the flexibility of the course. "I did a lot of projects, did my summer job at Jawaja in south Rajasthan and essentially converted the programme into a kind of a self-learning and development to the extent one can learn in theory".

But even after completing the programme, there was never the thought that "I must start something of my own." What Vijay did realise after years of volunteer work was this: the people behind NGOs were good-hearted but their organisations were not professionally run. So he chose to join an organisation called FAIR (Foundation to Aid Industrial Recovery) started by Dr NCB Nath.

FAIR's main objective was to revive sick industries and they had a bunch of IIMA graduates of the previous batch, involved in this effort. But Dr Nath was also interested in doing something on the development sector and he offered Vijay a role in that area.

"I was there for a year and undertook many studies. But my heart wasn't into it. I didn't want to be a consultant on development. I wanted to do something on the ground."

In 1982, Vijay got to know a Gandhian NGO called ASSEFA – (Association for Sarva Seva Farms). The organisation helped farmers who received land from Vinoba Bhave's *Bhoodan* movement to make a living. Vijay joined to provide 'technical and management assistance' which would make the donated land economically viable.

A lot of poor-quality land was given by landlords to landless labourers during the famous *Bhoodan* movement. Basically it was a *patta* or title which was handed over. But someone needs to invest in levelling the land, arranging for irrigation and then starting cultivation with seeds, plough and bullocks. Only then will a landless labourer get converted into a small farmer. And you are not doing this with one person at a time, but a whole community with sixty, eighty, sometimes a hundred people.

Vijay worked in 15-20 villages with around 1000 households, the idea being to use capital investment to bring the people to a level where they made a steady income. Over a period of time they would repay the loan and the capital would then be used to help other farmers. This would make the entire process a sustainable one.

Sounds very sensible but it was not at all easy!

"When I took over the Bihar projects, all the money had already been spent," recalls Vijay. "But there were no benefits because of poor planning and implementation."

> **"You go through several years of either nothing significant happening or you actually have setbacks. For me, there have been blockages in going forward rather than going back. But I know of several entrepreneurs who have had severe setbacks. Basically they bounce back."**

For example, they had put six borewells, but they had not put the last mile of pipeline. So there was no water. 95% of the investment had been made, but with 0% result. And it was a vicious circle. Since there was no water, the farmers had no incentive to level the land. And of course they were already facing the burden of taking a bank loan.

"When we turned up in those villages, they were ready to hit me. They wailed, '*Aapne to hamko dooba diya. Koi kaam bhi nahi hua aur karza bhi hua.*'"

Vijay and his team got down to work – identified the needs, basic issues and somehow managed to get additional funding to fix them. Once you do that, the whole virtuous cycle starts.

"In fact it was a very bad situation. I managed to turn around one village first. Once that happened, the word spread and I became more welcome in other villages."

It was an important lesson in how to tackle the grassroots reality of development. Simply wanting to 'do good' is no good until you approach a problem systematically and sustainably.

Even as he toiled with ASSEFA Vijay had in his mind the concept for an organisation called 'PRADAN' 'Professional Assistance for Development Action'. Along with the Mr Loganathan (founder of ASSEFA) and Deep Joshi, who worked with the Ford Foundation, Vijay developed the i dea further.

In 1983 PRADAN was born, to spread the idea of 'on ground technical and management assistance' to many more NGOs. Several professionals joined PRADAN, excited by this mission.

"Even in those days professionals were more expensive than volunteers, so we decided to take a one-third cut in our salary. Of the remaining amount half was paid by the institution using our services and half by PRADAN using a Ford Foundation grant."

"PRADAN was an attempt at helping NGOs do what they are doing more effectively. I didn't think of myself as an entrepreneur or a social entrepreneur. I merely thought of myself as a management and technical person. Solving problems, no doubt for poor people. In fact I used to call myself an action consultant.

But Vijay quickly realised that setting up an organisation of any kind involves the same set of basic issues – establishing credibility, getting minimum resources, financial accountability. Even if you haven't conceived it as an enterprise, it becomes one.

What PRADAN did beyond the actual technical assistance it provided was evangelise the idea of young professionals contributing to the development sector. Both the demand side and supply side started increasing. From two NGOs and four professionals on its rolls, PRADAN quickly expanded to 10 NGOs assisted by twenty-five professionals.

"PRADAN became an organisation or social enterprise in its own right without our quite thinking about it like that. There was no long-term business plan."

Of course, with growth came the problem of constantly garnering resources and building a team. All the standard enterprise management issues, started building up.

While PRADAN was definitely an early example of 'social entrepreneurship' ie an effort to tackle a longstanding social issue in a fresh and new way, it never became financially self-sustaining. It remains dependent on external funding.

"The communities that PRADAN works with are too poor to pay. So it still depends on grants from organisations like the Ford Foundation and of course, the government."

Suppose the state irrigation department is investing a crore in building borewells, you need ₹ 10-12 lakh to manage and implement it. That is what comes to PRADAN. 25 years since its inception, PRADAN remains a robust organisation with 250 professionals working for it.

> "I realised that if we continued to remain dependent on grants for our own functioning, and government loans for the community, it's going to be a very slow path. We won't be able to control anything."

Only, Vijay Mahajan has moved on.

Vijay left PRADAN on 31 December 1990. The reason he left is a long story.

For years, Vijay had given his heart and soul to development work. He travelled the length and breadth of the country, met with the poorest of the poor, worked on how to make their life better.

His own life, meanwhile, was falling apart.

Vijay had married Savita, a batchmate from IIMA. While he was mostly to be found in dusty Bihar, she was working in Delhi. It was a long-distance marriage, at best. In 1988, Savita got a fellowship to Princeton.

"Dr Kamla Chowdhary, former IIMA professor who knew us well, caught hold of my ear and said, 'You also go or else you can bid goodbye to your wife'. Plus, I was also very exhausted. Establishing the concept constantly – with professionals, with NGOs, with governments, and of course with communities with whom you are working. I am describing it in very few sentences but it was very hard work. Psychologically also."

So Vijay too decided to take a year off and also managed to get a fellowship at the same University. While in the US, he got a chance to think about what he had achieved so far. By that time, PRADAN had started working directly with communities, not just NGOs, and it became clear that credit or capital is a necessary input. But one which the rural and the marginalised find very hard to get from local banks.

When he returned from Princeton after a year, Vijay rejoined PRADAN but was restless. The work it did was no doubt good but it was not making enough of an impact, he now felt.

"I realised that if we continued to remain dependent on grants for our own functioning, and government loans for the community, it's going to be a very slow path. We won't be able to control anything."

He hadn't yet thought of an alternative but said, let me go out and explore. For a while he considered politics but then dismissed the idea.

"I couldn't figure out anything. So I said, okay. Livelihood *ke liye kuch karna hai* so I became a self-employed consultant. But I remained in the field of livelihood promotion, working for poor people."

His clients included the World Bank, UNDP, NABARD and the Ford Foundation. Vijay had already built a very good reputation in PRADAN so getting assignments was not very difficult. But what really charged Vijay up during this period was the chance to solve the bigger problem: the right and sustainable method to promote livelihood.

A space where 'nothing is happening' is actually just what you need to do some serious soul searching. And unlike many entrepreneurs, Vijay was actually able to walk away from the organisation he had given birth to and create this vacuum.

PRADAN was in safe hands with Deep Joshi at the helm. Vijay could 'move on' although he knew not exactly where. But he kept swimming in the seas of development, hoping to one day sight the shore.

In 1993, the Ford Foundation asked Vijay to do a study of the SEWA Bank. Interestingly, they had excess deposits and were struggling to deploy credit. It was the first time Vijay saw how a bank functioned, from the inside.

The SEWA bank was a co-operative, run by members of the organisation's trade union.

"That's when I learnt in a very detailed way, how we can actually build a peoples' organisation with their savings and use the accumulated savings to give loans. And I got fascinated by that."

Vijay went in search of similar organisations round the world. With the support of the Ford Foundation he studied Shore Bank in the US, Grameen Bank in Bangladesh, and Bank Rakkyat in Indonesia. He was also asked to do a study on 'financial services for the poor' by the World Bank. Vijay teamed up with IIMA batchmate Bharti Ramola of Price

> "The kind of things that one does in an organisation every five years, we were doing every six months. We thought *ki yeh fit ho gaya*. We have gone from a concept note to a local area bank in two years flat."

Waterhouse for this project. They handled the technical details while he provided the insight into the rural poor.

These two studies spread over 1993-95 became the 'intellectual capital' for Basix.

On requests from many quarters the studies were shared with numerous institutions, including RBI, NABARD and ICICI.

The end result was that Vijay finally saw a light at the end of the 'I don't know what to do' tunnel. With a better understanding of rural financial institutions and the confidence that he could run such an institution, he was now ready for the Next Big Thing.

There was also some comfort generated in the form of savings and mainstream contacts.

Savita and Vijay decided to shift from Delhi to 'somewhere in the south of India'. The city chosen was Hyderabad.

"It's interesting that when you make decisions, in retrospect they look like very wild decisions. But you make them for very casual reasons. Savita's sister was living in Hyderabad, so was my uncle. And it was not deep South, yet it was South."

In 1995, Vijay began writing a feasibility report to start a rural bank.

At that time, Dr Manmohan Singh was the Finance Minister. He too had been to Bangladesh. He came back and said, "We should have an institution like the Grameen Bank of Bangladesh". Vijay jumped at at that chance.

"NABARD, UTI, IDBI, ICICI and NDDB were several of the institutions that actually gave me high-level audiences. The FM is saying, 'Let's do a bank for the poor; you want to start a bank for the poor. Let's see what you have in mind.'"

But here is where Vijay committed a bit of a *faux pas*. In India it is very difficult to start a bank. At that time, you needed a minimum of ₹ 100 crore equity. Now it is ₹ 300 crore. And even if you have that, you don't get a licence quickly.

Vijay had no means of raising that 100 crore. In essence he wasted 6 months trying to set up a bank. Eventually Dr Dave, who was the chairman of UTI at that time, said to him, "I fully understand what you want to do. But you will not be able to raise the money necessary for a bank on day one."

He offered Vijay a chance to implement his idea within UTI instead. Similarly N Vaghul of ICICI said, "We will put up some equity. But I seriously doubt you will be able to start a bank."

So at one level there was high-level support and encouragement but when it came to actually putting in 100 crore that was too big a leap of faith. Finally on the advice of some friends and well-wishers Vijay decided it was time to stop talking about the project and *do* something.

There was a section 25 company set up by PRADAN called 'Indian Grameen Services' which was not being used for anything in particular. Vijay bought over the equity of ₹ 81,000 and took over the company.

This vehicle was used to launch 'pilot micro credit' in Raichur district in Karnataka, 4-5 hours drive from Hyderabad, and the neighbouring Kurnool district which is in Andhra Pradesh.

"The reason why I picked these two is that an IIMA batchmate of mine – Pramod Kulkarni – who first worked with me in PRADAN had later started an NGO called PRERNA in Raichur. And Kurnool was one of the districts where we had done the World Bank study. So I was familiar with the area and its problems."

Now the problem is, if you want to start credit, you need money to lend. That, we did not have.

At around the same time, the Sir Ratan Tata Trust had asked Vijay to do a five-year strategic plan for them. In the course of this work which took a year, he got to know the trustees well and even shared his own dream with them.

When he went to hand over the final plan, Deanna Jejeebhoy, Programme Advisor, asked me, "But what about your own plan?"

He said, "I am stuck."

She said, "How much do you need?"

He said, "A crore should be enough to prove the concept."

So she asked him to write a proposal to the Tata Trust. The catch was that in its 80-year history the trust had never given a loan – they only gave grants. And Vijay didn't want to take a grant. Because then, the concept was not proved. So the matter got stuck.

Finally, Mr Palkhivala, Trustee and Mr Soonawalla – Tatas Sons' Finance Director – said, "Let's give this young man a loan, although in our mind, we should treat it as a grant. If it doesn't come back, it doesn't matter."

Armed with this money, Basix finally started operating in June 1996 in Raichur.

By now it was clear that a bank was not possible, but it was also clear that it could not be a non-profit organisation either. So finally on the advice of his banker friend Anoop Seth and auditor Nagarajan, Vijay decided to set up a non-bank finance company, or NBFC.

In 1996, there was no need for either a licence or minimum capital to start an NBFC. What's more, NBFCs in those days could take deposits so they could operate almost like banks. Vijay's plan was to get the Ford Foundation and the Swiss Agency for Development Cooperation to put in 'quasi equity' of ₹ 15 crore which would act as the initial lending money.

"I was hoping that once I do that, it would convince Indian banks, and then they will take over." A business plan was formulated over the next few months. The Ford Foundation has an arm called Programme Related Investment Arm (PRI) which deals like a social investment banker. So for the first time in his life, Vijay started doing big spreadsheets with a lot of help from batchmate Bharti and auditor Nagarajan.

In October 1996 an NBFC called Bhartiya Samruddhi Finance Ltd came into existence. In January 1997, the Ford Foundation approved a loan. Meanwhile the idea of a LAB or Local Area Bank was also taking shape.

On a trip to Indonesia, Vijay and Bharti had seen the concept of 'Rural Private Banks' (BPRs) which had very low start-up equity, as little as $50,000. And there were 8,000 BPRs in Indonesia.

"We came back and made a presentation to RBI, and asked why don't we have small rural banks or Local Area Banks in the private sector? The Narasimha Rao government fell and Chidambaram became the Finance Minister in 1996. When they came to power, there was a common minimum programme. One of their agenda items was to double rural credit in five years."

Chidambaram asked RBI for suggestions on how to achieve this. The Mahajan idea of Local Area Banks (LABs) came to the Minister's notice. In August 1996, the LAB concept was approved. Basix applied for a LAB licence and received RBI's in- principle approval. The start up equity was an affordable ₹ 5 crore.

From an individual to a section 25 company to an NBFC to a LAB, the organisation had gone through an incredible amount of restructuring. "The kind of things that one does in an organisation every five years, we were doing every six months. We thought *ki yeh fit ho gaya*. We have gone from a concept note to a local area bank in two years flat."

All was going as per plan when a huge scam hit the world of finance. CRB Capital, an NBFC owned by one C R Bhansali went belly up. This prompted the RBI to impose registration as well as a minimum capital requirement of ₹ 2 crore for an NBFC. Thirdly, it prohibited NBFCs from taking deposits. What's more, the in-principle approval for Local Area Banks was also put on hold.

Vijay and his team were hit by a ton of bricks. In the meantime, there was a commitment to repay the Tata Trust loan since they would be transiting to NBFC status. "Thank you very much for helping us start. We don't want to mix charitable money with business," was the guiding principle set in stone by Bharti Ramola, who along with Deep Joshi became co-promoters of Basix.

In June '97, ₹ 1 crore was repaid to the Tata Trust, partly from money which came from the Ford Foundation. Overall, things were difficult and uncertain.

"We had around ₹ 3.5-4 crore at the time we returned the Tata Trust money. We had operations on the ground and could quadruple our lending. The problem was the entity became very hobbled. It couldn't take deposits, its future was not clear."

Finally in October 1997 money came in from the Swiss. There was now another 6-8 crore to lend and the venture started going from strength to strength. The beneficiaries were all very poor households.

"We were using all kinds of methodologies, self-help groups, joint liability groups and individual lending. On the ground, the work was really fantastic." With its unique insight into rural India built over so many years, Basix could service this market like no other. In terms of the variety of products, variety of channels, variety of services, and linking livelihood to lending, the organisation was unmatched.

Basix became the model for doing unique and innovative things and yet breaking even. This is significant because in the early years most microfinance institutions make huge losses. Basix avoided this by operating at a higher scale from the very beginning.

Secondly, because of the profile of its people, Basix could bag some consulting work. While the core business was moderately loss making, with the additional income, it achieved a break-even.

"By 1998-99 we were the darlings of the sector. Applauded for working with poor people, using innovative products and channels, and yet being sustainable. The problem was, Indian banks were still not willing to lend to us. We got very frustrated."

The crux of the matter was that banks lend against assets. For a lending institution, its only asset is its loan portfolio. That was just not considered a good enough collateral back then.

In 1999, Mr Ramesh Gelli's Global Trust Bank was the first Indian institution who gave Basix a loan of ₹ 50 lakh. The amount eventually went up to ₹ 2 crore. Vijay then went to RBI and lobbied for the cause.

Dr Bimal Jalan, RBI Governor at that time, appointed a task force on microfinance whose top recommendation was that banks should lend to MFIs. This was approved and in fact, such lending was classified under 'priority sector'.

All of a sudden banks were lined up at their doorstep, chasing Basix. "These same banks were sitting on our

proposals for three years, *andar ghusne nahin dete the*...."
Vijay muses. The fact is government institutions work on
directives. Whether they like your idea or not, see merit or
not, is not the issue. There is no incentive for them to take
unnecessary risks.

The trick then is to lobby at the highest level. Because if one
person at the very top accepts your idea it will be accepted all
the way down. No doubt this requires a lot of patience and
persuasion, but the effort is well worth it.

Now that Basix had access to capital from Indian banks, the
next issue was capital adequacy.

"You have ₹ 2 crore capital, and you have already borrowed
₹ 8 crore. So banks are already nervous, they don't want to
go beyond 1:4, 1:5. So we needed to enhance the equity in
the NBFC."

Once again Vijay began the task of networking and raising
capital.

"I went to 20 institutions. Of these, IFC, Shore Bank (US),
Triodos Bank (Netherlands) and our own ICICI and HDFC
agreed to put equity in Basix in the year 2000. In all, I raised
about ₹ 10 crore." As soon as that hurdle was crossed, the RBI
granted the Local Area Bank licence. The condition was that it
had to be a separate entity with its own equity of ₹ 5 crore.

What's more, the bank licence was valid for only three
districts. At that time, Basix as an NBFC was working in 15-
20 districts. But because a bank offers the advantage of
'saving', of collecting deposits, Vijay decided it was worth it. A
complex arrangement was worked out.

Bhartiya Samruddhi Finance pulled out from the two districts
where the bank would operate. A lot of effort went into undoing
one entity, establishing another and hence in that period the
organisation suffered. But eventually it was all sorted out. Then
came the real bombshell.

Five years after starting operations, Basix conducted an
impact assessment study. The results came out in 2002 and
they were shocking.

"We found that only half of our customers who had been
borrowing for 3 years and repaying successfully, said that they
had a positive increase in their income as compared to a

control group. A quarter said there was no change, and a quarter said we have had a decline."

The results shook the Basix team. What was happening?? They went and spoke to those who said they didn't benefit or had a decline. Vijay got deeply and personally involved.

"What I found was that basically the poorer the household, the more it suffers from risk. But that risk is not factored. If the buffalo dies, it is a disaster for the borrower. Then there are health issues. Secondly, their productivity was so low, that they hardly had any surplus. They had nothing to sell in the market. And the third was, if they actually managed a small surplus, they got the worst prices and the worst terms in the market."

Basix had always been aware that credit is a necessary but not a sufficient condition. So it did offer technical assistance and support services but it just wasn't adequate.

"We went through very major turmoil, debate, demotivation. I came close to thinking that *yeh sab bekaar hai*. My life was wasted doing all this. Eventually we gathered our wits and crafted a new operating strategy. We added a suite of insurance products. So now we are the country's largest micro-insurance provider."

Basix now provides life insurance for all its customers and their spouses, and a limited health insurance covering critical illness and permanent disability. In addition there is livestock insurance, crop insurance and asset insurance for equipment. And all these are done in partnership with the major insurance companies.

Over 20,000 claims adding up to ₹ 8 crore have already been settled. The average claim is only ₹ 4,000 but it has made all the difference.

"For the other two issues, we added agricultural and business development services, including market linkages. To do all this well, we bring customers together into groups and to make the groups work well, we offer institutional development services. This is what has become our new 'Livelihood Triad' strategy."

Which goes to show that an idea is only as good as its on-the-ground implementation. No matter how hard you try or how smart you are in going about it, you will make mistakes. An entrepreneur has to have the courage to look into the mirror and admit, "Yes, I made a mistake, now let's find out how to fix it!"

Cumulative lending by Basix crossed ₹ 1,000 crore in the year 2007 while bad debts are under 1%. As the organisation grows larger and larger, what keeps it going?

"In our case, it's the dual bottomline. When people join us they are not exceptionally motivated to do development work or work with the poor. Our salary structure is moderate. But within six months to a year, they start seeing that, 'Oh boy! I am truly helping some people to make their living.'"

And that's what kept Vijay going through some incredibly tough times. The tensions led to a cardiac problem three years ago. From an RBI meeting he went straight into an ICU, and had a bypass. He did slow down a bit, but bounced back after a year.

"If I wasn't doing Basix, I would have been doing something similar. Addressing the same issues, issues of how our world is configured. I think it is completely screwed up. I am not one of those who believes in absolute equality, I am quite happy with relative equality. But the fact that 400 million people are below such a subhuman level, that their human potential is completely snuffed out. To me, that's just not acceptable."

Yes, this commitment means he is 'missing in action' most of the time as far as his family is concerned.

"I think I have been a good son, a good father, a good husband. But if you are out five days a week or longer, you miss out on mundane day-to-day togetherness. It has been an issue with my wife, for my children. But they have been very generous with me, particularly my wife Savita. While she herself has had a mainstream career, she has always encouraged me to do what I want."

Savita Mahajan is currently the Associate Dean of ISB (Indian School of Business), Hyderabad. As we walk out of the library, where we held this whispered interview, he makes one final observation.

"And yeah, throughout our history, including today, she has always earned more than me. So that makes a difference."

And that's what it's all about ultimately – life, work, entrepreneurship. Making a difference.

ADVICE TO YOUNG ENTREPRENEURS

The single most important quality you need to have and cultivate further is to get up and walk every time you fall down. I am writing this the day after I turned down an equity investor from whom we have been seeking funding for the last several months, due to irreconcilable differences on terms. But while that deal broke off at 10 pm on Monday night and on Tuesday morning I was at a breakfast meeting with another prospective investor.

Likewise, one has to persist in terms of operational difficulties. Our expansion in Jharkhand state has seen many ups and downs due to the poor law and order situation there. In November, one of our field staff was shot dead by robbers. What did we do – we did not pull out. The day after the cremation, a hundred BASIX field staff, led by all of us in the senior team, went out doing our regular work – originating loans, collecting repayments, providing technical and marketing assistance to customers, etc.

But the second and equally important ability one needs to cultivate is the ability to learn – from experience, from critics, from competitors, from failures, from summer trainees, from mothers-in-law and from regulators! Expert knowledge is useful, but increasingly has a shorter and shorter shelf-life. So what is permanent is the ability to understand a new situation and respond appropriately, using both learning from the past but also a fresh appreciation of the situation. Some of this comes from the self and some from others.

This brings me to the third point. Entrepreneurship is widely misunderstood to be a personal trait. It is so, to some extent. But entrepreneurship is a social construction – it is a phenomenon where certain behaviours get expressed in certain individuals, due to the support of their 'eco-system' – colleagues, family members, investors, regulators, competitors and customers. All of these interactions, cooked in the skull of the entrepreneur, make for the heady mix that all of you are after. So nurturing this eco-system and interacting with it are extremely important.

Centre for Innovation Incubation and Entrepreneurship

ABOUT CIIE

The Centre for Innovation, Incubation and Entrepreneurship (CIIE) at IIM Ahmedabad aims at fostering innovation-driven entrepreneurship through incubation, research and dissemination of knowledge.

CIIE was set up by IIM Ahmedabad in 2001 and is supported by the Government of Gujarat and the Department of Science and Technology, Government of India. Since its inception, a host of organisations, professionals, academicians and networking partners within India and across the globe have been closely associated with the initiatives of CIIE.

Some of the ongoing projects are also being backed by the Wadhwani Foundation (set up by an IT entrepreneur in Silicon Valley, USA), Ministry of New and Renewable Energy (GoI), Piramal Foundation and Microsoft.

Ongoing programmes at CIIE include:

iAccelerator: A summer start-up camp for young IT professionals, students or web-developers with entrepreneurial ambitions.

Anveshan: A unique annual event held by CIIE. Anveshan is a nationwide proactive search by CIIE for hi-tech and high-impact innovators in public, private and informal sectors.

Selected innovators are invited to avail of CIIE's incubation facilities and become commercially viable. Other initiatives include IIMA Entrepreneurs' Conference, Solar Innovation Programme and Inventors of India workshop.

For more visit *www.ciieindia.org*

ABOUT WADHWANI
FOUNDATION

The Wadhwani Foundation funds not-for-profit efforts that inspire, educate and support new entrepreneurs, and create environments where they can succeed. Its mission is to help individuals achieve their full potential, regardless of background.

Launched in 2000, the Wadhwani Foundation is founded by Dr Romesh Wadhwani, an IT entrepreneur in Silicon Valley, California.

The Wadhwani Foundation believes entrepreneurship is a powerful tool for individuals to realise their potential. Entrepreneurship is more than starting a business; it is a way of thinking, and a critical driver of growth in any economy. Entrepreneurs bring to the market new products and services, and devise better and more efficient ways to operate.

In doing so they create valuable, productive new jobs. Successful entrepreneurs create wealth for themselves, their families, their communities and society.

For more log in to *www.wadhwani-foundation.org*

You can also visit the National Entrepreneurship Network (NEN), a resource for entrepreneurs, supported by the Wadhwani Foundation. NEN was co-founded by five of India's premier academic institutions: IIT Bombay, IIM Ahmedabad, SP Jain Institute, Bombay, IBAB, Bangalore and BITS Pilani. Over the past three years, NEN's focus has been to catalyse entrepreneurship on campuses across India.

www.nenonline.org

START UP RESOURCE

If you would like to contact any of the entrepreneurs featured in this book for help/advice, here are their email ids.

Do try and be specific in your queries and a little patient in getting a response!

1. **Sanjeev Bikhchandani**, Info Edge, *sbikh@naukri.com*
2. **Shantanu Prakash**, Educomp, *shantanu.prakash@educomp.com*
3. **Vinayak Chatterjee**, Feedback Ventures, *vinayak@feedbackventures.com*
4. **Ashank Desai**, Mastek, *ashankd@mastek.com*
5. **R Subramanian**, Subhiksha, *rs@subhiksha.biz*
6. **Narendra Murkumbi**, Renuka Sugars, *nm@renukasugars.com*
7. **Chender Baljee**, Royal Orchid Hotels, *cb@royalorchidhotels.com*
8. **Madan Mohanka,** TEGA Industries, *madan.mohanka@tegaindustries.com*
9. **Sunil Handa**, Eklavya Education Foundation, *sunilhanda@eklavya.org*
10. **Vardan Kabra**, Fountainhead School, *vardan.kabra@fountainheadschools.org*
11. **Deep Kalra**, MakeMyTrip, *dk@makemytrip.com*
12. **Rashesh Shah**, Edelweiss Capital, *rashesh@edelcap.com*
13. **Nirmal Jain**, India Infoline, *nirmal@indiainfoline.com*
14. **Vikram Talwar,** EXL Services, *vikram.talwar@exlservice.com*
15. **K Raghavendra Rao**, Orchid Pharmaceuticals, *krrao@orchidpharma.com*
16. **Jerry Rao**, Mphasis, *raojerry@hotmail.com*
17. **Shivraman Dugal**, ICRI, *srdugal@icriindia.com*
18. **Shankar Maruwada**, Marketics, *shankar@marketics.com*
19. **Ruby Ashraf**, Precious Formals, *ruby@promzstar.com*
20 **Deepta Rangarajan**, IRIS, *Deepta.rangarajan@irisindia.net*
21. **Cyrus Driver**, Calorie Care, *cyrus@caloriecare.com*
22. **Venkat Krishnan**, Give Foundation, *venkat@giveindia.org*
23. **Anand Halve**, chlorophyll, *anand@chlorophyll.in*
24. **S B Dangayach**, Sintex, *dangayach@sintex.co.in*
25. **Vijay Mahajan**, Basix, *vijay@basixindia.com*

Rashmi Bansal is a writer, entrepreneur and a youth expert. She is the author of four bestselling books on entrepreneurship - *Stay Hungry Stay Foolish, I Have a Dream,* and *Poor Little Rich Slum.* Her books have sold over half a million copies and been translated into 10 langauges.

Rashmi is the co-founder and editor of *JAM (Just Another Magazine).* She writes extensively on youth, careers and entrepreneurship on her blog Youth Curry.

Rashmi is a popular guest speaker at reputed business schools in India and the US.

She mentors numerous young entrepreneurs and also conducts motivational talks and youth insight seminars for corporates.

An economics graduate from Sophia College, Mumbai and an MBA from IIM Ahmedabad, she lives in Mumbai.

You can reach her at:

Email: mail@rashmibansal.in.

Facebook: www.facebook.com/rashmibansal

Twitter: www.twitter.com/rashmibansal

Also by Rashmi Bansal

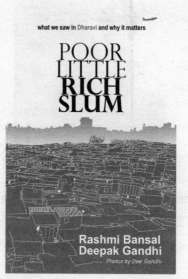